Elijah Nicholas Wilson

The Living Pulpit

Or Eighteen Sermons by Eminent Living Divines of the Presbyterian Church

Elijah Nicholas Wilson

The Living Pulpit
Or Eighteen Sermons by Eminent Living Divines of the Presbyterian Church

ISBN/EAN: 9783337088071

Printed in Europe, USA, Canada, Australia, Japan

Cover: Foto ©Lupo / pixelio.de

More available books at **www.hansebooks.com**

THE LIVING PULPIT,

OR

EIGHTEEN SERMONS

BY EMINENT LIVING DIVINES

OF

THE PRESBYTERIAN CHURCH.

WITH

A BIOGRAPHICAL SKETCH OF THE EDITOR,

BY GEO. W. BETHUNE, D.D.

EDITED AND PUBLISHED
BY REV. ELIJAH WILSON.

ELEVENTH EDITION.

PHILADELPHIA:
C. SHERMAN & SON, PRINTERS,
S. W. CORNER OF SEVENTH AND CHERRY STS.
1861.

CONTENTS.

	PAGE
THE FOLLY OF DOUBTING THE EXECUTION OF GOD'S THREATENINGS, ...	1
By Rev. E. Wilson, Editor.	
WORTH OF THE SOUL, ...	21
By J. T. Smith, D. D.	
THE FAITHFUL SAYING, ...	44
By Willis Lord, D. D.	
THE RULING PASSION, ...	63
By W. B. Sprague, D. D.	
SUPREMACY OF THE MORAL LAW, ...	93
By J. W. Yeomans, D. D.	
DISTRUST OF THE WORD, ...	109
By J. W. Alexander, D. D.	
CONSISTENCY OF THE DIVINE GOVERNMENT. . .	129
By Geo. Junkin, D. D.	
EFFICIENCY OF CHRISTIAN PRINCIPLE, . . .	157
By Thos. Smyth, D. D.	
THE GOOD MAN, ...	174
By John M'Dowell, D. D.	
THE HOUSE OF GOD, ...	188
By W. A. Scott, D. D.	

(iii)

CONTENTS.

		PAGE
PERPETUITY OF THE CHURCH,	. . . .	. 225
By J. C. Lord, D. D.		
SEEING THINGS INVISIBLE,	. . .	249
By J. H. Jones, D. D.		
CHRIST THE LIFE OF HIS PEOPLE,	. . .	. 263
By Robert J. Breckinridge, D.D., L.L.D.		
FAITH AND SIGHT CONTRASTED,	. . . .	. 299
By A. T. M'Gill, D. D.		
CATHOLICITY OF THE GOSPEL,	. . . .	. 319
By Chas. Hodge, D. D.		
CHRISTIAN SUBMISSION,	. . . . .	. 337
By H. A. Boardman, D. D.		
THE PRODIGAL,	. . . . . .	. 353
By John Leyburn, D. D.		
THE TREE KNOWN BY ITS FRUITS,	. . .	. 374
By E. P. Humphrey, D. D.		

PREFACE.

In presenting the LIVING PULPIT to the Public, the Editor feels that no apology is needed. The book presents a collection of Sermons by some of the most eminent living divines of the Presbyterian Church, whose names are a sufficient guaranty that the matter is essential truth, presented in the most attractive form.

The Sermons were furnished at the request of the Editor expressly for this volume, and are practical and didactic.

The design of the publication will be fully seen by a reference to the biographical sketch of the Editor, prepared by George W. Bethune, D. D.

Whilst the Editor, in common with others engaged in the dissemination of divine truth by the agency of the press, expects a pecuniary compensation for his labours, yet he trusts that his efforts in this department will meet with the approbation of Zion's King, and be abundantly blessed by *Him* to the promotion of his own glory, in the salvation of souls.

Should this volume meet with public favour, it may be followed by similar productions from eminent divines of other denominations.

The Editor would here most gratefully acknowledge his indebtedness to his brethren, for their kindness and courtesy in furnishing their valuable contributions for the work: and hopes that in the developments of eternity multitudes will be found before the throne of God, who were encouraged in their Christian course, or first directed to the Saviour, by these Sermons, and who will there rejoice with the authors over the hallowed influence of the *Living Pulpit.*

E. W.

Philadelphia, Oct. 1st, 1852.

BIOGRAPHICAL SKETCH

OF

THE EDITOR.

BY GEO. W. BETHUNE, D. D.

The severe trials of the Rev. Elijah Wilson, and the Christian patience with which he has struggled through them to usefulness, have won for him the sympathy and affectionate respect of many friends. As another method of doing good, and at the same time of honourably meeting unavoidable claims on his exertions, he has been led to publish this volume. The names of the good and able men who have cheerfully assisted his design, by contributing Discourses, give the best proof of the estimation in which he is held, and of the profit to be expected, under the Divine blessing, from the reading of the book. A slight sketch of his history may not be an uninteresting preface.

He was born in Philadelphia, the only child of James and Mary Wilson. His paternal grand parents were of Scotch-Irish blood, and came to this country a short time before the American Revolution, settling first in Haddonfield, New Jersey, but soon removing to Philadelphia, where James, the father of Elijah, was born in 1774.

His grand parents on the other side, whose name was Thomas, came from Wales after the close of the war, and settled on a farm in Montgomery County, Pennsylvania, where Mary, their only child, was born about 1788, and, at the age of 22, married to Mr. Wilson, who carried her to Philadelphia, in which city they spent their subsequent days.

Mr. Wilson's family were Episcopalians, but, for the

greater part of his life, he preferred worshipping with Presbyterians, though he never became a communicant. Mrs. Wilson continued in the principles of her parents, who belonged to the society of Friends; but her views of Christian doctrine were highly evangelical, and she strongly inculcated the truths of the Gospel on the growing mind of her son, whose delicate health during boyhood brought him more closely under her happy care and pious teachings.

From his early years Elijah was noted for an active, inquiring mind. To a great fondness for books, he added not a little mechanical genius, and a taste for art. This last tendency was more or less cultivated at different times, and he attained sufficient skill, especially in landscape painting, to defray the expense of his living and education for some time after death had deprived him (in his fifteenth year) of his father. Previously to this his studies had been interrupted by a severe dropsical affection, from which, after a twelvemonth's suffering, he was providentially restored by the skill of his physician, Dr. Hays, of Philadelphia.

Undiscouraged by such various hindrances and difficulties, he was determined to have a thoroughly classical education; and, when about eighteen, he entered the Academy at Kinderhook, New York, then under the able superintendence of Mr. Silas Metcalf. At Kinderhook it was his privilege to sit under the faithful, energetic ministry of the late Rev. Dr. Sickles, minister of the Reformed Dutch Church there; and, in the summer of 1831, he received, through the distinguishing grace of God his Saviour, the baptism of the Holy Ghost. He united with the Church in the following autumn. His earnest piety, ready talents, and thirst after knowledge, attracted the approving regard of Dr. Sickles, and other pious friends, who advised him to study for the sacred ministry; which counsel, after much anxious, prayerful deliberation, he followed, and diligently prepared himself for College. In the autumn of 1835 he was matriculated as a member of the Sophomore Class, in Rutgers' College, New Brunswick, New Jersey, and prosecuted his studies with credit and success for the next twelvemonth, supporting himself by his own industry, yet fully keeping up with his more favoured classmates. But the double tax upon his energies, physical and mental, was too great for a constitution never strong, and shaken by former disease. His nervous system being much impaired, he sought medical aid without success; yet continued, though feebly and at intervals, to pursue the course of the College, until towards the Christmas holidays. Already, however, he had had what he afterwards knew, though not then, to be the forebodings of the darkness which has since enveloped his life. About a year before this he lost his sense of smell, which he has never regained; and in November, 1836, when returning alone from evening prayers in the College Chapel to his lodgings, he was *suddenly* struck with total *blindness.*

For a little while he paused, wondering and alarmed in the darkness; then attempted to grope his way homeward, but could not. He opened his eyes wide, but they had no sight; after some moments he turned his face up to heaven and saw the blue sky, though the earth was veiled from him—then the heavy curtain slowly fell, and the world again was revealed to his view. The sense, so strangely suspended, had returned. He reached home, but greatly enfeebled by the stroke to body and mind. The next week, while at his studies, he again, and as suddenly, lost his sight; but after a few minutes it came back to him as before. Anxious as he was in consequence of these two attacks, he did not anticipate so terrible a calamity as utter, unrelieved blindness; but, though he relaxed his pursuits, the paroxysms became more and more frequent, until his retirement from College became necessary. His kind mother had been removed from earth a few years before this trial, which was severely aggravated by the loss of her affectionate care, and he sought at his second home, in Kinderhook, for rest and medical assistance. The physicians whom he consulted on his way in New York, encouraged him to hope for a cure when his general health should be recruited; and at Kinderhook he had the advantage of being under the able treatment of Dr. Dorr; but his seasons of darkness continued to return, his strength rapidly failed, and, though in the March following he was somewhat stronger, all objects were seen by him through a haze, which became more and more dim, until he could not distinguish one thing from another. One night, about the close of April, he went to bed and slept soundly; but on awaking in the morning he saw no light. He heard the inmates moving about the house—he approached the window of his chamber—the warm rays of the sun fell upon his hands and his face, but the brightness of its beams were not for him. He was *entirely blind*. He hoped, at the first, that the darkness would be only temporary and partial as before; but never since has he known the pleasantness of looking upon the face of nature or the smiles of friends. At the high noon of that sad day he felt that the eclipse was total. His spirit sank within him. He refused to eat bread, and would fain have died. He tried to look up and "see Him who is invisible." He shut himself apart from his sympathising friends, and bemoaned himself in solitude. He knelt to pray, but his very soul was in darkness, and he was constrained to cry, "My God! my God! why hast thou forsaken me?" The only scripture which spake to him, was the melancholy cry of the anguished prophet, "Is thy mercy clean gone for ever?" His agony of heart and mind continued for many days. He wrestled in prayer day and night. His little strength entirely failed. A pain on the top of his head, which he had felt from the beginning of his illness, became more and more acute; he lost for some time the sense of taste—so that those of touch and hearing only remained to him—his whole system was racked by frequent convulsions—his life was despaired of for more than a fortnight—and, though after that time his spiritual and physical energies were partially restored during a few succeeding months, he fell back into the same bodily distresses—but, through the blessing of God, not into the same mental distress, during the summer.

The faithful skill of Dr. Van Dyke was, however, rewarded by a kind Providence with the entire restoration of his general health, but with no hope that he would ever again receive his sight.

It is most pleasing to know that his spiritual faintness was the consequence not of unbelief, but bodily infirmity; for when his flesh rose from its weakness, and his brain recovered soundness, his heart again delighted itself in God. "The celestial light shone inward;" and his buoyant temper, animated by divine joy, showed itself superior to his trials. This happy Christian courage has ever since accompanied him, blessing his own life with a radiance from on high, and shedding from his cheerful, thankful example, an edifying pleasure upon all who have had the satisfaction of his society.

He still fondly clung to the hope of prosecuting his studies, but his friends persuaded him from attempting it; and abandoning his collegiate course, he, by their advice, entered the Institution for the Blind at Philadelphia, with a view of preparing himself to be a teacher of his brethren in affliction. But with limited means of improvement, through the slow process of reading by "raised letters," his ardent mind could not be content; and he remained at the Institution only from December, 1837, until the following spring. At that time a severe erysipelas in his head and eyes excited some hope that a favourable change had occurred, and that by skilful treatment his sight might yet be recovered; but, though he put himself into the experienced hands of Drs. Hays and Fox, of Philadelphia, his expectations were baffled.

Some kind friends (especially one Mr. W., of New York, for whose warm and active regard he has great reason to be grateful) thought that, with the aid of a partner, he might succeed in some branch of business, and had begun to make arrangements to that end. But the good Providence, which had chastened his spirit, intended better things; for, while on his way up the Hudson to visit Kinderhook, he fell in with the Rev. Sylvester Woodbridge, then the agent of the Auburn Theological Seminary, who advised him to go on with his studies for the ministry; and, to encourage him, cited the case of his cousin, the Rev. Timothy Woodbridge, who had become blind during his collegiate course, yet had continued his preparation, and was preaching with success as the pastor of a church.

Mr. Woodbridge suggested that an arrangement might be effected with some theological students to read the lessons in which they were engaged to him by turns. Mr. Wilson was favourably impressed with the plan, which Mr. Woodbridge promised his assistance to carry out. While awaiting Mr. Woodbridge's further communication, he was invited to visit the home of a college classmate, whose father, Captain John Steele, resided at Paradise, Pennsylvania. There, unwilling to be idle, he occupied and amused by teaching occasionally the two younger sons of his hospitable entertainer. Capt. Steele was so much pleased with the rapid improvement of his boys under Mr. Wilson's teaching, that he requested him to act as the private tutor of his children, which he did, and taught the two daughters, as well as the two sons of his host, with great success, until the March following, when Mr. Woodbridge wrote to him that he had made the arrangement, which he had promised, for Mr. Wilson's theological studies, at the seminary in Auburn, New York; and, not without many spoken blessings, accompanied by substantial evidence of esteem, from Capt. Steele, he left the home of that generous gentleman, to enter on his course at Auburn, in April 1839, and there continued his studies most profitably until the spring of 1841, practising his gifts as a public speaker by occasional exhortations in the religious meetings around, which were well received. In March of that year, after a close examination, he was regularly licensed as a candidate for the ministry, by the Presbytery of Cayuga, on which occasion he received from the members of that revered body many proofs of approbation and encouraging counsel.

Desirous of yet further improvement before entering upon the full labours of the sacred office, he, by the advice of a friend who was studying in the Theological Seminary at Princeton, and who engaged to make for him there an arrangement like that by which he had profited so much at Auburn, he determined to spend a year in the school of the prophets, under the wise superintendence of the Rev. Doctors Alexander, Miller and Hodge. In the meantime, he ventured to travel alone to visit his hospitable friend Capt. Steele, and preached frequently on the way; every where on the road and in the house meeting with attentive kindness. In September (having been detained by an illness of several weeks) he entered the Seminary at Princeton, and enjoyed regularly the opportunities of his class until May, 1842, when he was transferred from the Presbytery of New Brunswick (to which he had been dismissed from the Presbytery of Cayuga) to the Presbytery of New Castle, Delaware, by whom he was sent, in June, 1842, as a stated supply for the churches of Newark and Christiana. His services were so well received, that those churches, in the August following, united in giving him an unanimous call, and he was installed as their pastor on the 12th of the next October. Here he was blessed in winning the affections of a most estimable and intelligent young lady, Miss Ann Gray, daughter of Mr. Andrew Gray, of Chestnut Hill, Newark, whom he married on the 29th of November of the same year. Their union was eminently happy. Mr. Wilson continued in the charge of these churches, preaching regularly and doing the full duty of a pastor for four years. It is but just to say, that his labours were owned of God and the Church. They were richly blessed; scarcely a sacramental communion passed without the evidence of fruit, and, at one time, a considerable revival crowned his preaching of the Word. So much was he strengthened, notwithstanding his infirmity, that, in the spring of 1844, being invited to assist the pastor of the church at Wilmington, he preached for fourteen successive evenings, labouring the while throughout the day in visits of exhortation. This Mr. Wilson gratefully remembers as a most precious season of ingathering, when "many souls were added unto the Church."

For several reasons, which he considered sufficient, and his known "aptness to teach," Mr. Wilson was persuaded, in the spring of 1845, to take the superintendence of a "Female Seminary," at Newark, still retaining his pastoral care of the two churches which have been named. In this important school, about forty young ladies pursued a wide range of studies, and Mr. Wilson received high testimonials from most competent judges, to his fidelity as a preceptor, which was shown, at the examinations, by the scholars themselves. The written certificates given to Mr. Wilson speak of this sufficiently. His multiplied labours as a pastor of two churches and active principal of such a seminary were, however, too much for his strength.

In the spring of 1846 he was compelled to resign his pulpits; and in a year or two afterwards he gave up the charge of the school, which in the spring of 1847 had been moved to Wilmington. About this period of his life the Lord was pleased again to "bruise our brother, and put him to grief," visiting him with yet more and yet more bitter sorrows. His pecuniary fortunes suffered from some ill-advised changes in his school. Mrs. Wilson's health was shaken, and various circumstances led them to a more private life in the bosom of her father's family, whose residence was now at Wilmington. He was not, however, idle, but assisted Mr. Gayley of the Wilmington Academy, and preached to a feeble Church which had been begun in the outskirts of the city.

Now, July 1848, came upon him the saddest calamity of his life. His charming and devoted wife had been to him in every respect a helpmeet, enlivening darkness, cheering his labours, solacing his disappointments. God had given them two fair sons, Andrew Gray, (born December, 1844,) Chalmers, (August, 1847.) Their domestic content was full of sweetness—its chief charm the pious, cultivated, affectionate, clear minded, and strong hearted woman, who in every relation as a daughter, wife, mother, friend and member of Christ's Church, had won love from all who knew her, but especially from her blind, thankful husband. Yet she heard the voice of her Master calling her away, and died of the typhoid fever on the evening of the 10th of the month. "She was not, for God took her." Mr. Wilson sustained, as he could not but be, by the assurance of her sleep in Jesus, suffered far more from the absence of his bosom's comforter, than he had done from the loss of his sight. With her life, his second, better light went out. It was the deepest gloom of midnight to his heart; an irresistible melancholy came over his soul, which the sympathy of affectionate friends sought to alleviate, but could not chase away. He had to go on his way blind, without the gentle hand to lead him, which, by the gift of God, had been his ever careful, gentle guide.

But the children she had bequeathed him demanded his exertions, and the work of his Lord his zeal. His long tried, steadfast friend, the Rev. S. M. Gayley, was mindful of him, and, by generous influence, obtained for him the useful post of assistant chaplain to the Eastburn Mariners' Church of Philadelphia, the Rev. O. Douglass, the pastor (since gone to rest), having been compelled, by declining health, to leave the main duties in Mr. Wilson's hands. The labours of Mr. Wilson in this pleasing scene of missionary work were highly acceptable to the mariners, and those who had the superintendence of the church.

There he continued to serve, blessing and blest, until early in the spring of 1849, when he received a unanimous call from the Presbyterian Church at Wrightsville, York County, Pennsylvania, to become their pastor, which he accepted.

His entrance upon this new sphere of exertion was signalised by a copious rain of the Spirit, reviving the church, and causing many plants of righteousness to spring up within the garden of the Lord from the good seed of his word. The ministry of Mr. Wilson continued to be highly appreciated by the congregation of Wrightsville, and he exercised it, notwithstanding his physical disabilities, with ease and comfort. Several of his friends, however, with whose judgment his own agreed, adopted the opinion that his usefulness might be enhanced by his giving himself to the spread of the truth through the press; and, in order to the making of a full experiment, he resigned the pastoral charge of the Wrightsville Church in December, 1851, though, at the earnest request of the elders and congregation, he still continued to occupy their pulpit as the stated preacher until June 1852.

It was Mr. Wilson's first intention to publish some of his

own religious writings; but shrinking from what he modestly feared might be thought undue presumption, he has determined that his opening venture should be with the writings of others, who are widely known and approved throughout the Evangelical Church of this country. How well he has been assisted by his fathers and brethren, the contents of the present volume show. He sends it forth, hopeful of the divine blessing.

Such is the simple story of his afflicted yet favoured life. The general facts have been taken down from his own lips, as he told what the Lord had done for his soul, and "mentioned the loving kindness and great goodness" of the angel of the covenant, in leading him "by ways which he knew not, and paths he had not known." If some words of affectionate praise are found threaded throughout this narrative, it is because the writer of these pages could not deny himself the expression of his feelings. They have been written under the bias of a warm friendship; but that warmth of friendship has been the consequence of his acquaintance with Mr. Wilson's character and course, which have won for him a like esteem from all who knew him.

No doubt the trials of his experience induced a tenderness of judgment; but it is not less certain that his patience, and cheerfulness, and courageous perseverance compel towards him a rare respect and heartfelt good wishes. Nor must it be thought that this opinion of him as a Christian man and an Evangelical minister, has been formed only when considering his difficulties. Were he not blind, he would be entitled to an equal estimation. Pursuing his studies continuously and earnestly, by the help of readers, his memory and his power of attention have been strengthened by practice. His range of investigation has been wide; his acquaintance with standard authors in various departments of theological and general literature is familiar; his judgment, from the intensity of his thought, while listening to the friend at his side, has become unusually quick and sound, so that it may be said with truth, few of our working clergy are better stored with material for the pulpit than he. He thoroughly understands and faithfully expounds the system of truth set forth in the standards of the church to which he is loyally attached. His discourses are notable for their analytical arrangement; his definitions are apt; his illustrations happy; his mode of thought oftentimes fresh; his language easy and not devoid of *unction;* which, united to a demonstrative force, distinct enunciation, and a natural earnestness mingled with pathos, render him, through divine blessing, a forcible, pleasing preacher. The absence of sight interests his hearers for him, but occasions no awkwardness of manner, or unpleasant feelings; and he is listened to with emotions of thankfulness that it pleases God to bring such joyful light out of such darkness.

His story is instructive, confirming the evangelical doctrine, that we may, through grace, "glory in tribulation," be made strong by weakness, and "count it all joy when we fall into manifold temptations;" nay, that there are no impediments or obstacles insuperable to one who, trusting his Master's promise, is determined upon doing what his "hands find to do, with all his might."

THE FOLLY OF DOUBTING THE EXECUTION OF GOD'S THREATENINGS.

BY

THE REV. E. WILSON, EDITOR.

Knowing this first, that there shall come in the last days scoffers, walking after their own lusts, and saying, Where is the promise of his coming? for since the fathers fell asleep, all things continue as they were from the beginning of the creation.—2 PETER iii. 3, 4.

THIS is a prophetic declaration of an apostle, relative to the character and conduct of a class of men who would arise in the last days, that is, at the termination of the Jewish polity, and, affecting to discredit the promises and threatenings of God, by scoffing at religion, would walk after their own lusts.

The history of every age, since the days of the apostles, has furnished lamentable proof of the truth of this declaration. Even in this age, under the increasing light of the gospel, scoffers are increasing in number and daring profaneness. So true is the affirmation of Scripture, that "evil men and seducers shall wax worse and worse, deceiving and being deceived." "For, as in water face answereth to face, so the heart of man to man." In every age unbelief marks his character, and evinces the truth of Scripture, that "the heart is deceitful above all things, and desperately wicked." With affections thus averse to holiness, he refuses obedience to the divine commands, and yields to his wayward propensities. When urged to the duty of repentance and faith, he flies to some refuge of lies; and to still the voice of conscience, affects to doubt the truth of divine threatenings.

My object is to show the folly of those who doubt the execution of God's threatenings.

Their folly will appear evident from the following reasons:

1st. Because they demand an *immediate* fulfilment, saying, "Where is the promise of his coming?" The scoffer must see an immediate exhibition of retributive justice, or else he utterly refuses to believe the evidence which God has been pleased to give.

It needs no very extensive survey of the divine government, to discover that an immediate execution of threatenings is not a principle of its administration. For an apt illustration of this principle, refer to the history of Manasseh. The character of this prince was of the most detestable kind. He not only filled Jerusalem with innocent blood, but also caused Judah and Jerusalem to sin more grievously than any of the surrounding nations. Idolatry, through his influence, became the prevailing religion from the royal court to the meanest subject. In addition to these enormities, the warnings and admonitions by the prophets to this proud and idolatrous prince, were rejected by both prince and people with disdain.

Thus provoked by contempt, and by the violation of

every law of humanity, justice, and mercy, Jehovah threatens Manasseh and his people with a sweeping destruction, saying, "Because Manasseh, king of Judah, hath done these abominations, and hath done wickedly above all that the Amorites did which were before him, and hath made Judah also to sin with his idols; therefore, thus saith the Lord God of Israel, Behold, I am bringing such evil upon Jerusalem and Judah, that whosoever heareth of it both his ears shall tingle. And I will stretch over Jerusalem the line of Samaria, and the plummet of the house of Ahab; and I will wipe Jerusalem, as a man wipeth a dish, wiping it, and turning it upside down. And I will forsake the remnant of mine inheritance, and deliver them into the hand of their enemies, and they shall become a prey and a spoil to all their enemies; because they have done that which was evil in my sight, and have provoked me to anger since the day their fathers came forth out of Egypt, even unto this day." But did God, in this instance, immediately execute his threatenings? No, for the subsequent history shows that Manasseh himself died in peace, and the execution of it on his people was deferred to the reign of Zedekiah, about *one hundred years.*

Again, this principle of the divine government is more strikingly illustrated in the history of Amalek. This idolatrous nation made an attack on Israel when weary and enfeebled from their wanderings in the desert; but Jehovah wrought a complete victory for his chosen people.

This unprovoked attack brought on Amalek the displeasure of Jehovah. And as an expression of his righteous indignation, "the Lord said unto Moses, Write this for a memorial in a book, and rehearse it in the ears of Joshua; for I will utterly put out the remembrance of Amalek from under heaven." Here, again, is sentence against the transgressor immediately executed? By no means; for, notwithstanding this threatening, Amalek is, through the divine forbearance, preserved from *immediate* destruction. Still, lest it should be inferred from this delay that God had forgotten their sins, or indeed never intended to execute his sentence, he, after the lapse of nearly half a century, renews, with additional reasons, his command to the Israelites, the chosen instruments to inflict his wrath, saying, "Remember what Amalek did unto thee by the way, when ye were come forth out of Egypt, how he met thee by the way, and smote the hindmost of thee, even all that were feeble behind thee, when thou wast faint and weary; and he feared not God. Therefore it shall be, when the Lord thy God hath given thee rest from all thine enemies round about, in the land which the Lord thy God giveth thee for an inheritance to possess it, that thou shalt blot out the remembrance of Amalek from under heaven; thou shalt not forget it."

The subsequent history of this people shows that they continued, from age to age, to cherish towards Israel a hostile disposition, and like modern scoffers, perfectly secure in their sins, they hastened to fill up the measure of their iniquity.

The long-suffering of God having at length become exhausted, he delivers, *after the lapse of five hundred and forty-eight years,* his **final command,** through his prophet Samuel, saying to king Saul, "Now go and smite Amalek, and utterly destroy all that they have, and spare them not; but slay both man and woman, infant and suckling, ox and sheep, camel and ass." This threatening was now fully accomplished, and the remembrance of Amalek blotted out from under heaven.

It is true, that the history of Manasseh and Amalek gives but an imperfect view of the testimony which might be gathered, to prove that an IMMEDIATE execution of threatenings is not a principle of the divine administration. But if the testimony of Moses and the Prophets fails to convince the scoffer, that God will *finally* fulfil his word, then would he not be persuaded though one rose from the dead.

The reason of this long delay of judgment given by the apostle in the chapter whence our text is taken, is, that God is "long suffering to us ward, not willing that any should perish, but that all should come to repentance." And we would naturally infer, that such an exhibition of forbearance in the midst of deserved wrath, would induce the sinner to embrace this favourable moment to "seek the Lord while he may be found," and thus escape his judgment. But such is the madness of his heart, and the folly of his course, that in bold defiance of every threatening of the Almighty, he, sheltering himself beneath his unreasonable doubts, still persists in his rebellion, and asks, amidst the clearest evidence, "Where is the promise of his coming?" "Where is the God of judgment?"

II. But, again, their folly is more strikingly manifest, *because they utterly disregard the teachings of Providence.*

Every impenitent heart is prone to imagine that God is a being simply benevolent, overlooking his justice and holiness. This vain notion the sinner continues to cherish, though God, through the abundance of his mercy, has, in his providence, added instruction to instruction. But the greater the light—in which God exhibits his determined purpose inviolably to unite in his moral government, justice, mercy and holiness—the more obstinately blind does the sinner remain. And if nothing but an overwhelming exhibition of power, in executing the fierceness of his wrath, could arouse the scoffer from his willing stupidity, God has, even of *this*, condescended to give him abundant examples.

A moral lesson, irresistible in its impression on the reflecting mind, we have given us in the terrific destruction of the antediluvian world. One hundred and twenty years did divine justice, through the intercession of mercy in behalf of its guilty inhabitants, forbear to execute its denunciations of wrath. But like sinners of the present age, those incorrigible and stupid sons of violence suffered the time given them for repentance to pass unimproved. Divine justice, though forbearing, slumbered not. The unexpected, the fatal hour arrived. Mercy retired. The door of hope was closed, and justice, with the besom of destruction, swept a guilty race from the face of the earth. God, as if determined that this lesson of instruction should not be lost to any succeeding age, not only recorded it upon the sacred page, but also chronicled it upon the cornerstones of the world, inscribed it on every mountain top, left its impress on the surface of every valley, and transmitted it through the traditions of all nations.

But has the hand of divine justice been less truly manifested in the moral government of the world in any succeeding age? By no means. For where is Nineveh, that once humbled yet impenitent city? Where are the cities of the plain? We have the answer of the apostle, that "God, turning the cities of Sodom and Gomorrah into ashes, condemned them with an overthrow, making them an ensample unto those that after should live ungodly." The same inquiry and answer may be made in reference to Babylon, Tyre and Sidon, Carthage and Rome. These were among the most renowned cities of the world; long the subject of prophecy; distinguished alike for their extent and influence; the enormity and number of their crimes, and, finally, not less distinguished for the display of divine justice in their destruction.

But the moral lessons to be derived from the volume of providence, whether the instructive events be remote or near, appear alike inefficient in teaching the scoffer his true character, and in convincing him that the most high God ruleth in the kingdoms of men, and that he appointeth over them whomsoever he will.

Nebuchadnezzar, a proud and idolatrous monarch of Babylon, while walking in the palace of his kingdom, and being elated with the greatness of his capital, and the glory of his dominion, "spake, and said, Is not this great Babylon, that I have built for the house of the kingdom, by the might of my power, and for the honour of my majesty?" But how suddenly was he arrested in his career! "While the word was in the king's mouth, there fell a voice from heaven, saying, O king Nebuchadnezzar, to thee it is spoken, the kingdom is departed from thee; and they shall drive thee from men, and thy dwelling shall be with the beasts of the field! they shall make thee to eat grass as oxen; and seven times shall pass over thee, until thou know that the Most High ruleth in the kingdom of men, and giveth it to whomsoever he will. The same hour was the thing fulfilled upon Nebuchadnezzar."

Now Belshazzar, his grandson and possessor of his throne, though acquainted with this history of Nebuchadnezzar, yet rejecting all its evidence of the sovereignty of God, pursued a course still more aggravating in the sight of heaven; the more aggravating, because he had the greater means of instruction. But in the midst of his idolatrous feast "came forth fingers of a man's hand, writing on the wall of his palace—MENE, MENE, TEKEL, UPHARSIN," the sentence of his condemnation and execution.

Alarmed at this vision, the king finally brings in the servant of the true God, because he alone was found able to interpret the writing. So true is it that Jehovah will always put honour on his children in humbling his enemies.

Daniel, when admitted into the royal presence, briefly states the history of Nebuchadnezzar, his crimes, condemnation, humility, and restoration, and declares to the king, "Thou, his son, O Belshazzar, hast not humbled thy heart, though thou *knewest* all this."

It is true, that time has removed to a great distance all the events above specified, but the case of the Jewish nation is a standing miracle; evidencing, beyond reasonable doubt, that Jehovah is still the governor of the nations, the King of kings, and Lord of lords. For who can be ignorant of the fact, that the house of Israel, though long the favourite of heaven, yet has been for ages scattered among every nation of the earth. Cruelly oppressed in every way which human ingenuity could devise, and still preserved a distinct people; reserved, both as objects of wrath and mercy, to furnish some forthcoming age a signal exhibition of the divine glory.

But we need not depend for evidence exclusively on the history of nations, for we have ample proof in the life of each individual, that God, from the volume of providence, is giving every man impressive lessons for his immediate improvement.

What though some regard not the work of Jehovah, neither consider the operation of his hands, yet to every willing mind he is constantly exhibiting himself rich in mercy, glorious in holiness, wisdom, and power.

The harmony of our moral and physical constitution, with the laws of nature, proves beyond contradiction, that the Author of our being not only designs our happiness, but also that we should constantly associate in our minds obedience and happiness, disobedience and misery. For every man finds, from daily experience, that an infringement of these laws is followed, sooner or later, and generally instantly, by pain, disease, misery, and death. And equally indubitable is the testimony of individual experience, that a strict observance of these laws is followed by health and happiness. The full flow of animal spirits consequent on partaking of a cheerful meal, in strict accordance with the laws of health, as truly inculcates the doctrine as does the Bible itself, that God purposes in his dealings with us to unite inseparably in our minds obedience and happiness. But is the testimony of our experience, as to the effect of regarding or violating the moral law of our being, less certain than that of the physical? or is it consonant to reason to suppose that less harmony and order of sequence would exist in the moral world than in the physical?

The experience of every man fully accords with the doctrine of the Bible, that the work of righteousness shall be peace, and the effect of righteousness quietness and assurance for ever. Surely these instances are enough to convince every rational person that God, in his supervision of the world, is constantly furnishing lessons of moral instruction, and that he has not at any time left himself without a witness. What, then, must be the folly of those who utterly disregard the teachings of divine providence!

III. Those therefore, who, under such circumstances still continue to cherish their unbelief, *must evidently make their doubting the truth of God an excuse for their sin.* This conduct of the sinner is evidently nothing less than to offer one sin as a pretext for committing many more. But how absurd and vain is such a refuge!

Such, however, are the extremes of absurdity to which the sinner is driven by a love of sin; but let conscience awake, and remorse will arise in his mind, from a consciousness of personal guilt, and fear of condign punishment.

Hence, when the transgressor becomes truly conscious of personal guilt, he cannot but be tormented with that fearful looking for of judgment and fiery indignation which shall devour the adversaries. So long, therefore, as he continues under the dominion of Satan, and wedded to his lusts, the unequivocal sentence, that "the wicked shall be turned into hell," must pierce him with horror. Here we would infer, that the sinner, from a sense of his guilt and danger, would ground the weapons of his rebellion, and plead for pardon. But no—lest he should be compelled to close with the voice of God and of conscience, he makes lies his refuge, and under falsehood he hides himself.

Thus, when the conscience has been overpowered by continually resisting all its admonitions, then their wayward passions constitute their only guide, the gratification of their carnal desires the object and end of their being.

Are not the laws of God, and his plan of salvation by a Mediator, of such a character as to commend themselves to the judgment and conscience even of the impenitent? If not, why does sudden calamity and fear compel even the vilest of the wicked to implore divine assistance, and earnestly beseech our Lord and Saviour for mercy to avert His impending wrath, which in the day of prosperity they so affectedly disregard or despise? But let the long-suffering mercy of heaven withdraw His avenging hand, sheathe the sword of justice, and restore prosperity, how soon do their vain hopes revive, and they again resort to the same subterfuge of lies! Despising the riches of God's goodness, and forbearance, and long-suffering, they renew boldly and confidently their feeble strength to contend with Omnipotence; they stretch out their hand against God, and strengthen themselves against the Almighty; they run upon him, even on his neck, upon the thick bosses of his bucklers.

It is an old adage, and as true as it is old, "that experience keeps a dear school, but fools will learn in no other." Now, how wise these men become from experience, for though they have had repeated warnings, yet they seek peace and safety by again opposing their moral nature.

But does not this conduct evidently show that these men only pretend to disbelieve what they know is true, that they may furnish by doubting an excuse for sin? On what other conceivable principle can the fact be explained, that adversity does so effectually destroy their hopes, and compel them to close with the voice of God and of conscience? It is, therefore, evident that the scoffer's love of sin is so inveterate, that whenever urged to repentance and faith, he is necessitated, though he thus does violence to his moral nature, to shelter himself under the vain refuge of doubting the truth of God, that he may thereby have an excuse for continuing in sin.

Though the truth is attested by an overwhelming amount of evidence, when duly weighed, yet because this evidence is not given in such form as the sinner himself may capriciously choose, therefore he utterly refuses all evidence. So incredulous is he, as to reject the truth, though proved by the strongest evidence, and to embrace error though supported by the weakest. In this, his incredulity, he glories, because, in his opinion, it elevates him above the common herd of mankind, and evinces greatness and freedom of intellect. Women, children, and feeble-minded men may believe the word of God on the evidence which he has been pleased to give, but such credulity is beneath the dignity of great intellects and capacious minds. No, no. These persons cannot believe the truth when evinced to a certainty, but to show their incredulity must receive error, though disproved by all the evidence that boasted reason itself can adduce. To manifest their incredulity fully, it is necessary to take only one step more, and that is, to exhibit their principles in practice, which they do by "walking continually after their own lusts."

Thus their very practice furnishes no weak evidence of the truth which they affect to disbelieve. Having nothing but the subterfuge of a doubt to offer as an excuse for thus rebelling against God, yet they confidently demand, "Where is the promise of his coming?" "Where is the God of judgment?" But divine justice will not always slumber, and suffer these men to manifest this vain confidence; "for the day of the Lord will come as a thief in the night." "For when they shall say peace and safety, then sudden destruction cometh upon them, as travail upon a woman with child, and they shall not escape."

IV. Again, their folly will the more evidently appear, *because they suspend their highest interests on an unreasonable doubt.*

14   FOLLY OF DOUBTING GOD'S THREATENINGS.

Since "there is no work, nor device, nor knowledge, nor wisdom, in the grave," reason, as well as revelation, would teach us that every one should strive to make his calling and election sure, "while it is the accepted time and the day of salvation." But in opposition to the voice of God, of conscience, and of nature through all her works, the impenitent blindly, but wilfully, pursue their way of rebellion and death. "For if we sin wilfully after that we have received the knowledge of the truth, there remaineth no more sacrifice for sins, but a certain fearful looking for of judgment and fiery indignation, which shall devour the adversaries."

Man was created in knowledge, righteousness and holiness, and was endowed with these intellectual and moral powers, that he might, in all the works of creation and providence, behold and reflect the glory of his Creator, and find happiness in obeying his commands.

But the crown has fallen from his head, and all glory has departed from him. In consequence of the innate depravity of his heart, he now rejects the knowledge of the Most High, disregards the glory of his character, yields himself to the service of Satan and the dominion of sin, despises the Son of God and his salvation, and thus effectually destroys, not only his present, but eternal happiness.

While absorbed in the gratification of his passions, he esteems his own permanent well-being, the happiness of the universe, and the glory of the great Jehovah, as objects unworthy of rational pursuit—unworthy of the least regard. And when the gospel urges its claims on his attention, with all its power of appeal to the heart, he awakes from his lethargy only to doubt, and vainly wish for happiness in a course of disobedience and death. For if the gospel, with its promises and threatenings, is true, then the scoffer must perish; there is no alternative. But that it may eventually prove true is at least possible, and its bare possibility involves interests too important to be banished from the human mind, or for a moment to be neglected.

How great, then, must be the folly of those who doubt the execution of God's threatenings, and still more absurd does it appear, since on their very doubt the question turns of their eternal happiness.

But why is it, that the impenitent take so little interest in their permanent well-being, while they so zealously expend all their powers to lay up treasures on earth, "where moth and rust doth corrupt, and where thieves break through and steal." They never suffer a doubt to prevent their most strenuous efforts, while there is the least prospect of obtaining the objects of their carnal desires. A possibility of extending an empire will so arouse all the energies and ambitious hopes of an Alexander, or a Bonapart, that they will call into requisition all the resources of a nation, and jeopard the life of millions, merely to promote their own aggrandizement. Is there a possibility of the merchant increasing his means of earthly enjoyment by foreign commerce? Without reluctance he will expose all his property, though the product of his toil and exhausting labour for years, to the mercy of the raging storm and treacherous ocean. The same hope, excited by the success of others, inspires the heart of the poor and the oppressed, and calls into vigorous activity all their powers, to increase merely their present happiness.

What expense will the wicked, when assailed by disease, spare to secure their recovery, and prolong their life for self-indulgence? Such is their love of the world and fear of judgment, that a mere possibility of recovery elates them with hope, and makes them cling even to the last moment of life, as the wrecked mariner clings to a fragment of his shattered bark.

Now, can men of sane minds deem themselves wise, in sanctioning such conduct in respect to their temporal interests, and the preservation of their bodies, while they suffer an unreasonable doubt to blast the highest interests of their souls? Would not consistency of conduct absolutely demand, even on the mere possibility of the reality of religion, and of the truth of its promises and threatenings, that they should put forth vigorously their best directed efforts, to secure also their permanent wellbeing? But Christianity rests not on a bare possibility; its reality is attested by all the evidence which reason can ask for or desire. What, then, must be the inconsistency—nay, consummate folly, of those who not only suspend their own everlasting happiness on an unreasonable doubt, but also utterly disregard the well-being of the universe, and contemn the glory of the eternal God? "He that sitteth in the heavens shall laugh; the Lord shall have them in derision."

V. But this leads us to observe, finally, *that the doubting of the scoffer will not prevent the execution of God's threatenings.*

The punishment of the lawless and disobedient may be regarded as essential to the well-being of human government; and no principle of the divine government is more fully established than this, viz. that God will by no means clear the guilty. Both the law and the gospel declare that "the wicked shall be turned into hell, and all the nations that forget God." "According to their deeds accordingly he will repay fury to his adversaries, recompense to his enemies." "Though hand join in hand, the wicked shall not be unpunished. For he that believeth not the Son shall not see life, but the wrath of God abideth on him. He shall break them with a rod of iron; he shall dash them in pieces like a potter's vessel."

What, then, is the scoffer's strength, which he can exert in opposing himself to the truth and power of God? His feeble arm can oppose only a doubt and ridicule. With these he encourages himself to wage, as he fondly hopes, successful war against Jehovah, and the highest interests of his illimitable empire, as if Omnipotence was inadequate to crush every opposing power which the sinner can raise.

Oh what madness! what extreme folly! "He that planted the ear, shall he not hear? he that formed the eye, shall he not see? he that chastiseth the heathen, shall not he correct?"

But if the truth of revelation fails to enlighten and restrain the impenitent, they are nevertheless without excuse; for much of the nature of God, and of their duty, is revealed to them by the light of creation and providence. "Because that which may be known of God is manifest in them, for God hath showed it unto them." For the invisible things of Him, from the creation of the world, are clearly seen, being understood by the things that are made, even his eternal power and Godhead; so that they are without excuse. And if they regard neither the light of revelation nor providence, yet have they not the law of conscience, which is sufficient to establish the justice of their eternal condemnation? for all men do naturally the things that the law requires, which proves that they have a law in themselves, since they frequently act according to its rule. The work of the divine law is written in their hearts, by which they discern the difference between right and wrong—what is just and what is unjust.

If evidence can attest the truth, and facts evince the certainty, of the purpose of God to punish the disobedient, then the actual execution of all his denunciations could not furnish *stronger ground of certainty* than that which God has already given. Unless, therefore, one of two things can be proved, either that God does not intend to execute his threatenings, or that his power is inadequate, the destruction of the scoffer is inevitable. For if Jehovah has purposed by his only begotten Son to introduce and maintain his kingdom in the world, will he not, as all powers and agencies are under his control, roll onward unchecked the mighty wheels of his eternal government, though beneath them lie crushed his guilty feeble foes?

God's immutable justice, holiness, and truth demand the immediate and eternal punishment of the wicked, but through his abundant grace and mercy he condescends to expostulate with them, saying,

"As I live I have no pleasure in the death of the wicked, but that the wicked turn from his way and live; turn ye, turn ye from your evil ways, for why will ye die?" How strongly marked, therefore, is the folly of those who not only doubt the execution of God's threatenings, but also despise the riches of his goodness, and forbearance, and long-suffering, and dare to mock at every thing sacred.

God has predicted their fearful and eternal destiny, saying, "I also will laugh at your calamity; I will mock when your fear cometh; when your fear cometh as desolation, and your destruction cometh as a whirlwind; when distress and anguish cometh upon you." "Then shall ye return and discern between the righteous and the wicked, between him that serveth God, and him that serveth him not. For behold, the day cometh that shall burn as an oven; and all the proud, yea, and all that do wickedly shall be stubble, and the day that cometh shall burn them up, saith the Lord of hosts, that it shall leave them neither root nor branch. But unto you that fear my name shall the Sun of righteousness arise with healing in his wings."

Take heed, brethren, the professed disciples of the Lord Jesus, "lest there be in any of you an evil heart of unbelief in departing from the living God." "Stand, therefore, having your loins girt about with truth, and having on the breastplate of righteousness, and your feet shod with the preparation of the gospel of peace; *above all taking the shield of faith,* wherewith ye shall be able to quench all the fiery darts of the wicked." "Let your light so shine before men, that they may see your good works, and glorify your father which is in heaven." And in due time ye shall receive the fulfilment of the promise, that "they that be wise shall shine as the brightness of the firmament, and they that turn many to righteousness as the stars for ever and ever."

But, dear reader, are you still walking after your own lusts, and saying, in the language of the scoffer, "Where is the promise of his coming? Where is the God of judgment?" The riches of God's goodness and forbearance may be despised, his warnings and threatenings may be contemned, "but know thou that for all these things God will bring thee into judgment." Does not your own experience confirm the truth of God, that the way of transgressors is hard? If, therefore, your way is dark and portentous, what shall *the end* be?

Thus saith the Lord, "If I whet my glittering sword, and my hand take hold on judgment, I will render vengeance to mine enemies, and will reward them that hate me." Despise not thou the gracious invitations of redeeming love and mercy. Cease to incur the displeasure of Jehovah by doubting the execution of his threatenings. While it is the accepted time, fly to the Lord Jesus Christ, and secure, by repentance and faith, a refuge in him. For "he that believeth on the Son hath everlasting life, and he that believeth not the Son shall not see life, but the wrath of God abideth on him." If thou be wise, thou shalt be wise for thyself, but if thou *scornest*, thou alone shalt bear it.

THE WORTH OF THE SOUL.

BY

J. T. SMITH, D. D.

PASTOR OF THE SECOND PRESBYTERIAN CHURCH, BALTIMORE, MD.

For what shall it profit a man, if he shall gain the whole world and lose his own soul? Or what shall a man give in exchange for his soul?—MARK viii. 36, 37.

THESE questions are not of precisely the same import. They are addressed, indeed, to the same individuals, and relate to the same subject; but the individuals addressed are supposed to be placed in different circumstances, and the form of the question is modified accordingly. The first contemplates the condition of a man who has his chosen portion in this life, and demands of him the profit, "if he should gain the whole world and lose his own soul." The second contemplates the condition of a man in the world of despair, whose soul is already lost, and demands what he would be willing to give "in exchange for his soul." Both questions relate to the *comparative* worth of the soul. They affirm, in the most emphatic manner, that it is of *more* value than the whole world; and, upon the ground of its *surpassing* worth, they press the great duty of labouring *first* and *chiefly* after its welfare. I propose to detach the prominent idea of the text from the specific relations and connections in which it there stands, and to make THE WORTH OF THE SOUL, abstractly and absolutely considered, the subject of my discourse.

Need I here say one word to secure attention to this subject? You are proud of your extensive possessions, and you do not soon grow weary in telling over the sum of your riches. You have one treasure of great price, however, which you may never yet have rated at its full value. I propose, in this discourse, to estimate the worth of this treasure, and thus to show how rich you are. When such is my purpose, may I not hope for an earnest and interested attention?

Two distinct and independent tracks of illustration open up before us. We may enter upon a direct inspection of the soul itself, and from a survey of its nature, its capacities, its powers, and its destination, infer its value; and then we may take a wider range, and gather illustrations from without, and from the deep interest which higher orders of being take in its welfare; and from the high estimate which God places upon it; and from the history of its creation; and from the still more marvellous history of its redemption, demonstrate still further its value.

I. We are to sit in direct inspection upon the soul itself, to see if there be any thing in its nature, or its endowments, or its destination, which may serve our purpose. And

1. As to its Nature. Exhaustless variety is a striking characteristic of the works of God. It was

long ago remarked, that in the whole universe no two things can be found exactly alike. Resemblances we find every where, perfect similitude no where. And the remark holds good, not only of the external appearances of objects, but of their intrinsic worth. From the tiniest insect, one rank of being rises above another in excellence, till the whole terminates in that great sum of all excellence, that grand climax of all being—God. High up in this scale of value is found the human soul, standing at the head of all earthly existences, and ranking just a little lower than the angels.

The human body, delicately, curiously, and beautifully framed, is accounted the perfection of material nature—the very master-piece of the great Architect. But the body feels not, thinks not, wills not, acts not. It is but the blind tool of the agent within. Emotion, thought, hope, happiness, have their seat in the soul. The soul is yourself, the body is a mere appendage which you carry about with you, as you do your clothes. Your high prerogatives, as man, are all conferred upon you by the soul, and it alone elevates you above the dust. The body is built of the clay you tread beneath your feet. The eye, wonderful as is its mechanism, multiplied and spirit-like as are its uses, is nothing but painted dust; and the whole fabric is built of what you may see in the "deep damp grave." The confession so often on our lips, "we are but worms of the dust," is not the language of excessive humility. It is the plain, unvarnished truth. Whether we look to the origin or the end of these, our tabernacles of clay, we must own their fellowship with the worm.

What material object, then, can be compared, as to its value, with the soul? What utter insignificance does the apostle stamp on the whole material universe, when he tells us, "All these things shall be dissolved!"

Next above material organism comes animal instinct. And what are the instincts of animals but the reason of God? What teaches the bee to construct its cell, and the spider to weave its web, and the stork to build its nest on high? Who warns the birds of the approach of winter, and guides them, unerringly, in their long flights over trackless deserts and wide seas, without map or compass? The instinct of animals is the reason of God, prompting them to provide for their present and sensual wants. But the soul is endowed with an independent reason. Her instincts rise out of her own being, up towards God, and onward towards immortality—and over all, conscience, God's vicegerent, keeps watch and ward.

The soul introduces us into the higher walks of existence, giving us fellowship in the world of spirits, and companionship with God, and angels, and "just men made perfect," and partnership in their pleasures—the pleasures of intelligence and of virtue. If by the body we are linked to dust, by the soul we are allied to God. If by the body we say to the worm, "Thou art my sister," by the soul we are made the fellows of seraphim! What strange extremes unite in our being! The connecting link between God and the inferior creation. Our foundation in the dust, we aspire towards Divinity! The soul is of the *highest* order of existence—for God and angels are spirit. Immeasurably inferior to these, indeed, in the appendages and expansion of its being; in *nature* it is precisely the same. And across the wide chasm which now separates it from God, his voice is distinctly heard, and hopefully responded to—" Be ye perfect, even as your Father which is in heaven is perfect." What means the strange language—" Transformed from glory to glory into the image of the Lord"—" made partaker of the divine nature?" We can pardon the sublime dream of Plato, that the human soul is a portion of the divine essence—a fragment of Deity imprisoned in dust. It is of most excellent nature. Nothing on earth equals it—nothing in heaven surpasses it. Consider,

2. Its endowments. Activity, power, intelligence, moral agency, infinite progression, are among its higher attributes. Passing these, however, we would remark specially upon the capacity of happiness, perhaps the highest prerogative of spirit—" Man's chief end is to glorify God, and enjoy him for ever." If these ends of our being are not identical, they are at least inseparable; and the last grand purpose of our being is "to enjoy."

Happiness is a thing of which the visible world can furnish no emblem to those who have never experienced it. To be understood it must be felt. The gold which kindles such joy in the miser's heart, feels not the emotion it imparts. The heavens, which awaken the poet's fancy, and expand, to something of their own dimensions, the astronomer's intellect; which point the devotee upward to God, and scatter gladness, beauty, and life so lavishly over the earth, feel in themselves nothing of the glory or the gladness they impart. The sun is cold amidst his own beams—the stars are dark amidst their own radiance. Though so glorious to us, they are nothing to themselves. The earth is joyless, amidst all the pulses of joy which beat upon her surface. When the great Creator had made all—air, land, and sea, and filled them with exhaustless sources of happiness, he brings man, places him in the new made world, and says, The power to enjoy is yours; look around, above, beneath, all is exquisitely fitted to minister to your pleasure.

Every fountain of happiness in the outward world has some channel opened up, through which it empties itself into the soul. Has nature her harmonies?—the ear conveys them to the soul. The eye ranges over all that is beautiful and sublime in the universe of God, and carries back its discoveries to the soul. And thus, by her organs of sense, the soul ranges at will over the universe, and lays all nature under contribution to her happiness. But she has sources of joy, aye and of sorrow too, within herself; and it is when she shuts up the inlets of the external world, and retires within herself, that she finds the highest rapture or the profoundest despair. Uncover the soul of a saint, see his perfect peace, his high communings, his glorious hopes—there is a heaven there, were there none without! Uncover the soul of a sinner, see his remorse, his despair, his malignant passions, his fearful apprehensions of "wrath to come," there is a hell there, were there none without!

The soul's capacity to suffer and to enjoy we

cannot fathom. Do you ask, How much can I enjoy? We can but point you to those exhaustless materials of enjoyment provided; to your memories of all you have enjoyed; to your imagination, and your hopes; the many forms of happiness of which you can conceive, for which you hope, and of which you feel yourself capable. Nor can we tell how much you could suffer. Remember your head aches and heart aches; your pains and your sicknesses. Remember your disappointments, your fears, your despair. Have you ever felt remorse? But were the capacity of suffering filled to its full measure, we cannot tell, an angel's tongue cannot tell, how much you could suffer. And the capacity to enjoy and to suffer, stamps the soul with a value passing all calculation.

This is but our embryo state, and we cannot, even in imagination, fix any limit to the soul's progression. Give it a more delicately constructed—a *spiritual* body; give it senses more perfect in themselves, and in their adjustment to the objects of the outward world; let its eye have a wider range, a more piercing scrutiny; let its ear be more finely attuned, and its nerves increased in sensibility; give it new senses to discern those hidden elements of nature which now escape its closest scrutiny; remove its pride, its passions, its carnality; and then, when fitted for heaven, place it there. Afar from these earthly sources of pain and sorrow, surrounded with all heaven contains to happify, and who can tell what it shall become where its progress is ever accelerating, where every experience acquired enlarges the basis for future acquisitions, where every exertion put forth strengthens for a bolder and loftier attainment. Follow its ascending way on, and on, till imagination tires, and then think of it stretching on, and on, beyond that point out through the untold ages of eternity! Consider,

3. Its Destination. And here we might construct an impregnable argument for the immortality of the soul, out of the materials already collected in this discourse. The surpassing excellence of its nature, and its high endowments bespeak its immortality. For it consorts not with the wisdom or the known ways of God, to suppose him to endow it thus highly, and yet give it neither time nor facilities to develope and exercise its powers. Why give it capacities which are never unfolded? capabilities which are never called forth? powers which can go out into no adequate exercise? Its imperfect and undeveloped condition here is irrefragable evidence of its existence hereafter. Here it is the chrysalis—there the winged angel of light. This is its childhood—that its manhood. Did this life bound its being, it were but a gorgeous mockery, a solemn cheat.

The idea of eternity baffles and confounds conception. You are foiled in every attempt to compass it, because you have no measures by which to effect the computation. Take your own life as a measure; lay it along side of eternity, and it dwindles away to utter nothingness in the comparison. Take the six thousand years which have elapsed since the creation of the world; multiply them till numbers fail; still you have not reached a starting point in the computation. Conception is still at fault. Years, ages, cycles of ages, will not serve for measures of eternity. It absorbs all duration, and then stretches on, undiminished and unimpaired, to infinity beyond. No addition can increase it; no subtraction can lessen it. It has no measure, and it defies all conception.

It seems a long time to the prattling child to look forward to the gray hairs of eighty years. It seemed a long time to the spirits who first entered the land of darkness and despair, to look forward through the many ages of pain, and woe, and wailing which must elapse before the judgment of the great day. It seemed a long time to Abel, when he saw his name written first in heaven's register, to look forward through unnumbered ages till the last name should be written there. But these long periods of time all pass, and when looked back upon, seem but an hand-breadth. But there is no past in eternity; no future, no starting point, no goal, no beginning, no end. Now the existence of the soul merges into eternity; and here our conception of it is lost. It claims half the eternity of God. If not without beginning of days, it is without end of years. If not *from* everlasting, it is *to* everlasting.

How terrible the thought of an eternity of pain, an immortality in hell! The sting of the worm is, that it never dies! The fierceness of the fire is, that it is not quenched! How long eternity must seem when its every moment is lengthened out by misery! Imagine a lost soul ages hence, seated in its dungeon, or rolling in the fiery lake, and this may be its sad soliloquy:

"These limbs are not yet consumed. I feel no symptoms of death. I am stronger to suffer to-day than when I first felt these flames. And ever, as they burn higher and hotter, I feel my strength to endure, enlarging with them. I have tried to count the long years as they rolled by, but in vain. I cannot tell how many ages are gone; but eternity is still to come. I have wished, I have prayed, O! how earnestly, for death—but it mocks my prayer,

> 'I feel my immortality o'ersweep
> All pains, all fears, all time, all years;
> And, like th' eternal thunders of the deep,
> Proclaim this truth—Thou livest for ever.'"

Brethren, who among us shall dwell with the devouring fire? Who among us shall dwell with everlasting burnings? Shall it be yourself, or the neighbour, the friend, the child sitting by your side. Who shall it be *among us?*

How transporting the thought of an immortality in heaven! Imagine yourself for a moment there. With many of you it will be but anticipating what a few more days shall reveal. Sit down amidst the general assembly and church of the first born above—amidst patriarchs, and prophets, and apostles, and martyrs, the greatly good of every age and of every land, who are all contemporaries there. Go with Paul to his glorious mansion—standing near, perhaps next, to the throne; and look on the many mansions in your Father's house, stretching off on every hand in long perspective! Wander with Baxter along the banks of the river of life, as it comes gushing from the throne of God, and rolls its glad waters afar over the plains of heaven! Sit down with Payson under the shade of that tree, which bears twelve manner of fruits, and gives from its leaves healing and immortality to the nations! Rejoin the company of those who have gone up from your own fireside, and taken their crown! Among them all "there is no more death, neither sorrow, nor crying, nor pain." God himself has wiped away tears from off all faces. In the midst of the innumerable multitude, there is one "as it had been a Lamb slain." To him every eye is turned; before him every knee is bowed; at his feet every crown is cast; and from unnumbered harps, and from unnumbered voices, blended in heaven's loudest, sweetest song, swells high the anthem, "Worthy is the Lamb that was slain"—"unto him that loved us, and washed us from our sins in his own blood." To be ever "with the Lord"—this is the very heaven of heaven.

II. In passing to our second general topic, we notice,

1. The interest manifested for the soul by the higher orders of beings. We are not isolated or companionless in the universe. We are not alone, with God, even in the world. "Millions of spiritual beings walk the earth, both when we wake and when we sleep." Invisible to us, we are well known to them; and sharing a common spirituality, subjected to the same high authority, children of the same great Parent, they can have fellowship and family sympathy with us. The powers of darkness, with all their might and malignity, are leagued against us. Why did Satan tempt our first parents to their fall? Why does he so impiously usurp, and, as a strong man armed, so desperately defend, the empire of the soul? All along the way to heaven, is not every step contested? Are not all who travel

there called to the wrestling "with principalities, and powers, and spiritual wickednesses in high places?" Have you ever thought that the spirits of darkness hold a sleepless watch over you, and brave afresh the threatening thunders of Omnipotence, to maintain their mastery over you? When some subtle suggestion of evil has glided into your mind, or some sudden and lion-like temptation has fiercely sprung upon you, have you ever thought it came from hell— the result of counsel and deliberation there held?

And the holy angels—what wakeful sympathy and intense solicitude do they feel for us! Ministering spirits as they are, they leave heaven on no errand so gladly, as to minister to the heirs of salvation. "There is joy in heaven, among the angels of God, over one sinner that repenteth." The very first movement of repentance in the sinner's bosom, sends a wave of joy over all their bright and blissful abodes. "This our brother that was dead is alive again, the lost is found."

Were you, reader, while your eye is upon this page, to repent, we can tell you what would take place in heaven. The angels, who are watching around you, would send up some messenger with the glad tidings. As he sped upward with joyful haste, the band who stand at heaven's gate, or bend over its battlements, to receive messengers from distant worlds, would descry his approach, and come forth to meet him; and, as they learned the joyful tidings he bore, they would gather eagerly around him, and conduct him through the gates into the city, and over its golden streets, and amidst its trophied palaces, to the eternal throne. And all the inhabitants of heaven would be gathered, by proclamation, about him there; and your name and your repentance would be proclaimed aloud; for you are well known—known by name, in heaven; and they would call for the Book of life, and write, or rather read, there your name, and they would call for the book of God's remembrance, and blot out the record of your sins; and they would publish and proclaim your right to share with them, thenceforth, in the tree of life and in the holy city. And God, the eternal Father, would be well pleased that another rebel was subdued, another soul saved; and Jesus, the blessed Saviour, would see of the travail of his soul, and be satisfied; and the Holy Spirit would rejoice over his new and glorious creation; and angels would rejoice, that their brother, their younger brother, whom they had long mourned for as dead, was alive again; and the saints would raise high, and still higher, their anthem, "Worthy the Lamb that was slain." And perchance the mother who watched over your infancy, or the father who counselled your manhood, or the beloved friends who have gone before you to the spirit-world, would press through the throng, and Oh what speechless joy would thrill through their bosoms! And there would be joy in heaven, more joy in heaven over you, than over all those myriad hosts of bright and unransomed spirits who have kept their first estate. "There is joy in heaven over one sinner that repenteth, more than over ninety and nine just persons that need no repentance."

2. Let us take our stand upon another theatre—

amidst the opening scenes of creation. For long unchronicled ages, God dwelt alone, the sole inhabitant of space. From his solitary throne he beheld not an atom, nor a living thing; all was a mighty blank, a vast and empty void. God spake—and, responsive to his voice, planets, and suns, and systems sprang forth out of nothing. He poised the sun on its axis, balanced the planets in his hand, and marked out every star its pathway in the heavens; and the vast solitude of space, which but yesterday was empty, was filled with a universe of mighty, and moving, and peopled worlds. He spake, and the earth came forth out of nothing. It appeared in a hitherto empty place, without foundation, without support; suspended upon nothing—a huge, and formless, and floating chaos; and a thick darkness, a moonless, and rayless, and starless night, brooded over it. God spake—and there was light. And the wild waters flowed together into one place, and the dry land appeared, clothed with greenness and fertility, and order and beauty sprang forth from the very bosom of chaos; and the earth was fitted up as a well appointed mansion for living things; and exhaustless supplies were provided and garnered up for the provision of all their wants. But as yet there were no living things to partake or enjoy. God spake—and air, and land, and sea, were filled with a crowded population; the waters were stored with fishes, the fowls ascended on outspread wings towards heaven, and the dry land was covered with myriads upon myriads of living things, from the little insect which sports in a drop, or peoples a leaf, to the giant Behemoth which shakes the solid world with his tread. All these fed upon the bounty, and shared in the goodness, of the great Creator; and the hum of activity, and the voice of joy were heard over all the peopled earth. And the great Creator looked down upon the world which he had made, and filled with life, and sensation, and happiness, and said, "It is good!"

And shall the work of creation terminate here? Shall nature be furnished with no anointed priest? Shall God have no worshippers? Among all the myriad tribes of his creatures, shall there be none like himself? none to love, to reverence, and to adore him for all his goodness and his wonderful works? And was it for soulless creatures of dust, who are incapable of progression here, and whose existence must terminate for ever at death, that God reared up the mighty fabric of the universe? No. The work is not yet complete; the last and crowning product of creative power is yet to appear. "And God said, Let us make man." There was no consultation when the sun was made—none when the heavens were spread abroad as a curtain, and embroidered with stars. He just spake, and it was done; he commanded, and it stood fast. But now, when the lord and governor of earth is to be created, there is a pause, a preparation, a consultation. *Let us* make man. *So*, as the result of this counsel, *so* God created man. A simple word sufficed for the creation of all things else. A word called the earth out of nothing, and evoked order out of chaos, and the body of man out of dust. But a far higher instrumentality is employed in the creation of the soul. "God breathed into his nostrils the breath of life, and man became a living soul." A word is a thing foreign and external to the individual uttering it; a breath is an emanation of himself. And if all that God created by a word was alien from himself, the soul is the very "inspiration of the Almighty." And it is like God, modelled after him; a miniature likeness of him, as finite may be of infinite. "Let us make man in our image, after our likeness." If God had minded his power, his wisdom, and his goodness, in the other works of his hand, he would mirror himself entire in the human soul. For nothing but a spiritual and immortal nature could bear the full image and superscription of the Most High. His own image and representative, the soul, was invested with God's prerogatives —knowledge and dominion. Every where else the dominion of blind physical force was established, but the power of knowledge was conferred upon man. By this he was to disarm physical force; curb and direct the fury of the mightiest elements; subject the lower tribes of creation to his bidding; and have the dominion, not of the strong arm, but of the intelligent will over all the earth. Let them, (thus runs the great charter,) "let them have dominion over the fish of the sea, and over the fowl of the air, and over the cattle, and over all the earth." And when God had thus made man he said, "It is very good." And he blessed them, and "the morning stars sang together, and all the sons of God shouted for joy." With such high endowments, and in the midst of such august preparations, was man ushered into being, and proclaimed the lord and governor of earth—"a king and a priest unto God for ever and ever." Every circumstance connected with his creation, from the pause and the consultation which preceded, to the emphatic "very good" which crowned it, shows the high estimate which God placed upon the spiritual and immortal nature of man.

3. Let us take our stand upon another and a higher theatre; amidst the surpassing wonders of redemption. In creation the goodness of God operated freely without restraint or hindrance. No attribute of his own nature, and nothing without himself, interposed the slightest obstacle in the way of his breaking up the eternal silence and solitude of space, and peopling it with worlds. A simple volition, a naked putting forth of Omnipotence, was all it required to create. He spake to dust, and there rose up a human body. He breathed into that body, and man became a living soul; that is all man's creation cost him. But in redemption there were hindrances in the way; hindrances which Omnipotence alone could not remove. There was a compensation to be made, a satisfaction to be rendered, a harmony to be adjusted among the divine attributes, and a security to be obtained for the highest interests of all God's intelligent creation, before Omnipotence could stretch forth its arm to redeem. The very term *redemption* has a relation to price; and from the cost of the soul we may determine its real value. For it is a known law of divine action, that means are always accurately adjusted to ends—that more, or more costly means, are never employed than those which are necessary to effect

the end; and the price paid for the soul is thus a fair and an infallible index to its value.

Now, we know the cost of the soul's redemption. "Thou hast redeemed us to God by thy blood," is the song of the redeemed in heaven. "Ye were not redeemed with corruptible things, such as silver and gold, but with the precious blood of Christ." Where shall we find terms or illustrations wherewith to set forth the greatness of this price? Does not the apostle plainly intimate that we have no ideas at all adequate to this subject, when he tells us that we were not redeemed with corruptible things, such as silver and gold. It is by these "corruptible things" our ideas of value are represented. But "they that trust in their wealth, and boast themselves in the multitude of their riches"—the Barings and the Rostchilds of the earth—"none of them can by any means redeem his brother, or give to God a ransom for him." Let the princes of the earth heap their gold, and their silver, and their precious stones together; let the earth disembowel herself of her treasures, and the ocean give up her gems—and they cannot redeem a soul, for "the redemption of the soul is precious," too costly to be bought at such a price. It was himself the great Redeemer gave for us! Not a single act of obedience, or of suffering; not a treasure from his coffers, or a limb from his body, or a single pang of his Immanuel-mind—but *himself*. "He loved us, and *gave himself* for us."

Come, then, and view this "unspeakable gift." Come with angels, and see the great Redeemer stooping down from the throne of Godhead, laying aside his kingly crown, emptying himself of the worship and the blessedness of heaven. We know something of what he stooped *to*, but how little we know of what he stooped *from;* how little we know of what he *forsook!* Come with the shepherds to the manger of Bethlehem. And has the Lord of life and glory stooped so low? If an angel should voluntarily become a man, or a man a worm, it were for a wonder. But for Christ to descend so low— to cross the infinite chasm which separates him from the loftiest angel—to pass below angels—to descend the chain of being so far—to stoop from the majesty and blessedness of Deity down to the weakness and the infirmities of humanity—this passes wonder! God became man—a stable, a manger—not even a palace or a tapestried chamber. No wonder the shepherds said one to another, "Let us now go even to Bethlehem, and see this thing which has there come to pass." Come with the chosen disciples to Gethsemane. See the God-man stretched all night long in agony upon the ground! See the sweat, as it were great drops of blood, gushing forth and bathing his body. Listen to his cries of anguish, "My soul is exceeding sorrowful, even unto death." "O! my Father, if it be possible, let this cup pass from me!" "Was ever sorrow like unto his sorrow?" Come with the disciples to Calvary. See the victim, whom they have scourged and condemned to death, approach. A crown of thorns is pressed upon his bleeding brow—a heavy cross is laid upon his lacerated shoulders—and the rabble of Jerusalem are following him, with cruel mockings, as he is dragged along through the streets. "It is their hour, and the power of darkness!" They drive the nails into his hands, and feet, and then thrust the spear into his side. For six hours he hangs upon the accursed tree — bleeding, dying. There was not a friend to be near, or to comfort him then. Pharisees, and Sadducees, and Jewish priests, and Roman soldiers gathered, in stern array, around his cross, and wagged their heads upon him. He complains not of the friends who had forsaken him, nor of the enemies who so cruelly entreat him; nor of the nails or the spear, the vinegar or the gall. But one cry of anguish escapes him, "My God! my God! why hast thou forsaken me!" To be forsaken of God—that was the cup he trembled to drink—yet he did drink it to its very dregs.

But why all this? "God so loved the world as to give his only begotten Son" for its redemption. Not that he needed the world, for the word which created could destroy. His breath could have blotted it out of the universe, and called into being ten thousand other worlds, unblighted by the curse, and peopled by beings higher and holier than we. What was that world which God so loved? Not this material world, for it is but dust, and soon will be burned with fire. Not these bodies, for they too are dust, and soon will be nothing but food for grave-worms. What was that world which God so loved? That miniature world in your own bosom. In his estimation it was too precious to be lost—too precious to be annihilated; and he gave the most hoarded and priceless treasure in his whole empire to purchase it; and Christ from the throne of heaven stooped down to the pain and the ignominy of the cross to redeem your soul.

But the payment of the purchase-price alone cannot redeem the captive. It is the office of the Holy Spirit to embellish and beautify. He is at once the beautifying spirit of the material, and the sanctifying spirit of the moral, universe. Where he comes not, all is darkness and chaos; where he comes, all is light, and order, and beauty. In the first creation the earth "was without form and void," and "darkness was upon the face of the deep," until the Spirit came and brooded over the chaotic waters. In the new creation, he fits up a world of moral light and beauty out of darkness and chaos. The soul is in ruins; her jarring and discordant powers at war with each other, and with God; and the darkness of ignorance, of error, and of sin, broods gloomily over her. The Spirit descends, and moves upon this spiritual chaos; rebuilds and embellishes; and, though active voluntary resistance is put forth against him, though often grieved, and often quenched, never tires in his work, until the soul is crowned with more than its pristine honour and glory, and fitted for the "inheritance of the saints in light." Even in her deepest degradation the whole Godhead gather around the soul, to raise it up again to heavenly places; and in the mystery of its redemption we find the grand crowning evidence of the worth of the soul.

Allow me, in conclusion, to gather up this whole subject, and throw its entire weight, as an emphasis upon the question of our text — "What shall it profit a man, if he shall gain the whole world, and lose his own soul?". It is but a small portion of the world any one individual can hope to possess. You, however, are supposed to obtain the whole. The dream of universal dominion is realized by you. You are crowned a monarch; the broad earth is your empire, and you reign without a rival or a foe. Every land pours its treasures into your coffers. Gold and silver and precious stones glitter around you. The luxuries of every climate are spread profusely upon your table. Crowds of obsequious servants anticipate your slightest wish. When you appear, in your gilded equipage, among the multitude, they say, "It is a God." And to the remotest corner of your empire—in the snow huts of the pole, and under the spreading palms of the south—your praises are sung, and all delight to "do you reverence." They watch your slightest look, and chronicle your every word, and obey your every nod. Pleasure waits evermore in your train, and holds her enchanted cup continually to your lips; and you have no wish ungratified, no hope unfulfilled—for you have gained the whole world. And what will all this profit you, if you lose your own soul? Will it fill the aching void within? Will it ease you of a single pang? Will it rob death of his sting? Will it pour the light of life and immortality into the darkness of the grave? Will it buy you a single drop of water, when you are tormented in the quenchless flames? Will it bribe you an entrance, through the gates, into the city? And where will be your empire, when the world and all things therein shall be burned with fire? You may now feel but little solicitude about your salvation. Amidst the pressure of your business, and the hurry of your pursuits, and the tumult of your passions, heaven and hell may seem too far off to demand much attention. Amidst the clamourings of the appetites, and the distractions of the outward world, the soul may seem too impalpable—its wants and its aspirations too ethereal—its rewards and its punishments too spiritual, to share largely in your thoughts. There is a strange madness in the human heart. While all heaven and all hell are bending over you with unutterable solicitude, and enlisting their sympathies and their mighty activities in your cause, shall you alone be thoughtless and indifferent amidst all the movements which are circling around you? Have you alone no interest at stake? Why stand you here all the day idle? Just starving for the bread of life, wherefore "spend your money for that which is not bread?" Your eternal salvation to work out, wherefore "spend your labour for that which satisfieth not?" Can you sleep under the uplifted thunderbolts of angry Omnipotence? Can you go smiling and sportive onward, when " your way is dark and leads to hell?" "Awake, thou that sleepest, and arise from the dead, and Christ shall give thee light."

THE FAITHFUL SAYING.

BY

WILLIS LORD, D. D.

PROFESSOR IN THE THEOLOGICAL SEMINARY, CINCINNATI, OHIO.

This is a faithful saying, and worthy of all acceptation, that Christ Jesus came into the world to save sinners.—1 TIM. i. 15.

LET us analyze this saying. Let us separate its ideas, that we may give to each a distinct, though brief, consideration. Let us seriously mark their aspect and bearing with reference to our own character, course and destiny.

I. "*Christ Jesus* came." We bid you notice this fact as essential to the power and glory of the evangelic doctrine. The grandeur of the person gives grandeur to the truth affirmed concerning him.

For whom do the words "Christ Jesus" designate? Beyond question, the Son of God. They do indeed express only the name he bore after the incarnation; but by constant usage of the scriptures, they then denote the person who became incarnate. Differing modes of existence and manifestation did not destroy the divine and eternal personality. The Word was made flesh, but in the flesh thus made he was still the word.

The affirmation, then, is of a divine person—the Son of God—second in the mysterious subsistence of the infinite three. *He* came. Not an angel of light; not a saint in glory; not Gabriel, who ministered peradventure nearest the burning throne; not Moses or Isaiah, most exalted perhaps among the redeemed. No—not they; but *He* came by whose power Gabriel and his angelic associates were created, and by whose blood the lawgiver and the prophet alike were saved. At that sublime moment, when the eternal counsels were about to be expressed in the great acts of redemption, and because the exigencies of lost men transcended the wisdom and power of all creatures, it was the voice of Christ Jesus which broke upon the silence of heaven— "Lo, I come to do thy will, O God!"

The fact is incontestable—its importance and grandeur infinite. For how can the purpose and endeavours of such an one fail? What possible contingencies can arise, not foreseen by his omniscience? What combination of difficulties so great, that they must not vanish before his wisdom and power? If God undertake for the lost, no matter how extreme and appalling their state, they will be rescued.

This truth, we repeat, is essential. It is the foundation of the Christian system. If the victim on Calvary was not the incarnate Word—God though man, and man though God—the hope of salvation, by his obedience and death, is a dream. It may be thought by some consoling, inspiring, joyous, but it is a dream, to be dissipated for ever when we enter the grave. There never was a more absurd notion, than that salvation can be achieved for sinners by a creature. Show me that Christ Jesus was not truly divine, and, by the same argument, I will show you that he cannot be a Saviour. And if he be not, who is? What shall dying men do, if they may not rest their souls on Christ, as the Son of God—the brightness of the divine glory, and the express image of the divine person? What can they do, but die without hope—yea, die for ever!

II. This divine Being came, continues the text, *into the world;* i. e. into this world.

Very many worlds God has made, of still greater extent and magnificence than this, to circle with it, in its majestic course around the centre of the system; but in no other have been enacted the scenes of redemption. It is an exclusive distinction of this world, that by the Church redeemed and existing on its bosom, is made known unto principalities and powers in heavenly places, the manifold wisdom of God, according to the eternal purpose, which he purposed in Christ Jesus our Lord. Bethlehem and Calvary are here. The garden of that untold agony—the sepulchre, hewn out in the rock, where the Prince of life lay in the embrace of death—the Mount of Olives, whence he ascended, leading captivity captive—all these are here.

The influences of the cross doubtless, indeed, reach to the outmost limits of God's vast creation, making manifest, as could have been done by nothing else, the wisdom, love, power and glory of Jehovah. But here the cross was reared. Its base was imbedded in the soil of earth; its top was fanned by the air and bathed in the light which fall upon us. Christ Jesus came into *this* world!

How did he come?

Not merely, does the apostle mean to say, in his essential and universal presence, as God. In this sense our world has been his dwelling-place from the morning of creation. His arm has upheld the stupendous structure. His power has constantly renewed the face of the earth, and carried forward all the processes and operations of nature. For as he created, so does he sustain all things by the word of his power; by him all things consist.

Nor did he come, does the apostle mean to say, in the form and presence, which anciently he so often assumed, as the angel of the covenant. It was thus he appeared to the patriarchs and saints of former dispensations. It was thus he was present with Abraham at that strange sacrifice on Moriah, and the day before the fiery overthrow of Sodom and Gomorrah. It was thus he revealed himself to Jacob at Peniel, in that wondrous conflict wherein the patriarch prevailed with God. It was thus he went before his people in the wilderness, when he said, Surely they are my people, they will not lie; so he was their Saviour. In all their affliction he was afflicted, and the angel of his presence saved them, and he bore them, and carried them all the days of old.

It was another and more marvellous presence of the Son of God the apostle contemplates—his presence by incarnation in the son of Mary, in reference to which the angel said to the shepherds, "Unto you is born this day a Saviour, which is Christ the Lord." "Who being in the form of God, and thought it not robbery to be equal with God, made himself of no reputation, and took upon him the form of a servant, and was made in the likeness of men." For "forasmuch as the children are partakers of flesh and blood, he also himself likewise took part of the same." And so " the Word which was in the beginning with God, the Word which was God, by whom all things were made, and without whom was nothing made which was made; the Word became flesh, and dwelt among us, and we saw his glory, the glory as of the only begotten of the Father, full of grace and truth."

In this manner "Christ Jesus came into the world." It is a stupendous truth. It would exceed belief, as it does comprehension, did it not rest on the testimony of God; and if, furthermore, immeasurably vast and mysterious as it is, we could not see its divine adaptation and imperative necessity in reference to us as sinners. We have been startled, my brethren, at recent and passing political events. They seem to us great—momentous. To see kings abdicating; thrones and princedoms falling; the masses, so long trampled beneath the hoofs of power, rising; and then the re-action, the crushing again of hope, the re-ascendance of despotism, and the suppressed heavings of outraged humanity, while the whole aspect of human things becomes dark and perilous—oh, how all this engrosses the minds of thoughtful men! And yet inexpressibly tame, trivial, empty, are these things, in comparison with the unique, unparalleled, infinite truth, that "Christ Jesus came into the world;" that being God, he was found in fashion as a man; that occupying the throne, and receiving the adorations of the universe, he came down to the dependance of a creature and the reproach of worms; that the source of all authority, he made himself subject to law; and the fountain of all life, he came under the power of death; that, compelled by no perils that were invading his presence, but moved by the miseries which were overwhelming us, he came; that, the King of kings, and the Lord of lords, he came to raise us to his own blessedness, to invest us with his own glory, to make us kings and priests unto God for ever!

For mark, now, the complete statement of the text, that,

III. "Christ Jesus came into the world *to save sinners!*" We must form our estimate of Christianity from its real nature and design. If we conceive of it wrongly, we shall judge of it unfairly. In its influence indeed on all the faculties, and all the interests of men, it bears the proof of its divine source, and of its power for good. It has ameliorated the physical condition of the race; it has given impulse and expansion to the mental powers; it has imparted tenderness and purity to the social and domestic affections. Civilization has followed in its progress. Commerce and the arts have flourished in its presence. Literature and science have felt no other influence so genial and enriching. Where it has reigned, law has become the expression of justice, and government the safeguard of liberty. It is impossible to over-estimate the legitimate and benign effects of the gospel of Christ, on the entire condition of men, as the denizens of this world, as well as the heirs of immortality.

But, then, these effects have all been indirect and secondary, as compared with the main purpose for which "Christ Jesus came into this world." That purpose was "*to save sinners.*" If you contemplate his mission and work apart from the light of this vast central truth, you may yet see much in them to admire, but you will fail to comprehend their real grandeur and glory. Jesus Christ, my brethren, was far more than a social or civil reformer, attempting to dry up the streams of human degradation and misery, while he left untouched their prolific and inexhaustible fountain. He was far more than a master in philosophy, who came to solve the problems of science, and elaborate systems of morals and metaphysics, after the manner of Plato or Aristotle. He was far more than a jurisconsult or statesman, whose mission it was to announce legal and political maxims, and propose models of constitutions and governments. He was a Saviour! The objects of his grace were sinners. They had broken the law of God. They had incurred his holy displeasure. They had yielded themselves as the bond-slaves of Satan. They were therefore sinking, helpless and hopeless, to eternal ruin. Christ Jesus came to *save* them.

How save them? In the evangelic sense, what is salvation? The inquiry is important. In the scriptures themselves the term is relative. It is sometimes used without any reference to that great spiritual and eternal deliverance contemplated here. A man may be saved from sickness, danger, fear; from a great variety of evils, merely temporal. The term, therefore, must have its meaning in each several instance, from that of which it is the contrast. Christ Jesus came to save *sinners.* Salvation, then, in this case, must be understood by the present character and condition of those who are to be its subjects.

Who, then, and what are sinners? In what condition are they? They are those who have apostatized from God, and broken his law. That law is perfect, eternal, unchanging. Its demands can never be mitigated—its sanctions must be enforced. It is preposterous to think of any other alternative. The earth and the heavens may pass away, but the law of God, in its undiminished authority and extent, and its retributive power, must remain for ever. It cannot pass away.

The effect of this violation of the law is twofold.

In the first place, it changes the *relations* of men to the divine government. They are thenceforth condemned. The fearful penalty of sin is denounced against them. Its execution may be delayed, but at length it must come. From the absolute perfection of the law, there is no possibility, for one who has sinned, of regaining his position and immunities as an innocent man. Guilty he must remain. The penalty, therefore, must be exacted. It is eternal death.

In the second place, it changes the *affections* of men towards God. The very nature of the soul is vitiated by sin. What was pure and perfect becomes defaced and polluted. Love to God gives place to aversion and hate. All the moral faculties are perverted and defiled. Selfishness becomes the master principle or affection. Self, the reigning God. If the divine law, therefore, did not for ever bar sinners from heaven, and subject them to woe, their own depraved nature and sinful passions would.

The salvation of sinners, consequently, has respect to their legal condemnation, and their moral depravity.

To be effectual, it must remove the curse of the law which is upon them, and it must form them anew in the likeness of God. Under this conception of it, "Christ Jesus came into the world to save sinners." Immense, we repeat, and never enough valued, are the benign influences of his coming and work on the social, intellectual, and political condition and prospects of men. He gave the most salutary precepts. He enjoined and exemplified the most pure and heavenly affections. He announced the essential principles of truth and righteousness, and demanded of all men, through all time, affectionate and holy submission. His words have been light to the mind, and life to the soul. Wherever they have been permitted to go forth in their fulness and purity, they have regenerated society, and remodelled governments. They are achieving social and civil results now, in view of which hoary oppression trembles. O! if while they are giving to the masses the knowledge of their rights, they shall also be received far enough to awaken within them the sense of their responsibilities—to lead them to identify rational and enduring liberty with the spirit and principles of the government of God—who can express what scenes of prosperity and happiness may yet appear! If men will obey the gospel—Europe, yes, the world shall be gloriously free. If they will not do this, agitation and revolution are in vain. Despotism may indeed give place, at every now and then, but only to a more desolating anarchy. And anarchy, after a little, will lash itself into exhaustion, and subside in the embrace of a still more absolute despotism. The essential elements and means of social well-being, mental elevation, and political freedom, are in the instructions and institutions of Jesus Christ.

The mission, however, of the divine Redeemer related directly and chiefly to the souls of men. He came to save *sinners*. Is it inquired again, How save them? The answer is, by delivering them from the condemnation of the broken law, and by renewing them after the image of God, in righteousness and true holiness. This is salvation. Less than this is not salvation.

But this question, thus answered, throws us back on a greater question. How can sinful men be delivered from the curse of the law? Helpless they are. They cannot meet its demands. They cannot satisfy, except by enduring its terrific penalty. While they are condemned by it, and utterly without strength, it must remain, in its precepts and its sanctions, unchanging and eternal. How, then, can sinners be saved?

In the verdict of enlightened reason, two conditions must concur in order to this result.

The principle of substitution must have a place in the government of God. As by no possibility those who are condemned by the law, can deliver themselves from its curse, it results, that if they are saved at all, it must be by the interposition of some one not thus condemned, in their behalf, who can and will meet for them its claims and its penalties. If in their case there can be no substitution, there can be no salvation.

This substitution, moreover, must be made by one whose personal character is not only holy, as for instance, an unfallen angel, but who also is not originally subject to the law. It would be manifestly impossible for any one, whose own obedience was demanded, and to the extent (as from the essential perfection of the law it must be) of *all* his affections and faculties, to render an obedience in behalf of others. This condition, therefore, excludes every creature, whether man or angel, from the work of saving sinners; for every creature is under law—under law which exacts and exhausts his whole powers in obedience for himself. To find that a qualified substitute for the guilty, we must go beyond the sphere where the law of God has jurisdiction! And where is that? Oh! where is that? No where, except within the splendors of the uncreated glory! No where, except with reference to Him who sits upon Godhead's throne! The result is clear and irresistable. There must be a divine Saviour, or there can be no Saviour!

The inquiry was one of infinite moment; will God interpose? Will He, whom we have sinned against, and by whom we are so righteously condemned, will he, can he, interpose? Thanks unto his name, grateful as we can render and eternal as our being, God has interposed! "Christ Jesus came into the world to save sinners!" The simple, yet wonderful announcement, involves all that we have thus represented as indispensable to salvation. For gather up now into one view what it does involve.

The Word was God. He was God before he came in the flesh. He remained God after he thus came. The two natures, in mysterious union, constituted one divine person, Jesus Christ. He owed no obedience to the law, therefore, on his own account.

He was the supreme Lawgiver. His subjection to it was voluntary, even when he became incarnate. He was made under the law, not as the inseparable result of his being born of a woman, but according to his own will, that he might redeem them which were under the law. His whole obedience, therefore, and his whole endurance, were available for those for whom he obeyed and suffered.

For this interposition of the divine Redeemer was not for himself. It was vicarious. It was made on the declared principle of substitution—the just for the unjust. Indeed, as it could not be on his own account, who had never sinned, and needed no salvation, it must have been for the sake of others. And so the constant testimony is, " he bore *our* griefs and carried *our* sorrows. The chastisement of our peace was *upon* him." " He bare *our* sins in his own body on the tree."

Substitution involves imputation. The two are inseparable. They are essential parts of one whole. If Christ obeyed the divine law, and endured its penalty in my stead, and for my benefit, that obedience and endurance are mine, by being set to my account; or what is precisely the same thing, by being imputed to me. And this truth is perfectly intelligible. Men recognise it, and act in accordance with it, in the most common, as well as the most weighty, affairs of life. The principle on which it rests is incorporated in all law, and exemplified in all government. It is worse than folly to attempt to expel it from the word and government of God. Despite all human opinions and reasonings it will remain eternally true, that " as by one man's disobedience many were made sinners, so by the obedience of one many shall be made righteous;" that God "hath made Him who knew no sin, to be sin for us, that we might be made the righteousness of God in him!"

The result now of these truths is indeed glorious. In his incarnation, in his obedience, in his unexampled sufferings and death, Jesus Christ was the substitute for sinners. Who can express then the hope that thus comes to the lost? For though he became man, that he might obey and might die, Jesus Christ was yet God. The worth, therefore, and the sufficiency of his atonement are immeasurable; as much so as is his divinity. Contemplated in its essential nature and intrinsic efficacy, it is absolutely without limit. You may compare it to the horizon, which, as you approach it, ever recedes and widens. Or you may compare it to an ocean, whose depths reach no bottom, and whose waves break on no shore. But all comparisons fail, all language, and all thought, are beggared in the attempt to express or conceive the illimitable fulness and sufficiency of the atonement.

But there arises a difficulty here—a difficulty which at times presses on serious and thoughtful minds. The penalty of the law is death. To meet and endure that was requisite in order to atonement. How could Christ Jesus endure this penalty?

It *is* a difficulty, and perhaps it were both more wise and reverent to recognise the impracticableness of its full solution now, and silently wait for the light of eternity. Thus much, however, is obvious, that a penalty must adapt itself in its actual infliction to the nature, and be affected by the dignity, of the being on whom it may fall. So the penalty of the divine law, while remaining the same in its own nature, must manifestly become different in some respects when inflicted on different orders of creatures, as on angels, and on men. Hence this point has sometimes been represented thus: "All creatures must endure the penalty of the law, if it fall on them, for ever, because they are finite. The eternity of their woe is thus incidental; i. e., it results, not of necessity from the law, but from their nature. The duration of suffering, therefore, is not absolutely necessary to the proper infliction of the penalty by *whomsoever* endured, but it is thus necessary when endured by those who are finite; i. e., by creatures. The Son of God, however, was not a creature. By virtue of his divine, and, therefore, infinite nature, or being, he could exhaust in a limited period that penalty which a creature could never exhaust. It indeed assailed him. It beat upon his humanity. It bore him to the very gates of hell, but his divinity broke the fierceness of its power. It cried out for blood. Its cry was inexorable—unceasing. Along the flight of weary centuries, it had made even the altar and the temple of Jehovah's worship the place of slaughter. Nor could it be satisfied with the life of beasts. It kindled on the souls of men. It drank up their spirits. It burned on from generation to generation. But when it reached the sacrifice on Calvary, the son of man, yet also the Son of God, its rage was spent, its power destroyed. It could not long grapple for the mastery with an uncreated arm. It kindled fiercely on his humanity, and wasted it. It burned towards his divinity, and expired!" "He hath redeemed us from the curse of the law, *being made a curse for us!*"

It is thus, brethren, that Christ Jesus saved sinners from the condemnation of the law. The remaining exigency of their condition he meets by sending into their souls the Holy Spirit. By his presence and power they are made alive from the dead; they exercise new and sacred affections; they become partakers of vast and immortal hopes; in every taste and susceptibility of their moral being; they are formed and fitted for the glorious and eternal kingdom of God. So great, so entire, so enduring is the salvation by Jesus Christ.

IV. In reference to all this we now add, "*it is a faithful saying.*" It is no more immense and wonderful than it is true. It is to be believed, therefore, without fear and without hesitation. Every sinner this side of death may rest his soul on it securely.

The *testimony* of God demonstrates its truth. Over and over again the Scriptures present us with the doctrine of atonement by Jesus Christ. Every where they reveal him as a divine person; though now, for the purposes of redemption, in mysterious but real association with humanity. Every where they represent his obedience even unto death, and in death as vicarious, as in the place and for the benefit of sinners. With the clearness and vividness of a sunbeam they trace these words, and such as these— "He was wounded for our transgressions, he was bruised for our iniquities; on him was laid the iniquity of us all." In the view of his cross, and as the divine solution of the appalling sacrifice there, they exclaim, "Herein is love, not that we loved God, but that he loved us, and sent his Son to be the propitiation for our sins!" Yea, that "God so loved the world, that he gave his only begotten Son, that whosoever believeth in him should not perish, but have everlasting life!"

The *influence*, moreover, of this blessed doctrine, when it is really received, demonstrates its truth. All those effects which it is designed to produce are realized. The sinner is forgiven. He has peace with God. He has the witness of the Spirit. His affections are changed. The objects of his supreme desire and pursuit are new and sacred. He takes pleasure in spiritual things. He becomes increasingly like Christ. His life is a service to God. His death even is a victory over death, and his eternity is heaven.

Yes, beloved brethren, it is a faithful saying. Patriarchs believed it, though to them the great sacrifice was still in the distant future. Prophets foretold it in their most glowing and majestic strains, and they trusted in what they thus foretold. Apostles proclaimed it, and rejoiced that they might seal their testimony with their blood. Martyrs confessed it, and its celestial power was that which took their terror from the fiercest flames. Multitudes in every age have borne witness by lives of holiness and deaths of triumph, that "Christ Jesus came into the world to save sinners!" Oh! men and brethren, must the sacred succession stop? Shall this faithful saying have no more witnesses here? Is it possible that you should feel you do not need the blood of atonement? Or can you suppose for a moment, that in the flow of ages its fulness is exhausted? You do not need it if you have never sinned. It is exhausted, if that which is infinite can fail. But neither the one nor the other of these things is true. You have sinned—often, long, fearfully. The atonement of Christ remains, and will remain, in its undiminished fulness and glory; and, therefore, worthy,

V. As the apostle finally adds, "*worthy of all acceptation.*" The meaning is, it is worthy of a prompt, cordial, grateful, whole-souled reception by sinners, and by all sinners.

Shall we stop to say, that *all sinners need* this salvation? They do need it. No necessity can be more obvious or more imperative. Under the divine government, where there is sin, there must be atonement, or there must be death. This necessity grounds itself in the divine nature. Justice is an essential, and therefore immutable attribute of God. It is inseparable from his being, as much so as his spirituality — his infinity — his almighty power. Should he therefore cease to be just, he would cease to be God. For him, therefore, to pass by or forgive sin, on the ground of mere sovereignty, or expediency, or general benevolence, irrespective of the great principles and claims of justice, we hold to be impossible; as clearly and inexorably so, as it would be for him to be unjust. The necessity of atonement, therefore, in the case of sin, and if it be pardoned, is absolute. Where it is not found, the sinner must die. Are you sinners? You need then an atonement. You all need it. There are no creatures in the wide universe who have a more personal or a deeper interest in the saying — that "Christ Jesus came into the world to save sinners." In the truth of his atoning sacrifice is your only hope for eternity. In your acceptance of and reliance on that sacrifice, by faith, is all your salvation!

Or shall we detain you to repeat that this salvation is *sufficient* for all sinners? It certainly is thus sufficient. We speak, of course, of its essential nature and fulness. Viewed in itself, the sacrifice on the cross has a worth, and adequacy absolutely unlimited. They are restricted only by the revealed purpose of God to apply the atonement to those alone who believe. This purpose does indeed exist; and, like God himself, it is immutable. How could it be otherwise? No remedy can be effective, unless it be applied. It may possess the most unquestionable and powerful healing properties—but what will these avail, if the diseased and the sick will not use it? God gave his Son, that whosoever *believeth* in him may have everlasting life. But, wonderful as was this gift, illimitable as were the virtue and merit of the sacrifice so made, he that believeth not must perish. It is God's own averment. The atonement itself, with all its fulness of grace, power and glory, cannot save those, who by unbelief persist in rejecting it as the ground and means of salvation. That there are such persons, and will continue to be, the history of men and the word of God render certain. But the limitation of the atonement so resulting, is from causes external to itself. It remains still in its own glorious all-sufficiency. If sinful men will receive it and rely on it, no matter who they are, nor how many, nor how multiplied or grievous their sins, it will be effectual; it will save them. If they will not receive it, the die is cast; there is no atonement for them; they must perish in their iniquities. It is a result certain as the being of God. It is a result demanded and secured by every principle of fitness and right, by the perfection of the divine character, and the inviolability of the divine government.

Do you, then, believe in Christ? Will you believe in Christ? In this case the atonement is divinely sufficient. There is not a sin against you, in the book of God, which, in view of it, will not be forgiven. There is not a stain of guilt upon your soul, which, through its efficacy, will not be washed out. There is not a want of your immortal being, which, for the Redeemer's sake, will not be freely and for ever supplied. Oh, it is indeed "a faithful saying, and worthy of all acceptation, that Christ Jesus came into the world to save sinners!"

My brethren, worldly themes occupy you. Truths like these seem to you perhaps foreign, unattractive, spiritless. The scenes of time, which ever flit by you, like shadows, are in your view real and important. Well, they are so. They have a significance deeper than you are aware. They have a relation to eternity, solemn and fearful. They have an imperishable record before God; a record to be read in the judgment. But forgetful of this significance and this relation, you contemplate these scenes in only their present aspect. Such is their power over you, that we fear you will still turn away from the cross, but if you do, remember, "Christ dieth no more!" We fear you will still close your hearts to the glorious truth, that "Christ Jesus came into the world to save sinners;" but if you do, remember "there remaineth no more sacrifice for sins!" The great work of expiation is finished. It stands before you God's amazing provision for the wants of men; unexampled—sufficient—alone. In view of it, he demands now your decision. It is for you to receive Jesus Christ and live—or to reject Jesus Christ and die.

THE RULING PASSION.

A SERMON TO YOUNG MEN.

BY

W. B. SPRAGUE, D.D.

PASTOR OF THE SECOND PRESBYTERIAN CHURCH, ALBANY, N. Y.

The heart of the sons of men is fully set in them to do evil.—ECCL. viii. 11.

In connection with

Thou shalt love the Lord thy God with all thy heart, and with all thy soul, and with all thy mind.—MATT. xxii. 37.

THERE is scarcely any thing in relation to which men are so jealous as their own rights; and scarcely any question, which they scan with such severe scrutiny, as who shall be their rulers. Let some important post of civil authority be about to be filled, and you will hardly find a man in the community who is indifferent to the pending question; and not improbably there may be a tempest raised, that will make the very foundations of society rock. And so, too, men are eagle-eyed to discern the first symptoms of oppression. If rulers are disposed to be tyrants, their subjects quickly find it out; and even if they have not the courage to resist, or complain, they are still galled by the yoke, and would make an effort to throw it off, if they could. Liberty every man regards as his dearest possession; and whoever discovers a disposition to trifle with it, need not marvel, if he is met with the spirit of resistance.

But it happens, a little strangely, that those who are so jealous of any external encroachment upon their rights, too often manifest little or no concern in respect to the more important dominion in their own bosoms. They will spare no pains to investigate the character of the candidate for some paltry office, the influence of which may only slightly affect them, while yet the world within may be completely subject to one tyrant or another, without their ever taking note of the fact that they are oppressed. In the hope of disturbing carelessness, and enlightening ignorance, on this subject, I design to address you on THE RULING PASSION—*its nature—its origin and growth—its influence.*

The general topic upon which I am to dwell obviously connects itself with each of the passages which I have cited. The first—"the heart of the sons of men is fully set in them to do evil"—is a declaration that mankind not only, on the whole, prefer the wrong, but that they choose it, and pursue it, with the utmost intensity of purpose. The latter —" Thou shalt love the Lord thy God with all thy heart, and with all thy soul, and with all thy mind" —is God's requisition upon the children of men, to give Him their supreme and perpetual homage. I have brought together the two passages, because one exhibits the ruling passion for evil—the other, the ruling passion for good; and both will necessarily be brought into view, in the contemplation of the general subject.

I. Our first inquiry respects the *nature* of the ruling passion. What is it that we designate by this appellation?

The ruling passion, in the most general sense, may be defined—*the concentrated energy of the soul.* I am aware that this is a legitimate subject for philosophical disquisition; and that, viewed in this light, much might be said upon it, that would be both true and useful; while yet the well-defined boundaries of human knowledge should not be passed. But the time, the place, every thing connected with the occasion, limits me to the more practical view. The definition that I have given, is perhaps as plain as the nature of the subject will admit; but be that as it may, every individual may know infallibly what it is, if he will make suitable observation upon his own experience.

The ruling passion may be considered in a more general, or a more restricted sense.

In the more general sense, it consists in the prevalence of a sinful or a holy temper; in other words, in that state of the soul which constitutes man either the enemy or the friend of God.

It is obvious, alike from Scripture and from experience, that man, in an unrenewed state, lives chiefly for his own gratification; that his chosen element is amidst the things that are seen and are temporal. This the Saviour expresses, by "loving darkness rather than light;" and the Apostle, by "minding earthly things;" and the wise man in our text, by "the hearts of the sons of men being fully set in them to do evil." And who need be told that all experience coincides with this record? While there are many professing to be Christians, who belie their profession by an apparently supreme devotedness to the world, how manifest is it that the multitude who make no profession, are actual idolaters of the world in some form or other! Their thoughts, their affections, the combined energies of their souls, are employed upon, actually fastened to, the things that must perish with the using. It is by no means necessarily implied that they are profane, or dishonest, or immoral in any sense; or that they are destitute of naturally amiable and benevolent dispositions; or that they may not perform many acts that shall have an auspicious bearing upon the welfare of society, and even upon the interests of the church; but after all, they are lovers of the world more than lovers of God. Their ruling passion is towards the earth. They have no heart to relish, nor even an eye to discern, the things that are spiritual. Such is the condition of man—of every man in his unrenewed state.

But when the renovating act has once passed upon him, new objects of affection and pursuit rise before his mind, and its energies receive a new and correspondingly noble direction. From having had a heart fully set in him to do evil, his ruling desire now is to love the Lord his God with all his heart, and all his soul, and all his mind. True, he is yet a miserably imperfect being, and he often has occasion to lament that when he would do good evil is present with him; and sometimes, perhaps, he is in doubt whether he is not still in unbroken bondage to his lusts. But whatever may be his imperfections, or his apprehensions, or his conflicts, the current of his soul is really moving towards God; his strongest desire is, that God may be glorified in him and by him. And this desire discovers itself in a new course of action. It may not, indeed, be new in every sense; it may not be new to the undiscerning eye of man; for it is quite possible that the external deportment of an unrenewed person, under the more general influences of Christianity, may be scarcely distinguishable from that of the true Christian; but it *is* new to the heart-searching eye of God, because it is prompted by a new principle, and directed to a new end.

I have said that the ruling passion, considered in a more general sense, is that sinful or holy temper which constitutes the moral state of man as the friend or enemy of God—in a more restricted sense, it is the particular form which that temper assumes— the channel through which the energies of the mind, whether working for good or evil, chiefly operate.

On this point I may be contented to refer you to the results of your own observation. Whether you look into the world, or into the church, or, I may add, into your own hearts, provided you will compare your experience with that of others, you will find a diversity in the ruling passion corresponding to the variety of human pursuits. All bad men are alike in general—that is, in being supremely devoted to their own selfish gratification; but they differ endlessly in respect to the form in which the evil tendency develops itself. In one, the ruling passion is the love of wealth—in another, the love of praise— in another, the love of pleasure—in all, the love of the world. And the same remark applies to *good* men—while love to God and man is the great principle that presides over all their actions, and gives the general complexion to their character, even this principle discovers itself in a variety of forms—one may be more serious and devout, another more active and philanthropic; one may become absorbed in one field of benevolent operation, another in another; and the energies of each may be directed, possibly too exclusively, in his own particular channel; while yet the actions of all, when they come to be referred to the remoter cause, are found to be dictated by the same spirit. So much for the nature of the ruling passion.

II. Our second inquiry relates to its *origin and growth*. We shall still keep in view the distinction already recognised, considering it in a more general and a more restricted sense.

If we consider the ruling passion as consisting in the general temper of the soul, constituting the individual a sinner or a saint, we shall find, of course, that it has a different origin, as it partakes of a sinful or a holy character.

In the former case, it is evidently to be referred to man's original apostacy. That mankind are born with a propensity to evil, is proved by the same kind of evidence that proves their original propensity to eat and drink; for if the latter is developed a little earlier, the former discovers itself as soon as the nature of the case will admit—namely, with the first indications of moral agency. If there are any who choose to deny this fact, our appeal is to universal experience—even to those very cases which are brought to prove the opposite doctrine; for amidst the utmost sweetness and loveliness that early childhood ever exhibits, if you watch narrowly, you will find the workings of an evil propensity—evidence that the spoiler has been there, sowing the seeds of moral death. For the reason of this state of things, we can go no farther back than Paul carries us, when he says, "As by one man sin entered into the world, and death by sin, so death hath passed upon all men, for that all have sinned." Any other theory of the origin and transmission of human depravity than this declaration clearly implies, is unphilosophical, and inconsistent with palpable facts. I say then, man derives his sinful nature, his ruling passion for evil, directly from the great ancestor of the race. In the shock of the apostacy the gold became dim, and the fine gold was changed.

And whence does the Christian derive *his* ruling passion for good? I have, in a measure, anticipated the answer under the preceding head—from the renovating, life-giving agency of the Holy Spirit. The Bible every where attributes this work to the Spirit, without, however, explaining minutely the manner in which it is performed. It is this to which the Prophet refers, when he says, "Not by might, nor by power, but by my Spirit, saith the Lord." And again, "A new heart will I give you, and a new spirit will I put within you; and I will take away the stony heart out of your flesh, and I will give you an heart of flesh." To this also the Saviour refers, when he says, "Except a man be born of the Spirit, he cannot see the kingdom of God;" and the Apostle also, when he speaks of being saved, "by the washing of regeneration, and the renewing of the Holy

Ghost." The amount of all that we know on this subject is, that the Spirit of God operates in some mysterious way, by means of the truth, and in accordance with the laws of our moral nature, to the production of a new moral state of the soul, a new ruling passion, a strong relish for those spiritual objects which the individual once regarded with indifference or disgust. He is himself conscious of the change, from an inspection of his own inward exercises; and others take knowledge of him that he has been the subject of the change, as both his words and actions breathe a new and heavenly spirit. You may impute the change to something else than a divine agency; you may say that there is some mysterious power that resides in man's own will, by which spiritual life rises out of spiritual death; but the subject of the change repudiates such an intimation. He will tell you that he is a monument of divine grace, a living witness to God's mercy and power in the transforming work; and that *but* for this gracious interposition, his heart would still have been fully set in him to do evil.

But if such be the origin of the prevailing temper or habit of the soul, both for good and evil, whence originates the particular form which the good or evil temper assumes? In other words, whence originates the ruling passion, considered in a restricted sense?

Doubtless it is to be traced in most instances, primarily, to the original constitution of the mind—to the elements of the intellectual and moral nature, as they are supplied by the Creator Himself. No doubt there is a diversity in the original character of men's minds, corresponding to the variety which we see in their external appearance; and hence we find that children of the same parents, educated by the same teachers, and subjected, so far as possible, to precisely the same training, not unfrequently become widely different in their characters; and *that*, irrespective of that radical change which may, or may not, have been wrought in them by the Spirit of God. Here, no doubt, in all ordinary cases, is the seed of the ruling passion; and the mother, if she is watchful, may not unfrequently detect its incipient growth, while the child is yet in the nursery. If you will write the history of the man, who, in a fit of revengeful passion, shed his brother's blood, and has had his own blood poured out as an offering to public justice—his mother, if she still survives to tell the story of his childhood, and if she could bring herself to speak out all that is lodged in her memory, would not improbably tell you that she saw that terrible passion in her son, while it was yet in embryo; and that nothing has happened to him that was not shadowed forth to her anxious spirit almost before he left the cradle. And so, on the other hand, if you will trace the history of some individual whose life has been but an unbroken succession of deeds of mercy, and whose name quickens the pulsations, and draws forth the tears, of the inmate of many a hovel, you will not improbably learn, that those who watched over his earliest years had often admired the beamings of a kindly and generous spirit in his infantile smiles. Not that there is any thing here to excuse vice; for these evil propensities belong to a moral agent, and he is bound to see that they are eradicated, instead of being indulged. Nor is there any thing, on the other hand, of which the good man has occasion to glory; for the graces of nature, not less than the Christian virtues, are from above—the former are the production of a creating, the latter, of a new creating agency.

I have spoken of the origin of the ruling passion —let us now, for a moment, contemplate its *growth*. This is to be referred to the influence of habit and to the power of circumstances.

It is a law of our nature that the repetition of any act increases the facility with which it is performed; and hence, we find that that which is originally difficult soon becomes easy, and that which is, at first, indifferent, becomes, at no distant period, like a second nature. Notice the operations of this principle wherever you will, and you will always arrive at the same conclusion. I point you to the poor drunkard, who stands before you completely brutalized, though immortal; whose nearest friends cannot bear to look upon him, because he is the very personification of idiocy or loathsomeness. There was a time when he was first conscious of the existence of that deadly appetite, and when he began to indulge it, he dreamed not how fearfully strong it was destined to become; but each successive act of indulgence strengthened the propensity, till now, as you see, it holds him with a giant's grasp. Look, too, at the miser! The passion for accumulating and hoarding up may have originally had a prominence in his moral constitution; but it was not *so* prominent, but that, in the earlier part of his career, he could sometimes show himself public-spirited, and perhaps even devise liberal things. By long continued indulgence, however, this sordid passion has gained the complete mastery over him, so that he is as deaf as an adder to the claims of charity, and even to the cries of absolute distress. And the same principle is illustrated in the growth of a habit of philanthropy. Wilberforce was originally possessed of warm and generous sensibilities; but it was the fact of those sensibilities being always kept awake—the fact of his devoting his life to the cause of the negro's freedom—that made him tower into such a glorious example of benevolence as the world has rarely seen. And if we consider the ruling passion in the more general sense, as denoting the sinful or holy nature, it is by this same influence—the influence of repetition, that the sinner becomes more and more a sinner, the saint more and more a saint. Possibly, to the eye of man, there may be no very perceptible change, either in the one case or the other; but to the Omniscient eye the moral state of the soul is changing continually; not an action is performed, not a volition exerted, not a thought cherished, for good or evil, but it has some bearing upon the permanent state of the soul—that which emphatically constitutes its character.

The other influence, to which is to be referred the growth of the ruling passion, is that of circumstances. It is a familiar but true remark, that men's characters are formed, in a great degree, by circumstances; and this effect is produced chiefly through the development of the ruling passion. True, as we have already seen, this passion grows immediately by succcessive acts of indulgence, but then there is the remoter influence of circumstances, in which these acts of indulgence usually have their origin; and where the favourable circumstances do not exist of themselves, the ruling passion not unfrequently creates them, and then acts itself out by means of facilities of its own devising; and, on the other hand, circumstances not unfrequently exert an influence to neutralize, even to change, the ruling passion. Let a child, in the first developments of its moral nature, betray a prevailing inclination to some particular form of vice, and then let it be placed in a condition which furnishes little or no temptation to that species of indulgence, and it is quite likely that some other propensity, originally of less strength than that, may gain the controlling power of the soul, and may keep it till the end of life. There is a tradition that Robespierre was originally of a gentle and sympathetic turn; and that it was owing to his infidel and bloody training that those horrible passions, which finally made him the terror of all history, gained such a malignant ascendancy in his bosom. But whether this tradition be correct or not, it admits of no question that circumstances often decide what passion is to be in the ascendant; and that they sometimes decide in favour of one which, in its earliest actings, had betrayed no indications of uncommon strength.

III. I pass now to the third and last general topic, viz: the *influence* of the ruling passion.

And my first remark, in illustration of this, is, that this passion has the mastery of the whole intellectual, moral and physical man.

It has the *intellectual* faculties completely under

its dominion. It has its own ends to accomplish, and it employs these faculties as servants to aid in their accomplishment. See how this remark is illustrated in particular cases. Mark that individual, whose heart is supremely set upon the honour that cometh from men, and observe how his intellectual powers are all laid under contribution for the attainment of it. His perception and judgment are always in a wakeful state, that he may be able to avoid every thing that is adverse, to avail himself of every thing that is favourable, to his particular object. His memory is continually tasked, that he may take advantage of the lessons that are furnished by the past—perhaps by his own past experience, whether for good or evil. His reasoning faculty, his power of invention, is put into vigorous exercise, that he may, if possible, devise some new facilities for securing to himself the plaudits of his fellow men. And when you have noticed how completely the whole intellectual man is brought into subjection, where the ruling passion is for the honour that cometh from man, look at another individual, and see how the same thing is accomplished, where the ruling passion is for the honour that cometh from God only. What that devoted Christian is striving after, is a crown of immortal glory; and which of his intellectual faculties, think you, finds a dispensation from the glorious work on which his heart is supremely set? Is it the perceptive faculty? But the eye of his mind is continually open to behold the truth, not only in its reality, but in its excellence and glory. Is it the judgment? But without this in constant exercise, how is he to ascertain what is true and right; in other words, what he is to believe, and what he is to do? Is it the memory? But it is the memory that supplies him with his materials for gratitude and humiliation, for meditation and devotion. Is it the reasoning faculty? But it is by means of this that he is constantly growing in spiritual knowledge, and without it he could never be more than a babe in Christ. Believe me, the ruling passion for the heavenly crown allows no one of the faculties of the mind to remain unoccupied. I do not mean that they are occupied to the extent tha they might be or ought to be, for that would be to make no allowance for an only partially sanctified state; but I mean that they all act *prevailingly* under the influence of the controlling desire of the renovated heart—the desire to glorify God in the attainment of immortal glory.

But the ruling passion extends its dominion to the *moral* man, as truly as to the intellectual; in other words, it controls all the subordinate passions, including also the animal appetites, together with the higher principle of conscience.

Observe, first, the influence which it exerts in neutralizing, or keeping in check, those passions or appetites which, if their operation were not restrained, would be found to conflict with it. If you were to judge of the miser by the coarse fare upon which he subsists, and the miserable tattered garments in which he clothes himself, you would say that he had no taste to distinguish between the coarsest and most delicious food; and that, as for his clothing, he would as soon appear in rags as in robes. But the truth is, he has, just like other men, his own natural preference for at least decent food and clothing, and possibly he may have had originally strong sensual or ostentatious tendencies; but the ruling passion for hoarding up is keeping these other tendencies in check, so that you would scarcely know that they belonged to his original constitution. And you might arrive at a similar conclusion in respect to the devoted Christian. If you were to judge of him by the moderation which he discovers in respect to all worldly enjoyments, you might conclude that he had naturally little or no relish for them; whereas he may naturally possess a very strong relish for them; but his ruling passion for spiritual and heavenly enjoyments has so far prevailed, that it has brought him to look upon them with comparative indifference. No matter what form this passion may take, it will always show itself mighty to keep the other passions in subjection.

Nay, it does more than this; it exerts an influence of a yet more positive kind, in rendering the other passions and appetites even subservient to its own ends. Let the love of fame, for instance, be supreme in the bosom, and see how it will employ the love of money in aid of its own gratification; for great wealth confers a kind of distinction that ambition often greatly covets. Or let the love of God be supreme, and see how the naturally benevolent dispositions and sympathies, even the admiration of whatever is graceful, or beautiful, or sublime in nature, are all brought into exercise in aid of the homage that is due to the Almighty Parent. In every case, indeed, in which there is not an absolute contrariety between the ruling passion and the subordinate principles of our moral nature, the former bends the latter to its purposes, constituting them, according to its own character, a good or evil ministration.

Moreover, the ruling passion acts with mighty power upon the *conscience*—that principle of man's nature which confers upon him his highest dignity. And it does this in two ways—as it gives complexion to the testimony which the conscience renders, and as it affects the character of the conscience itself.

I may appeal to the experience of every one for the fact, that conscience has a mighty influence in rendering man happy or miserable; and whether the one effect or the other is to be produced, depends upon its decisions in regard, either to particular actions, or the general moral state of the soul. As the ruling passion is, indeed, nothing less than the moral state of the soul, from which also the particular actions of the life take their complexion, it is obvious that this must supply the materials from which the decisions of conscience are formed; and that, as this has a good or evil direction, supposing conscience to perform its legitimate office, the soul is the seat of peace and joy on the one hand, or of tumult and terror on the other. Who is that wretched being, who is holding a communion of agony with himself, in some solitude which man's eye does not pierce? Ah! it is a man, who, in obedience to the strongest impulse of his nature, has murdered his fellow, or done some other desperate deed, which at present is known only to himself; and there is not a single circumstance that would seem to indicate the least danger of exposure; and yet conscience mocks all his efforts to be at rest, by filling his ear with sounds concerning the terrible future. And who is he that feels and evinces such a heavenly tranquillity, amidst the vicissitudes of life—that is not only patient, but even joyful in tribulation? Why, it is a man who knows no desire so strong as that of glorifying God, and benefiting his fellow creatures; and as he travels on from day to day, in his beneficent and upward course, he is cheered continually by the whisper of an approving conscience, and tormenting fears find no lodgment in his bosom. In each case, this mighty inward agent has been moved to diffuse terror or peace through the soul, by the ruling passion.

But this is not all; for the ruling passion affects the character of the conscience itself. What if the heart of an individual be fully set in him to do evil— do you believe that the conscience will be in no danger of sustaining an injury from such an influence? When the ruling passion first begins to operate in a course of sinful indulgence, conscience of course remonstrates; and as these remonstrances give pain, the mind is put upon devising some means of relief, without yielding up the favourite indulgence. And, generally, it does this by at first palliating, and afterwards excusing altogether the course upon which it is bent, calling evil good and good evil, putting bitter for sweet and sweet for bitter. And this process, especially when long continued, is found to act upon the terrors of remorse like a charm, and conscience at length becomes so torpid, that the ruling passion can act with the fury of a whirlwind, and not awaken it. The conscience is not dead, after all, but it has become diseased, lethargic, insensible. And, then, on the other hand, what if the individual be under the controlling influence of a principle of love to God and man—do you imagine that there will be no effect exerted upon the conscience by the operation of *this* principle? I tell you there will be a mighty effect. While the conscience will bear testimony in favour of the ruling passion, and of the course of action to which it prompts, the ruling passion will, in turn, enlighten, and quicken, and purify the conscience. So we find it in actual experience. The farther the Christian advances in the spiritual life, the longer he has yielded obedience to the impulses of his regenerate nature, the keener his discernment becomes for the nicest shades of both good and evil. He walks in a region of spiritual light, and he is in little danger of mistaking the character of the objects which appear in it. He is in intimate communion with the Lord of the conscience, and by such intercourse surely the conscience must be elevated and improved.

I only add, under this article, that the power of the ruling passion extends to the *physical* nature. I have already intimated that it extends to all the animal appetites, unless indeed it may chance itself to be identified with one of them; and then it will in some way exercise control over the rest, either by keeping them in check, so that they shall not interfere with itself, or else by making them minister to its own gratification. It extends also to the whole body—the hands, the feet, the lips, move in obedience to its dictates. It extends not unfrequently even to the bodily health, for where it happens to be identified with any one of the animal propensities, it takes but little time for it to make perfect shipwreck of the body. And even where it is seated more directly in the mind—where, for instance, it is ambition, or covetousness, or revenge, it not unfrequently acts with a consuming energy upon the bodily constitution; while, on the other hand, where it takes a virtuous and benevolent character, operating in kindly affections and philanthropic deeds, it ministers to the general health of the body, and even verifies the declaration of the wise man concerning Wisdom, that "length of days is in her right hand."

A second general thought, illustrative of the influence of the ruling passion, is, that it decides both the character and the destiny.

It decides the *character*, inasmuch as it makes the man what he is; for though the original materials, of which the character is formed, are supplied by the Creator, yet they are worked into one form or another, according to the direction which the ruling passion may happen to take. It is the ruling passion for evil that constitutes the sinner—it is the ruling passion for good that constitutes the saint; and conversion is nothing else than a change of the ruling passion from evil to good. If we consider virtue and vice as operating through particular channels, then we may say that it is the ruling passion that constitutes the traitor and the tyrant on the one hand, the patriot and the philanthropist on the other. That this *must* decide the character in view of God, who searches the heart, is self-evident; for as it constitutes man what he really is, so Omniscience cannot but see things just as they are. And it decides the character also in the view of men. In all ordinary cases, it is so manifest as to preclude all just reason for doubt; and even where there is a studied and constant effort to conceal it, it will be almost sure to work itself out through innumerable channels. Those even who attempt to practise the greatest duplicity—such are the arrangements of Providence —generally pass on the whole for nothing more than they are worth; for though it may never have occurred to you to inquire what the ruling passion is, it is from your observation of the operation of that passion, in their daily conduct, that you form your estimate of their character.

And if it decides the character, it decides the destiny, of course; for man's destiny is nothing more than the condition in which his character places him. In the present life, it must be acknowledged, that a man's external circumstances are, to some extent, independent of his character; and he who lives only to curse society, and treasure up wrath against the day of wrath, may be surrounded by the splendours and luxuries of life; may have every thing at his command to minister to a sensual or ambitious spirit. But the truth is, there is an illusion about this; there is not the happiness here that there would seem to be; and perhaps there are as many in these circumstances who find thorns in their pillows, as there are in the humbler walks of life. But if a man's earthly condition is to be estimated by the amount of happiness which he finds in it, then, as a general rule, the character decides the destiny even here; for there is that in virtue that will find sources of enjoyment in adversity; there is that in vice that will transmute the richest temporal blessings into a curse. And if this connection between character and destiny is manifest even in this life, much more will it be so in the future. Nothing less than this, surely, can be conveyed by the language of the apostle—" They that sow to the flesh, shall of the flesh reap corruption; and they that sow to the Spirit, shall of the Spirit reap life everlasting;" and by that declaration of the Saviour, which He makes as Judge of the world, "These," *i. e.* the wicked, "shall go away into everlasting punishment, but the righteous into life eternal." The ruling passion then constitutes the character; the character decides the destiny; the destiny beyond the grave never changes. Who can estimate the influence of the ruling passion, when it is to decide the condition of both soul and body for ever?

The power of the ruling passion may further be seen in the influence which it exerts upon other minds—upon a community—upon the world.

There are various channels through which men exert an influence upon each other, and upon society at large. There is persuasion, here addressed to the private ear of a friend, and there, moving and melting an immense assembly. There is example, which, though it operates silently as the dew, and by an influence not unfrequently unperceived by the individual who is the subject of it, yet often accomplishes its ends, where all other influences would fail. There is pecuniary contribution, which can assist largely in causing order and beauty to come forth where there was desolation, or in causing desolation to take the place of order and beauty. There is civil polity and military prowess, by which the destinies of states and nations are often settled. There is the press, all powerful to bless, all powerful to curse. There is prayer, that takes hold even of the Almighty arm. Now all these are but the instruments by which the ruling passion operates for the accomplishment of its purposes. It does not, indeed, always work directly; and it may sometimes seem to be operating in one direction, when it is really operating in another; as, for instance, the love of fame may possibly make a man appear exceedingly humble, or self-denied, or benevolent, when in his heart he is an utter stranger to all these qualities. But, either directly or indirectly, the ruling passion exerts an influence upon the whole tenor of the life; and when an individual finishes his earthly course, if you could get at the complete history of his ruling passion, you would have the record of whatever he had done for the benefit or the injury of his race.

Would you see what the ruling passion has been able to accomplish in some memorable instances? Look, then, at Napoleon. His ruling passion was the lust of dominion. And it nerved his arm till his arm became a rod of iron. It hardened his heart till his heart became a rock of adamant. It constructed yokes for the nations, as if they had been but cattle. He moved his hand, and a mighty city was swept off as with the besom of destruction; he moved it again, and an immense army was struggling in smoke and blood; and again, and the great ones of the earth came bending to him to take the chain. His career marked a new epoch in history. His influence was like the whirlwind, except that the whirlwind is the thing of a moment, but his influence will last for ever. Look at Washington. His ruling passion was that of a patriot—it was the desire to see his country free, and good, and great; and under its influence, he became the very personification of wisdom, and valour, and magnanimity; and while he broke the chain that bound us, bequeathing to us our inheritance in these glorious institutions, he set an example to the world, which has done more than any thing else to render the throne of the tyrant, at this hour, an insecure and uncertain thing, and which is destined to tell with mighty power on the ultimate civil regeneration of the world. And, finally, look at Paul, whose ruling passion was pre-eminently a desire to glorify his Master, and save the souls of his fellow men. How intrepid it rendered him in danger, how patient in suffering, how untiring in labour, how glorious in death! And who shall tell how much he achieved for the benefit of the church and the world? It was through his influence especially that Christianity darted abroad among the nations like the beams of the morning; that light came out of darkness, and life out of death, where darkness and death had for ages held their undisputed empire. And wherever, to this hour, Christianity has set up her dominion, it is not too much to say that the hand of Paul has in some sense been in it; for it is only the carrying forward of the work which he had the honour so gloriously to begin. Had he been constituted with the same powers that he actually possessed, and had his ruling passion been for blood and conquest—instead of being remembered in the thanksgivings of earth, and the yet higher thanksgivings of Heaven, his name might have appeared only on some dark page of history, as the name of a scourge and a destroyer.

I only add, in illustration of this point, that the ruling passion is for ever growing stronger. It may indeed be changed from one direction to another—considered in the more extended sense, it always *is* changed in every case of genuine conversion; and considered in the more particular sense, it is sometimes changed, independently of conversion; but it still remains true that, so long as it holds the ascendancy in the soul, it is, on the whole, always increasing in strength—the only even seeming exception to this remark arising from the decay of the faculties in which it may happen to be seated. Its operation in certain forms may indeed be temporarily suspended, through the influence of circumstances; but let the circumstances change, and if the ruling passion be not changed, it will be found to have gathered fresh strength from the check that has, for a time, been imposed upon it. I have marvelled sometimes to see how strong it has been in adversity, and even in death. I have seen the drunkard turning himself into a beast, when his own wife lay in her dying agony. I have known the gambler turn away from his mother's new made grave, to his accustomed haunts of delirious revelry. I have known the miser's very death dream to be about gold; and he has seemed to dread death chiefly because it must separate him from his earthly treasures. And even where the terrors of adversity, or the glooms of the last hour, may, for a moment, silence the sinner's ruling passion, unless God's Spirit interpose to change it, it will certainly re-appear, and act with more than its former energy.

And this leads me to say that the ruling passion will grow stronger in the next world. Admit, if you will, that it may be modified in respect to its particular character; modified by the new circumstances and objects by which it is surrounded. Be it so, that the miser may no longer care for his gold, nor the sensualist for his cups, nor the ambitious man for his laurels; and, on the other hand, we *know* there will be no objects in the abodes of the blessed to awaken or to demand the exercise of a spirit of compassion; nevertheless, the concentrated energy of the soul, for good or evil, will remain unchanged—the sinner will be reaching a more dreadful stature in sin, the saint a more glorious stature in holiness, through all the ages of an eternal existence.

But who, after all, can say that the ruling passion of the sinner *may* not exist in the next world, in precisely the same form that it does in this, with this terrible difference, however, that there shall be no object to minister to it? Suppose the craving appetite for sensual indulgence, the burning thirst for power, the sordid desire for wealth, to have gathered a thousand fold deeper intensity than the voluptuary, the ambitious man, the miser, ever felt on earth; and suppose each to be shut out from all the means of gratification; and suppose the ungratified passion to be for ever growing stronger as the ages of eternity roll away—Oh! tell me, ye who have known something here of the bitterness of cherishing desires that could not be met, tell me whether any thing beyond this is necessary to complete the idea of hell.

Oh how terribly, how gloriously, this thought, that the ruling passion is to grow stronger for ever, bears upon the future! How it magnifies, beyond any measure that our conceptions can reach, the misery of the lost—the happiness of the saved!

Fix your eye upon a man whose outward demonstrations are such, that you cannot even doubt that his ruling passion is for evil. Possibly, he may appear decent enough in his ordinary intercourse; but whoever knows him well, knows that he is revengeful—that it is in his heart to pursue the man who he imagines has injured him, even to the death; knows that he is profane—that he will, even in cool blood, insult the majesty, and defy the vengeance, of Heaven. If you could see him at certain times, when his passions are wrought up into a tempest, the mixture of rage and blasphemy that you would witness, would make you turn from him with shuddering, as from an incarnate fiend. All this, while he is yet in the body, and subject to the numerous restraints incident to the present state of existence. Keep your eye upon him a little while, and you shall find him a lost spirit; and now mark how that ruling passion for evil, which before seemed so strong, has gathered a degree of strength that mocks at the imbecility of all its previous operations. Mark off a million of ages from his existence, and see how you find the ruling passion then. You may talk of a giant's power, but that conveys no idea of the actual reality. You may collect every image of overpowering strength, and of unqualified horror; you may combine the darkness of midnight with the fury of the storm, and let the flashing of the lightning, and the rolling of the thunder, be the terrible accompaniment, and still you will have nothing that will more than faintly shadow forth the might and the misery seated in that sinner's bosom. And who has thoughts far reaching enough to overtake eternity? And yet eternity, eternity is the field on which the ruling passion is to have its perpetual development! I know not all the ingredients in the cup of trembling, which is put into the hands of the wicked in the next world; but it is enough for me to know, that the ruling passion for evil, whose operations sometimes terrify me here on earth, will not only be an everlasting inmate of the bosom, but will wax more fierce, and strong, and terrible, for ever.

Now, look at the man whose ruling passion is for good, and take the measure, if you can, of the happiness which he enjoys, of the good which he accomplishes, in its progressive and eternal development. As you see him here, bearing afflictions with undisturbed tranquillity, encountering difficulties with an overcoming faith, traversing the dark valley with an unfaltering step, you feel that the upward tendencies of his spirit are strong; and you are not afraid to see him die, because you are satisfied that his is the good man's death. But, even in all this, you have seen the ruling passion of only an imperfect Christian. Wait a little, till he has passed the heavenly portals, and you may contemplate that of a glorified saint. Lay every thing else, that may enter into the idea of future bliss, entirely out of view—

I am sure you will not doubt that here, in the saint's own bosom, and at the first moment after he has entered Heaven, is enough to constitute the eternal weight of glory. But, here again, look ye down through the vista of future centuries, fasten upon the remotest point to which even your imagination can reach, and the ruling passion for doing good and glorifying God, shall be acting with an energy that is the result of the steady growth of all the millions of ages that have intervened. And that shall be the starting point for a new course of development that shall make all that has preceded appear feeble and infantile. Saint in heaven, I lose myself in the contemplation of thy destiny! Be thou where thou wilt in God's dominions, that ruling passion of thy soul, ever active and ever growing, will keep thee entranced with the glories of Heaven.

Oh that I could write, as with the point of a diamond, on the memories and hearts of all our young men, the great practical lessons which this subject suggests to *them;* that I could show them how intimately it connects itself with all their responsibilities and prospects. Many of you, I doubt not, have already set your affections on the things that are above, and are running for the heavenly prize; but others of you, I have reason to fear, are making haste for the accomplishment of your own ruin. You are dreaming that the present is the time for indulgence, and that the future will be the time for repentance; that it matters little what you do now, in the days of your youth, as there will be time enough to retrieve your errors in the graver period of your maturity. As to the probability of your ever seeing that period, I leave it to your own reflection, after you have walked through any burying ground you please, and noticed how large a proportion of the grave stones mark the departure of the young; but the point which I wish to urge upon you is, that you are, imperceptibly to yourselves, forming a habit of indifference to religion; that each successive act of indulgence, or even procrastination, lessens your power to resist temptation, and increases the probability that you will never repent; and that, when the anticipated period for giving your hearts to God shall come, you may find yourselves so entirely under the dominion of your own lusts, as to be discouraged even from any attempt to escape. I say, then, your own dignity, your own safety, your own immortality, protests against this habit of delay; and if you open your eyes you will see "Danger," "Danger," written in letters of fire upon every unhallowed object to which your affections incline. But you are not merely to be happy or miserable yourselves—you are to exert a mighty influence in rendering others so; and that influence will operate in the one direction or the other, according to the character of your own ruling passion. Particularly your country's interests are, to a great extent, bound up in you; and the wise and far-seeing, at this moment, have their eyes upon you, as they would discern what are the signs of the times. Nay, there is an imploring voice that comes up from the depths of the future—the voice of unborn generations, reminding you that you are the depositories of *their* interests, and that the period is rapidly passing away in which you can earn their grateful benedictions.

What, then, is to be done? I answer, see to it, first, that your own ruling passion be right—that it be for truth and goodness, for conscience and for God. If the great work of making it right is yet to be performed, come penitently, and confidingly, and obediently, and bow down to the Holy Ghost, and you shall receive the clean heart at his hands. And then go abroad and try to change the ruling passion of the world. Labour, with all your might, in dependance on God's grace, to give to men's thoughts and affections an upward direction. Thus you will not only save yourselves, but be your country's benefactors through all successive generations; and when the ransomed shall all be gathered home, and shall be joining, under the influence of the ruling passion of Heaven, in a common song to Him who hath redeemed them, how ecstatic will be your joy to recognise among them, not one, but many, whose ruling passion, through your instrumentality, has been changed from sin to holiness, and whose eternal destiny has undergone a corresponding change from wo to bliss—from hell to Heaven!

SUPREMACY OF THE MORAL LAW.

BY

J. W. YEOMANS, D. D.

PASTOR OF THE PRESBYTERIAN CHURCH, DANVILLE, PA.

It is easier for heaven and earth to pass than one tittle of the law to fail.—LUKE xvi. 17.

WHEN the Saviour was derided by covetous Pharisees, for teaching that men could not serve God and mammon, he reminds them of an universal and unchangeable law, by which the actions and characters of all moral creatures were to be tried. He warns them that, easily as they might justify themselves before men, there was yet a tribunal where not actions only, but hearts would be judged; and the verdict of the degenerate sentiment around them could be no safe criterion to prove their manners blameless, and their prospects fair. Many things highly esteemed among men are abomination in the sight of God; and the judgment of God is the decision of a last appeal. It decides by a rule which is, by eminence, "THE LAW." And, however men may evade an honest and fair conformity, by glossing or wresting the letter, they cannot change or annul the law itself. That law underlies the scheme of the universe. It came out into clear view in the decalogue. It inspirited the ceremonials of the ancient church. It breathed in all the prophets until John. And now that the kingdom of God is preached, and every man rusheth into it, that same immutable law remains and pervades the whole system. "It is easier for heaven and earth to pass than one tittle of the law to fail."

The rank thus given to "the law," above other laws of the universe, may be traced by infallible signs in the course of divine dispensations. Indeed, it is the fair presumption, that if the principle of this supremacy of the law belongs to the system of created things, it will reveal itself in the operation of the system, and, most of all, at those points where the finger of God most immediately appears.

It is common to speak of moral law as most properly the law of God, in distinction from the laws of nature. But all the laws of the creation are both laws of God and laws of nature—laws of God, because God is their author—laws of nature, because conceived to reside in the nature of created things. By *law*, in the widest sense, we mean the principle conceived as determining the states and actions of persons and things. In this broad use it is applied alike to matter and spirit, even to God himself; in matter, regulating force and motion; in spirit, controlling thought and feeling, reason and conscience. It is in connection with reason and conscience that this principle takes the name of moral law. Expressed in words, it becomes, as in the Scriptures, a body of precepts, defining and enjoining what is right, and forbidding what is wrong; and is received as the written will of God, to be the guide of our life. This moral law is the kind of law which can never fail; and the signs which God has given of his supreme regard for moral law, are to be the subject of our consideration in this discourse. "It is easier for heaven and earth to pass, than one tittle of the law to fail."

1. Of all possible signs of the supremacy of moral law, one of the most comprehensive and impressive, is the dominion given to man over the rest of the earthly creation. God said, Let us make man in our own image, after our likeness, and let him have dominion over the fish of the sea, and over the fowl of the air, and over all the earth, and over every creeping thing that creepeth upon the earth. Thus to man, a moral creature, and the only moral inhabitant of the earth, is given dominion over all the earth. And this donation is made to his rational and moral nature; to the image and likeness of God in him. All things else on the earth are put under him. He may use them all for his benefit. Whatever has the capacity of serving him he may employ in his service. He is not required to prefer the life or the enjoyment of any other earthly creatures to his own; but when their labour or suffering may be useful to him, he may exact it. When their death will promote his well being, he is at liberty to take their life.

This gift of dominion over all the earth shows the high esteem of the Creator for the moral principle in the creation, and the rank he has given to moral law. A creature who, without these divine endowments of reason and conscience, would be no way superior to the other living creatures of the earth, is invested with an authority claimed solely for his moral nature. The living tribes present themselves before him to receive their names, as if to offer their obeisance and their service. All take their places at his feet. And while he keeps his purity, which is really the condition of his power, he holds an easy and honourable sway. This exaltation over other creatures comes not from an arbitrary decree, to be enforced by outward power, against the nature of things. It rises from the nature of man; from the moral image of God within him; from the essential supremacy of the moral principle in the universe. It signifies, that in the realm of God morality is not to be subservient, but supreme; that the natural must serve the moral; that no power can arrest or change the course of moral law; that every valley shall be raised, and every mountain and hill shall be brought low, and that the way shall be every where prepared for fulfilling the moral purposes of God.

2. It is another impressive proof of the supremacy of moral law, that the other laws of earth and heaven are so evidently used for moral ends.

In that portion of the history of the world which is contained in the Holy Scriptures, we find the pleasure and displeasure of God with the righteousness and unrighteousness of men very commonly expressed through the changes in the material world. Sunshine and rain, cold and heat, all the various properties and motions of the elements, are so freely used to convey the blessing or the curse of God to men, as to suggest the thought that they were made for nothing else. Hence that natural expectation which so widely prevails among men, that a people with whom God is well pleased will have fruitful seasons, health, success in their labours, and order and peace in their society; and that a people with whom God is displeased will suffer from famine, or pestilence, or the failure of their favourite enterprises, or the distraction and ruin of their social state. And as of communities, so of individuals. However the course of providence may seem, at times, to depart from this rule, we still find that this subserviency of physical laws to moral ends is one of the most common matters of national expectation among men.

We cannot know how far these laws are thus applied in fact, except by intelligent and constant observation, with the eye of religious faith. Do you believe in a particular providence? Do you see the hand of a moral ruler at all in the changes of nature around you? Then do you hear the earth, with her fields of barrenness and fertility; the ocean, with its calms and its storms; the seasons, with their riches and their poverty; the living tribes, with their services and their depredations; the very hearts of men, with their friendships and their enmities, all uttering, with a majestic and overwhelming elocution, the moral sentiments of God. The moral events of the kingdom of God are brought to their issue by the natural operation of physical laws. Is there a famine in Egypt and Canaan? It occasions the promotion of Joseph in the government of Egypt, the preservation of his father's family, their removal into Egypt, the long and grievous bondage of the Hebrews there, their deliverance by a mighty hand, their wonderful pilgrimage through the wilderness, their establishment in the land of promise; together with all the moral effects which followed those events, and which will follow them to the end of time. When we consider the event, which issued in all these consequences, as a result of the natural operation of the laws of matter, we can hardly resist the conviction that those laws had these effects for their object, and were an important link in the chain of causes for filling the earth with the moral glory of the Lord.

This instance of natural laws resulting in moral effects, is rendered unquestionable and illustrious by having been recorded and explained in the book of inspiration. The history of the events is written by the infallible pen, and the events are placed in their true relation to each other. But suppose all history to be written by inspiration of God; what but that same infallible discernment would be needed to trace all physical changes to moral effects? Would not all nature then seem instinct with the moral designs of her Maker? Who could then doubt that the unconscious, as well as the conscious, being of the world, is geared into the spiritual kingdom, and forms one system with it, and is moving always, under the guidance of God, towards his moral ends? Thus all the changes of the world become illustrations and supports of moral character and moral law. Each contributes to its appropriate moral effect, as each ray of converging light contributes to form the bright and burning focus. Not that each separate event must have, by itself, a moral significancy, any more than each letter in a volume of history must have a distinct historical signification; but the series, as a whole, is an inscription of the moral law, and the moral character of God on the material tables of the universe.

Now it is not at all essential to the authority and power of moral law, that it should always have this form of expression. It may, for the present, be convenient; it may suit the circumstances of the subjects who dwell on the earth, and who, like ourselves, are interwoven with a material and temporary system; but for subjects under other circumstances, these same spiritual laws may be better expressed in other characters. It is convenient for English people that their laws should be written in the English tongue; but for people of other languages, the English law books would be useless, an incumbrance, fit only for burning, while the laws themselves, in their spirit, might suit other people, and remain to be expressed in other forms. Thus will the time come when the heavens and the earth, as books of moral law, will have no further use; when these forms of moral expression will become obsolete, superfluous, fit only for the fire; when the heavens shall be rolled together as a scroll, and, being on fire, shall be dissolved, and the elements shall melt with fervent heat; the earth also, and all the works that are therein shall be burned up; while the laws of truth and righteousness, which the heavens and the earth have so long been used to explain and enforce, shall remain in their authority and glory for ever. "It is easier for heaven and earth to pass than one tittle of the law to fail."

3. Yet more shall we feel the force of this truth

when we observe, how often and signally God has, for moral purposes, actually interrupted the order of nature.

Aiming at a moral impression on the world, he does mighty works in Egypt; and, beginning with Moses, he shows a bush burning with fire, but not consumed; he changes a rod into a serpent, and the serpent again into a rod; he makes the hand of Moses, at one moment, leprous—at another, whole; then, turning upon Egypt, he changes the waters into blood, covers the land with darkness, with flies, and with frogs—afflicts the people with a storm of hail, with murrain upon their cattle, with boils and blains upon themselves, and, finally, with the death of the first born of every family; and all this by a professed departure from the ordinary course of nature. Thus awfully were earth and heaven confounded, to give Egypt and the world an impression of the true God; and, as the Hebrews went forth from bondage, *they* also must be confirmed in the knowledge and fear of the Lord; and, for this purpose, a path for them is made through the sea, and their pursuers are destroyed in the returning waters. Forty years long was nature turned out of her ordinary course, six days of every seven, to supply that people with their daily bread; and every day of the seven to form a cloud for their guidance by day and their defence by night. Water flows from the rock for their thirst; quails flock to their camp as a supply of meat; the Jordan parts its overflowing waters, as of its own accord, to give them a dry passage. At their entrance on the land of promise the walls of Jericho, as of themselves, fall down to give them possession. The Lord thus led that people through a wilderness of miracle, to teach them and the world his name and will; to establish with them the practical supremacy of moral law; to show that people that the natural is made for the spiritual; that the world, in all its other departments of law and of life, must yield to disruption, dislocation, nay, to utter confusion and destruction, to exalt the laws of the Spirit. Behold how the Creator will prepare the way of his moral authority and power, through the solid mountains of his physical dominions, wherever they cross his path, and may help forward his moral work. The sun and moon stop in their courses, at the word of one of his servants; those great lights leave their apparent place in the firmament to convince men that the God of Israel is Jehovah. The heavens might be deranged, but the world must not be without the knowledge of the living and true God. It was easier for the heavens to be thrown into disorder, than for an impression in favour of moral law to be lost. It was " easier for heaven and earth to pass than one tittle of the law to fail."

But, of all the illustrations of this branch of our subject, the most commanding is given in the incarnation of the Son of God. In the person of the Mediator between God and man, there was an amazing departure from the established course of nature. And what lifts this case immeasurably above all others, which either have been or can be, is the fact, that it involves, not only deviation from the established laws of human nature, but also a mysterious and astonishing departure from the mode of the divine existence itself, as previously known. In other cases, God has taken creatures out of the course which he had established for them; in this case, he himself steps out of the previous mode of his existence and action. He gives what may be called, in a peculiar sense, a miraculous manifestation of himself, and takes a relation to humanity altogether extraordinary—the only case of the kind in the history of his self-revelations. He takes humanity to himself as a personal constituent, with even an earthly body. The nature of God becomes joined to the nature of man, not as God is joined to other beings, who live, and move, and have their being in him, but as a constitutional part of a person, as the body is the part of the man.

Although man had fallen from the law of the Spirit of life, yet must he not be allowed wholly to fail of this glorious property and end of his being. It must be restored to him; and, to accomplish this, the Creator produces a new creation, and sets himself before the world in a person and a relation which we know not how to describe. The very sight of this wonder, with the eye of an enlightened faith, is overwhelming. Man had the laws of his formation established from the first, and uniformly observed, by the Author of human generations, till the appearance of the Son of God in the flesh. God had his modes of existence and of revelation, which had appeared to be established from the time that man existed to behold them, and which had never before, in the whole course of divine manifestations, presented such a form as this. But an interest of the spiritual kingdom is to be secured. Now the way of God in saving men is no longer to be pursued invisibly, but is to be fully declared, that its impression may be fixed in the hearts of angels and of men, and that it may bear its part in the constitution and advancement of the church. And what were the laws of the human nature now? What were now the laws (for so we may here call them) which had controlled before the modes of the Divine existence, and determined the previous relations of God to created things? To make men believe his word, and accept his favour, he takes away both the human nature and the divine from the course of their previous and accustomed manifestations, and presents them in an extraordinary, a miraculous, relation to each other. It was easier for the established law of human generations to be given up, than for the violated law of spiritual life in man to be suffered utterly to fail; it was easier for a man to be conceived by the power of the Holy Ghost, and to be born of a virgin, than for one tittle of that law of spiritual life to fail; it was easier for God to be born of a woman, to be made under the law of humanity, to become properly and truly a man, to grow up in body and in mind like a human child, to think, feel, and act as a man, to labor, suffer, and die as a man, than for one tittle of that law to fail. When we behold God clothed in the form, and subject to the conditions, of humanity, and a man pervaded by the nature of God; when we see the hand of that mysterious person parting the net work of nature wherever he would have a passage through it to his moral ends; when we see him walking on the sea, stilling the tempest, causing the blind to see, the deaf to hear, the dumb to speak, and the dead to live; when we see Him, who only hath immortality, sinking under mortal pains, and giving up the ghost like a dying man, and continuing under the power of death for a time, while the sun is darkened, the rocks are rent, graves are opened, and the earth quakes to its centre; we then behold what confusion may come to the material laws of earth and heaven, rather than that one tittle of the spiritual law should fail.

This wonder, wrought for the introduction of the gospel, is but the beginning of wonders. The whole work of redemption, as carried on in the church, and in the souls of individual believers, is, as it were, a propagation of this miracle. The natural powers of heaven and earth are wrought into the system, and made subservient to redemption at the pleasure of the Redeemer; while the efficient power which works through them, to the perfection of the new creation, is the Holy Ghost. Thus the law of life is restored. God may condescend, in all the forms of his manifestation, as Father, Son, and Holy Ghost, to dwell in his people. The entire fashion of the old creation may pass away. God, the Eternal, the Infinite, may bring earth and heaven together to form for himself an abode among men, but not a tittle of the law can fail.

4. We may finally observe, how this supremacy of moral law in the universe finds acceptance with the reason and conscience of man. We feel a natural agreement with it, and act in conformity with it, when we follow the higher dictates of our nature.

If the moral sentiments of men vary with their

different degrees of cultivation, this fact is strongly to our point; for it shows that the more a man is cultivated, according to the laws of his nature, the more does he exalt the moral above the physical. Among savages, where physical power is law, the strongest man is the greatest man. The progress of culture elevates reason and intelligence, in the estimation of men, and assigns to mere bodily strength a lower place. And when the moral sentiments of a community begin to share in the judgments of reason, the moral qualities rise, at once, above all others; and the maxim is established, that the good alone are truly great. Hence every man, of the true moral culture, makes no account of bodily comfort, of property, or of intellectual reputation and influence, when his moral character is at stake. Hence all people, sufficiently enlightened to distinguish the physical, the intellectual, and the moral in man, instinctively regard the moral as the crown of human nature; the part of man for which the other parts were made; the foundation of all the real improvement and happiness of the race. This preference for moral excellence rises from the constitution of man. It appears wherever man has any just development; and wherever it thus appears, it exemplifies and illustrates the supremacy of moral law in the universe.

Suppose, now, this order of things in the world reversed. Let the moral kingdom be made for the physical; let it be once proclaimed that man was made for the horse, the sparrow the worm; for the cedar, the thorn and the thistle; that men are to be reared as food for the lion, or as nourishment for the oak; that their reason must be trained to secure that end; that the conscience must be employed only to prevent, or to detect and punish all deviations from that course; let it once be enjoined on men to obey their bodily appetites alone, subjecting reason and conscience wholly to their sway, and holding the spirit in bondage to the flesh in all things; could such an order of things be received by man? What a war would it raise between the world without and the world within! Without, the natural claiming supremacy—within, the moral; the facts of observation without at constant strife with reason and conscience within. To make such a world, and put such a creature as man upon it, would show such want of natural adaptation in the parts of the creation, it would be so unlike God as we now know him, that we could not believe its possibility. To us it must ever seem a thing impossible with God, so imperiously does the moral sense of mankind demand the supremacy of moral law. And such a decision is worthy of our moral nature. Those high powers which make us the kindred of angels and of God, however we degrade them in practice, we cannot disparage in theory. Men challenge honour for reason and conscience, though they may not follow their counsel. We are the natural and necessary advocates of the supremacy of moral law, and whenever the principle is asserted in the hearing of our higher nature, we say, Amen; let it be "easier for heaven and earth to pass than one tittle of the law to fail."

Of the practical suggestions which arise from this view of the supremacy of moral law, I mention,

1. The natural necessity of ruin as a consequence of sin. We are familiar with the consequences of breaking the physical laws of our being. If a man will not sow, he cannot reap; if a man will not consider, he must fall into trouble; if he walks among pits, with his eyes shut, he must fall; the sluggard must see his poverty come as one that travelleth, and his wants as an armed man; the drunkard must abide his poverty, his broken health, his shattered intellect, his premature death. From such penalties of physical transgression how shall he escape; but sooner, far sooner, may the sluggard grow rich, the careless and imprudent prosper, the drunkard drink health, wealth, long life, and mental power and splendor from his cups, than the breaker of the least commandment of the moral law escape the threatened punishment. Not a tittle of the law can fail.

2. In the light of this inviolable law, how precious is the gospel. Jesus Christ came to seek and to save them that are lost; but how hopelessly lost are the transgressors of such a law. Think of those bonds of nature which hold the rivers in their course to the ocean; which hold the ocean in its bed, and the mountain on its base, and preserve the harmony of the celestial world. The planet, falling by an inward infirmity from its orbit, what power of nature can restore it? What can save it from being a wandering star, to which is reserved the blackness of darkness for ever? But all the stars of heaven, once fallen, might easier rise again, by a self-restoring power, than a man, fallen from the guidance of his moral nature, by an inward infirmity, restore him-

self to righteousness and happiness. How mighty and merciful the hand which redeems from such a fall! Let every sinner lay hold upon it; for how shall he escape if he neglect so great salvation?

3. In the light of this subject, the value of our spiritual interests appears altogether inestimable. What is the brief welfare of the present life in the comparison? Even the lawful pursuits of this life, and those most important to our earthly happiness, have only a superficial and transient worth. The true basis of our prosperity, for time and eternity, is the law of our moral nature. Seek first the kingdom of God. Lay up your treasures in heaven. Build on the rock which forms the basis of the universe. The loose and dissoluble masses which have been collected on that rock, and which the weight of temporal interests seems almost to have petrified upon it, will not continue. A catastrophe is coming. The imperishable foundations of the moral world will rise, heaving from their surface the dissolving rubbish of a temporal economy, and thenceforth remaining only the glorious support of perfect righteousness for ever.

DISTRUST OF THE WORD.

BY

J. W. ALEXANDER, D. D.

PASTOR OF THE DUANE STREET CHURCH, NEW YORK.

The children of Ephraim, being armed, and carrying bows, turned back in the day of battle.—PSALM LXVIII. 9.

THIS ill conduct of the Ephraimites, in turning their backs upon the enemy, is referred by expositors to various events. It is by no means unnatural to consider the Psalmist as alluding to the surrender of the ark to the Philistines; for Shiloh, then the seat of the tabernacle, was within the tribe of Ephraim. 1 Sam. iv. 4. Whenever and wherever it occurred, it presented the mortifying spectacle of a host in retreat, and this when amply furnished with weapons of war. Ephraim, being armed, and carrying bows, turned back in the day of battle. The passage stands in the midst of rehearsals of victories and deliverances, and of rebukes for unbelief and doubt. It was "written for our learning," and we cannot meditate on it, without a sad reflection that we, as a part of God's Israel, are engaged in a warfare, and summoned to "fight the good fight of faith;" that *we* are armed with the grand weapon of faith—the WORD OF GOD; that we too have sometimes turned to flight, or proved cowards in Christ's cause; and that the shame of our sin is the greater, inasmuch as the weapon which we have distrusted is of divine power. Believing Israel to be a type of the church, and the words of the text to be for all ages of Christianity, I do not consider it in the least opposed to the analogy of New Testament precedent, to give this general principle of the Hebrew psalm a particular application. Dismissing the figure, therefore, let us seriously meditate on what it represents.

It is true of multitudes who are engaged in the Christian warfare, that they are distrustful of their own weapons. For a soldier, there could hardly be a more unfortunate prepossession. His blows must be half-delivered, and his disposition to parley or to flee, exceedingly subversive of bold fighting. The grand weapon of the Christian soldier is thus expressed, in the most general terms, and in a metaphor—"*the sword of the Spirit,* which is the Word of God." This is the great instrument of assault against the world and against himself; for it is a peculiarity of our warfare, that some of our most obstinate battles take place within the walls. The truth of God, however largely understood, is the name of our whole offensive armour. This truth in general, and certain prominent truths in particular, are precisely what the Captain of Salvation has put into our hands, to be used against the adversary. It is a firm confidence in the temper, strength, and edge of these weapons, which makes the brave combatant. And it is the distrust of our unbelieving minds in these qualities of the Word of God, which I would endeavour to stigmatise and remove. The fault here pointed out is not the fault of one and another merely, but in some degree of us all; of ministers as well as people; of societies and churches, as well as of humble individuals.

I shall endeavour to show how this distrust of divine truth is exhibited; how it operates against the success of Christian effort, and how it may be removed.

I. DISTRUST OF DIVINE TRUTH, AS THE MAIN OFFENSIVE WEAPON OF THE CHRISTIAN WAR, IS EVINCED IN A VARIETY OF WAYS.

1. *By the disposition common to us all, to resort to other instruments* than those which God has appointed. Not error merely, in opposition to truth; but sundry agencies, of a purely secular kind, are employed by Christians to accomplish those very ends for which the Scriptures are put into their hands. If the world is to be reformed, we fly to arrangements and causes which are external, economical, patriotic, literary, or simply moral, rather than to that which is spiritual. Things good in themselves, and pre-eminently good when subordinated to the gospel, become usurpations, malign and dangerous, when they supplant God's ordinance. The world is to be reformed, and, under God, we are to reform it; but in God's way, and by his methods. The corrupt mass of mankind, tending, by virtue of internal maladies, to a catastrophe of disorder, vice and woe, is to be regulated, purified and blessed by a certain prescribed agency, set forth in all its details in this book. In the midst of the great self-destroying mass is placed a small but mighty engine, to accomplish an end for which philanthropists and politicians are sighing and labouring in vain. This energy within,

which is to change the face of human society, and insure universal brotherhood, is the Church: the Church, my brethren; not of Rome, of England, or of Geneva, but the Church of the first-born of God; namely, the family of true believers, sanctified by the truth called out of all nations, washed in the blood of the Lamb, and enclosing an infant generation baptized into the Lord's name. The means by which this community is to effect so gigantic a result is one and simple; it is the truth revealed in the Scripture. To substitute for this any other agency, for the same ends, and not in subordination to this divine principle, is to change the whole method of warfare, and to forsake our own professions and standards. If the Church could be proved insufficient for what it proposes, this would afford a just reason for trying other means; but it would, at the same time, prove the claims of Christianity to be groundless. If other ends, not contemplated by the gospel methods, are proposed, they may indeed be sought by other means; but such ends are, by the very supposition, temporal, and therefore inferior. The great moral changes which would make our world a happy world, are exactly what the Church is ordained to effect, by means of the truth; and for all these ends the Church is sufficient. When wisdom has fully considered the line between these two classes of results, and allotted to Christianity those which are her part, it is a sort of disrespect to the system we profess, to use for the same purpose other machinery than that which God has prescribed; and to do so is to manifest distrust of God's way.

2. The same distrust is evinced *by a proneness in*

many of us to modify or conceal the statements of revealed truth. All truths are not alike fundamental, nor applicable alike to all cases and at all times; but every truth of this record has its place and season of application, and is then and there to be applied without reserve or tampering—for this plain reason, that it is the God of truth who utters it. But how often does it happen, that in addresses to the body of believers, in exhortations to the unawakened, in counsel to the inquiring, or appeals to our own hearts, we falter in delivering the pure, unadulterated word, and feel half afraid that it may do more harm than good! How often does worldly fear seal up the lips which were ready to pronounce the doctrine of God's sovereign election; or worldly policy drive back the free current of gracious invitation! More watchful against momentary offence, and occasional abuse, than against the permanent and destructive influence of ignorance and all error, we seal up the very fountains which God has caused to flow from the smitten rock. Hence we shudder when the preacher declares the statements of Jehovah himself, respecting his own awful decrees, or the irrevocable damnation of the dying hypocrite; and, on the other hand, stand ready, when he publishes the grace of Calvary, to hang chains and weights on the freedom of an offer which flies far and high above all legal preparations and conditions. Thus have a thousand errors and heresies arisen. Men have thought themselves more prudent than the All-wise. The Law has been lowered lest sinners should call it hard; the way has been hedged up, lest the blind, and the halt, and the lame, should find it too easy;

the Church has been barricaded with walls of ceremony, and garrisoned with ranks of officials, lest some of its riches should be pilfered by dissent; and the blessed Gospel, free as the air of Paradise, has been laden with conditions and restrictions, lest faith should be too simple. In every one of these, and in a thousand like ways, men show their distrust of divine revelation.

3. *Another proof of distrust in regard to the truth of God, is the small measure and lukewarm temper in which we actually use it.* If it is what we profess to believe, it is an instrument suited to an infinite diversity of objects, all included in the one result of making men better and happier. With this persuasion deeply fixed in our minds, we should be perpetually employing it for these ends; we should bring it forth, and apply it to the daily emergencies of labour, study, trade, and domestic life; we should use it for a standard, as we use the familiar standards of our common business, when we measure, weigh, or calculate. We should bring to this test the morality and expediency of many an act, and the purity of many a motive. That we do not, is only a proof how little we are Christians. It shows at how low a rate we estimate the cogency of scriptural principle; that there are so many things in commerce, in study, in politics, in education, and in social reform, (all involving moral relations,) which we never bring into the light of God's word. We carry on our affairs, and dispose of our property, and plan our amusements, and execute great changes in life, and bring up our children, and make our wills, without once turning to God's book to find how these

several steps, which really make up the aggregate of our lives, are regarded in heaven.

He who trusts in God's word as an infallible directory, will never find a day in which he can live without its guidance. He cannot rise from sleep, without a query how the day's plan may be laid so as to find him, like Enoch, walking with God; or take his early meal, without a purpose that it be sanctified by the word of God and prayer. He cannot receive his dues, without considering how much he oweth unto his Lord, and how much he is in danger from the mammon of unrighteousness. He cannot meet a friend, without casting about for a scripture maxim which may sanctify their union; or an enemy, without guarding his temper by the precept of forgiveness. Nor can he close his doors, and "go up to the habitation of his bed," until he has looked back over the journey of the day, and applied to it the lesson of God's statutes. And the fact that all this is unknown in the days of any professing Christians, is too conclusive an argument of their habitual distrust of heavenly truth as the instrument of their sanctification.

4. One evidence more will suffice to show our distrust of divine truth. It is *our neglect of this volume.* The soldier who has a favourite weapon is apt to be very much engaged in exercising it, and preparing to wield it. We have read of the knights in the days of chivalry, and of their trusty swords, many of which had inscriptions of honour and names of endearment. Many were the hours spent in sharpening and polishing these blades; many more in brandishing them by way of preparation, so as to

learn their qualities, and how to make them effectual. All this proved how truly they valued their arms, and it tended towards valorous conflict and easy victory. But we have a sword which we treat after a different fashion. It lies on our pulpits, perhaps on our tables. We bring it forth on special occasions, and never mention it but with devotion. We enshrine it, and praise it—would fight for it, but not with it. It lies, like the sword of Goliath the Philistine, at the dwelling of the priest Abimelech, "wrapped in a cloth behind the ephod." 1 Sam. xxi. 9. Whereas we should say of it, as did David: "*There is none like that: give it me.*" The sword of the Spirit, which is the Word of God, requires to be taken up in the way of daily exercise. It will be so handled by those who rely on it. The Scriptures, as the great magazine of truth, available for all the demands of life, will be resorted to in serious meditation by every man who is convinced that his own life and salvation, and the life and salvation of millions, depend on it; and he who is little engaged in close examination of the Bible, gives the best evidence possible that he has little practical belief in its amazing power. It is vain, and all but ludicrous, for any one to avow his supreme reverence for the Scriptures as the means of regenerating society and opening heaven, when he spends hours over the daily journal, or the book of gaiety, for minutes bestowed on prophets and apostles, and the words of Jesus, the Son of God. Let us change our practice or abate our professions; let us cease to applaud Moses, Isaiah and Paul, unless we mean to read them; for while we neglect our chief weapon, we plainly tell the world that we have no confidence in its virtues. If these marks are of any value, they show, my brethren, that in a greater or a less degree we are all guilty of ascribing less than is just to the chosen instrument of the Holy Ghost, the truth of revelation; and if we are conscious of the fault, we are in a good condition to deepen our sense of its folly, by contemplating, in the second place,

II. THE OPERATION OF THIS DISTRUST, IN REGARD TO CHRISTIAN ACTIVITY. The activity here meant is that which concerns our enemies, and the enemies of the Church, who are more numerous, and more malignant, and more formidable, than all human foes; and though fellow mortals may be sometimes "God's sword," and are often the devil's hirelings, you will behold, if your eyes are opened, an array yet more fearful, and a battle yet more bloody; for we wrestle not as with flesh and blood, but against princes, against powers, and the rulers of the darkness of this world, and against spiritual wickedness in high places. The odds would be fearful were not He that is for us greater than they that are against us. But divine aid in this contest, like all divine aid, is ordered and prescribed. God has provided armour, both on the right hand and on the left; that is to say, both sword and shield—both offensive and defensive. Every piece is named; the inventory is here—helmet, breastplate, girdle, buckler, and shoes; but all in vain, unless the warrior endue himself with the harness, and utterly ineffectual without the weapon of attack—the sword of the Spirit. This we have found reason to believe has been, with some, rusting in the scabbard; its heavenly temper is disallowed; and of this distrust the effect is manifold disability, weakness, fear and defeat. Let us more closely examine these effects.

1. Distrust of the Word of God, as an instrument, *indisposes the soul for spiritual warfare.* He who doubts his bow will avoid the conflict. Let me not be misunderstood, as if what I meant was religious controversy, in its common acceptation. Controversy there is indeed; but not the war of words, or simple battling for opinions. The war which rages under our banners is a war for life or death; it began when sin entered; it will end when sin is eternally expelled. In the individual soul, it begins when grace enters; it ends when glory is made sure. It is the flesh lusting against the Spirit, and the Spirit against the flesh. The new nature, like God its author, is essentially the antagonist of sin, in its principle and its acts. From the soul, that is, from the centre outwards, it urges an influence of opposition which is penetrating, expulsive, and destroying. It struggles to bring all things to its own likeness, and therefore to annul all that is unlike it; this is the law of the kingdom of heaven, which is leaven, and salt, and light. While this process goes on in the individual soul, it goes on also in communities. That which the seed of grace does in one, the piety of God's people does in many in the world at large; and both in one case and in the other, it is truth which is the instrument. To make it accomplish this, its office, there is need of constant, restless activity. Let this cease in the soul, and sin gains ground; let it cease in the Church, and Christianity makes no progress —which will account for a number of painful phe-

nomena, such as backsliding, the loss of comfort, the decline of revivals, the decay of missionary spirit, the arrest of reformation work, in a word, the "turning back in the day of battle." But you perceive at once, that a cause could scarcely be named more certain to produce this result, than distrust of the truth. Undervalue the power of this means, and you will be indisposed to war; you will love the shades of carnal peace; you will have a Christianity which is tamed down to servile acquiescence in all that sin proposes, and all that the world allows. Distrust of the armour of truth must needs indispose for the spiritual warfare.

2. Distrust of the Word of God, as an instrument, *makes the soul weak when forced into the struggle.* He who doubts his bow will fight feebly. This applies to those who actually contend against sin in some degree; but they contend at a disadvantage.

It was not the least of the causes of primitive success, that the apostles and martyrs confided in the Gospel as an instrument of irresistible force. They were not ashamed of it. It had transformed them; it could transform others. It was the power of God unto salvation, whether wielded against Jewish prejudice or Greek philosophy. In their hands it destroyed the wisdom of the wise, and brought to nothing the understanding of the prudent. They spoke in words which the Holy Ghost teacheth. This was their confidence; this made them strong in the battle—good soldiers of Jesus Christ. They dealt no doubtful blows; they ran not as uncertainly; they fought not as one that beateth the air. Even Paul, who, in presence among the Corinthians, could say that he was "base" among them, could also say of his Christian valour, "We do not war after the flesh, casting down imaginations and every high thing that exalteth itself against the knowledge of God." Nay, such was his estimate of this weapon, that he cries, "I count all things but loss for the excellency of the knowledge of Christ." And, my brethren, if you will turn over all the books of church history, and all your recollections of good men, you will not find an individual, ancient or modern, in the pulpit or out of it, remarkable for great success in promoting religion, who had not, at the same time, a high confidence in the truth of the Gospel to produce this very result.

How different the spectacle in our day! There are enemies enough to fight, but we sit still; or when we contend, how feebly is it! Vice triumphs around us—error stalks abroad; but our blows are scarcely felt, because we ourselves think them impotent. The remedy would be for us to acquire such a holy admiration for the Bible, as the instrument of invasion and victory, as should lead the feeblest woman, and the youngest Sabbath school teacher, to shout, "*The sword of the Lord and of Gideon!*" Then should our success be such, that the church would renew the exclamation of Habakkuk, "Thy bow was made quite naked, according to the oaths of the tribes—*even thy word!*" Hab. iii. 9. How can we shame and intimidate our foe when we doubt our very arms?

3. Distrust of the Word of God, as an instrument, *tends to make the soul retreat before its enemies.* He who distrusts his bow will flee.

Grant that you do not avoid conflict; grant that you ply your adversary, the devil, with some showers of arrows; yet any diffidence, in regard to the instrument you employ, will suggest cessation and flight. To begin a battle is not to conquer. In the evil day you are *to stand*, to war courageously, "and, having done all, *to stand*." Cowardice is certain, if you feel no strength; to doubt your armour is to be unarmed. David went out between two lines of fierce array, holding up his ruddy countenance with elation, though he carried only a shepherd's staff, a sling, and five smooth stones out of the brook; but he was strong in the Lord, and in the power of his might. "Thou comest to me with a sword, and with a spear, and with a shield; but I am come to thee in the name of the Lord of hosts, whom thou hast defied."

Our grand business is to carry on a warfare which our predecessors began. The world is to be subdued, and every Christian is in the ranks. You know your weapon of attack; you ought to know its power. But if, when assaulted, you have misgivings about this, and if these misgivings continue, you will faint, you will fly. Hence, when error has come into the church, and ministers and people have used the truth, as men use a bow which they expect to break, or a piece of ordnance which they fear will burst, the result has been according to that threatening against Israel: "The Lord shall cause thee to be smitten before thine enemies; thou shalt go out one way against them, and flee seven ways before them." Deut. xxviii. 25. In every engagement, in the heart or in the world, doubt as to the efficacy of the means will produce fearfulness and retreat.

4. Distrust, in regard to God's truth, *will be likely to cause defeat.* He who doubts his bow will generally be conquered. I admit that, in the great concern, namely, personal salvation, every regenerate man is safe; he cannot be defeated; his redemption is sure; but it is because he is in Christ's hands; because no one can pluck him thence; because the believer *abides* in him, John xv. 6, and Christ's words abide in the believer. It is by the *truth* that even saints persevere; but even saints may be repulsed in those lesser engagements which precede their final conquest. Israel may be chased by the Amorites, and destroyed by them in Seir, Deut. i. 44, though they are eventually to cross Jordan; they may be smitten before Ai, so that Joshua may say, "O Lord, what shall I say when Israel turneth their backs before their enemies?" Josh. vii. 8, though they are eventually to possess the land. Private Christians may lose the field, and, for a time, be subject to the world; congregations may lose the savour of divine things, and cease to influence the mass around them; public enterprises may fail, by reason of declining faith, in such as should support them; branches of the visible church may fall back before their adversaries, dwindle, and even disappear. All these are temporary conquests by the enemy. Thus Shiloh, once the seat of the ark, became a proverb of desertion. Jer. vii. 12, 14; 1 Sam. iv. 11; Psa. lxxviii. 60. Wittenberg, the cradle of the Reformation, is profaned by rationalism; Geneva, where Calvin taught, is held by bap-

tised infidels; and Cambridge, where the Puritan fathers rejoiced in a divine Saviour, is the citadel of Socinianism. Distrust of the truth, failure to employ it, substitution of something in its place—these are the causes of the dire reverse. And it may be that Protestant America, unless she take a manlier hold on the Scriptures, may become the western ally of the Beast, and shine with the splendid jewels, and crosses, and mitres of subjugation. In a word, if we would have the blessings of religion we must prize its means; and if we would be victorious against sin, Satan, worldly fashion, error, infidelity, Popery, idolatry, and vice, we must feel that the Bible is an instrument, which, in God's hand, shall bring them all to destruction. It is the lamentable want of this persuasion which makes us, though armed, to turn back in the day of battle; and it is *the remedy for this disease of the soul*, to which I call your attention; it is the third and last head of my discourse.

III. Before stating THE MEANS OF RECOVERY, let us look once again at the evil, and its opposite good. The evil is distrust of God's word; the opposite good is a high estimate of divine truth as the weapon of our warfare. The question is, How shall this just valuation of the truth be increased in us? And the answer to this may be comprised in a few simple, but I trust important particulars.

1. It will be our duty to consider *what this weapon has already achieved*. This was the method taken by the Psalmist in the context. He recounts the victories of Israel. It had been their sin that "they forgat God's works, and his wonders that he

showed them." v. 11. He rehearses these works and wonders—"They believed not in God, and trusted not in his salvation." v. 22. The Psalmist goes over the pilgrimage in the desert—"They remembered not his hand, nor the day when he delivered them from the enemy." v. 42. The sacred poet accumulates the trophies of God's host; in like manner, my brethren, let us look back at the conquests of truth. Whatever Christianity has done, has been done by the Word. This is the weapon which, in God's hand, routed the hosts of heathenism, razed the ancient temples, struck the oracles dumb, quenched the fire of altars, staunched the flow of human blood, broke the chains of slavery, raised the feebler sex to membership with Christ, and fortified ten thousand citadels with virtuous bulwarks; and when Christianity had grown corrupt, and superstition and idolatry threatened once more to come in like a flood, under a Christian name, the Lord lifted up a standard against them. It was this divine truth which effected the Reformation; it was this book which, found in the convent at Erfurt, became in the hands of Luther a sword to pierce the vitals of the Beast; it is this instrument which forced a way for our fathers into this western continent, and which their sons are carrying to the uttermost parts of the earth; it is a consideration which may be administered as a cordial to the fainting Ephraimite.

2. Nor is it in the past only that we find such encouragement. Consider, I pray you, *what this weapon is accomplishing this day.* From a thousand high places in Zion, in this Sabbath hour, the bow

is drawn at a venture, and the arrows of Messiah are sharp in the hearts of the king's enemies, whereby the people fall under him. God's people are still like Joseph—"the archers have sorely grieved him, and shot at him, and hated him; but his bow abode in strength, and the arms of his hands are still made strong by the hands of the mighty God of Jacob." Gen. xlix. 24. The Word, read and heard, is awakening sinners, comforting sufferers, supporting the weak, confirming the strong, and sanctifying the imperfect. While I speak, it is urging on to victory part of the host, who are this moment struggling on the verge of the river; and from whose lips I hear the voice of the last battle-cry—"O death, where is thy sting? O grave, where is thy victory?" Beloved, let us not distrust our weapons, until they shall cease to do such things as these.

3. But this is not all; the half has not been told you; for consider *what this instrument is yet to achieve.* It is the triumphal song of all the prophecies. They so illuminate the future, as that it becomes to the past and present what the noonday is to the morning-watch. Let me reserve for other Sabbaths the fuller recital of what holy seers have told us of that latter glory; enough for us to-day, that all these glories are the effects of truth. In other words, the triumph of Christianity is the triumph of faith. Our Captain of Salvation is leading us on to a victory, of which the philosophers of this world have not dreamt. He addresses us, in view of the coming onset, as he addressed Joshua thirty-two centuries ago; he so addresses us, as if he solemnly put our hands upon the

sword and on the bow—"*This book of the law* shall not depart out of thy mouth, but thou shalt meditate therein day and night; for then thou shalt make thy way prosperous, and then thou shalt have good success; have not I commanded thee? Be strong, and of a good courage; be not afraid, neither be thou dismayed, for the Lord thy God is with thee, whithersoever thou goest." Josh. i. 8, 9.

We learn, then, to confide in our weapons, by considering what they have done, what they are doing, and what they are yet to do.

4. Is it not then a plain duty, for the very end proposed, *to make ourselves familiar with this blessed volume,* in a degree which we have never yet known? Surely the Mohammedan will rise in judgment against us; for he cleaves to his Koran, he studies it, he passes days over it, he commits it to his memory. If our Christianity is destined, as I hope it is, greatly to revive in this age; if the Lord's battle is to be fought with unexampled vigour, it will not be until we give new attention to the scriptures of truth. Then, when this Bible takes its due place in colleges, in schools, in social circles, in families, in counting rooms, in ships upon the sea; when it is craved and called for by thousands, as in the days of the reformers, we shall behold a reformation of which that from Popery was but the type. Then shall heathen sages, if such remain, exclaim of the Church, as did Balaam concerning Israel, "The Lord his God is with him, and the shout of a king is among them!" Num. xxiii. 21. Then shall heathenism, and rationalism, and communism, and Romanism, and all the battalions of errorism, leave the field. "One shall chase a thousand,

and two put ten thousand to flight!" Deut. xxxii. 30. What, O, brethren, is the instrument in these certain changes? It is truth, before which all that is corrupt shall burn, and all that is stubborn shall be broken. "Is not my *word* like as a fire, saith the Lord, and like a hammer that breaketh the rock in pieces?" Jer. xxiii. 29.

5. Once more; as a remedy for distrust, *place yourselves in circumstances in which you will have to observe the energy of this weapon.* This truth, whether you are aware of it or not, is even now working wonders. It is healing hard hearts; it is transforming lions to lambs; it is pulling down strong holds. To behold all this, be persuaded, Christian professors, to enter the ranks yourselves. Draw forth the bow; put the arrow upon your string; engage in actual service; leave the world for a little to whirl without you, and venture out of winter quarters to do something for God. Even if your own army be asleep, steal forth and survey the enemy's camp, as did Gideon and his servant Phurah, and perhaps you will have cause to say with him, "Arise, for the Lord hath delivered into your hand the host of Midian!" Judg. vii. 15. Attain the mastery of your bow by practice, and you shall no longer turn your backs in the day of battle.

6. There is one further suggestion, and the series will have an end. Of all means of gaining confidence in the truth, none can be compared to this: *to become personally experienced in its power.* It can wound, and it can heal. Open your bosom to its efficacy. Ye who have meditated in the word, day and night, have no distrust of its power. It has

made you what you are; it is yet to make you wiser, purer, stronger, and happier. Pray, without ceasing, that God would fulfil in you "all the good pleasure of his goodness, and the work of faith with power." 2 Thess. i. 11. All the conquests of religion are so many new steps of Christian experience; new exercises or new subjects; and all experience is by faith. Say continually, "*Lord increase our faith!*" This is the victory that overcometh the world, even our faith. 1 John v. 4. Thus exercised, you will rise above all doubt as to the armour and the bow; believing, you will wonder at your foregoing timidity; and when all the church shall thus deeply feel the energy of the Word, the closing words of this passage shall come true: "Then Jehovah awaked as one out of sleep, and like a mighty man that shouteth by reason of wine. And he smote his enemies in their retreat; he put them to a perpetual reproach."

CONSISTENCY OF THE DIVINE GOVERNMENT.

BY

GEO. JUNKIN, D. D.

PRESIDENT OF WASHINGTON COLLEGE, VIRGINIA.

For it became Him, for whom are all things, and by whom are all things, in bringing many sons unto glory, to make the Captain of their salvation perfect through sufferings.—HEB. ii. 10.

MAN is a creature of sensation before he is capable of reasoning and moralizing. His first pains and pleasures are those resulting from the exercise of his merely animal senses. His ear, his eye, his taste, his touch, his smell, first awake his soul to consciousness, and let in the light of joy upon the hitherto darkened mind. After these he is competent to reason, and then capable of moral sensibilities. What period of time, and what amount of enjoyment, are written out in the records of his conscious felicities, before he experiences the higher happiness of his rational and moral nature, it is impracticable to determine. They will vary according to the infinitely varying characteristics of the physical organization and of the mental and moral structure. It is obvious, however, that in all cases they are very considerable. Infant humanity reaps a large harvest of harmless joys from the wide fields of nature, and habits of reliance upon these, as its chief good, become strongly fixed at an early period. These habits are often encountered in subsequent efforts to develope the higher faculties of the soul. We find it extremely difficult to give a reflective turn to the current of thought; to lead the mind away from the external to the internal; to divert the affections from the pleasures of mere sense, to the deeper flow, and more enduring satisfaction, of spiritual contemplations.

Here lies the philosophy of the general fact, that within the sphere of religion, the externals, the mere outward drapery, dazzles the eye and arrests the attention, whilst the inner, spiritual substance, passes unnoticed. Children in years and knowledge see with the eye and hear with the ear, while with the heart they understand not. Let religion put on an outward gorgeous ceremonial; let her appear arrayed in purple and scarlet; let her head wear the jewelled coronet; let her majestic service be accompanied with all the enchantments of choral and instrumental harmonies, and the undeveloped mind will hail her with exquisite delight; but let her appear meek and lowly, humble and unadorned, and there is no beauty seen in her; she is as a root out of a dry ground, despised and rejected of men.

Thus the Church, in the period of her nonage, was attracted by the splendid and imposing ritual of the Levitical dispensation. The visible symbols, the gorgeous embellishments, the outward solemn pomp and parade, filled the eye and the ear, and captivated the imagination of a people not yet grown to maturity in the things of the Spirit. From this state of necessary pupilage, under tutors and governors, the Church must, however, pass; but the transition will, of course, be accompanied with strong emotions and a violent struggle. Like the incipient efforts of the youthful mind to take in an abstract thought, and to reflect upon its own actions, the Israelite turns away with difficulty from the venerable and long venerated rites prescribed by Moses, to the unostentatious simplicity of Gospel institutions. David's Lord, in becoming David's Son, has laid aside the external appliances and trappings of worldly grandeur; and, therefore, to the carnal Jew, he is what he seems to be, and consequently is treated with contempt. "Can any good thing come out of Nazareth?" This is the stumbling stone, this the rock of offence over which the great body of the Israelites fell and were broken. We have Abraham to our father, we had Moses as our leader, and David as our king: the brazen altar, the golden candlestick, the gilded tabernacle, the glorious ark of the testimony, the gorgeous temple, the outstretched wings of the golden cherubim, the solemn choirs, and all the majesty of that magnificent service—oh, how shall we abandon this, all this, for Him who was born in a stable, cradled in a manger, crucified at Golgotha!

Entrenched behind these prejudices lie the great body of the Hebrew people, Paul's brethren according to the flesh. Behind these fearful barriers had the apostle himself lain, in all the confident security of individual and national self-righteousness. Therefore did he feel and fear for them; and, therefore, against these apparently impregnable bulwarks did he direct the first discharge of his heavenly artillery. Well aware that, whilst these prejudices remained, no arrow could penetrate the breast, he opens up to them at once the true dignity of the king Messiah, as found in his personal character, not in his external decorations. By presenting the pre-eminent grandeur and glory of the Son of God he aims to remove the offence of the cross. This he does in the first chapter, where he introduces him as Prophet, Creator, and King, and demonstrates, by abundant testimonies of Scripture, his lordship over the universe.

Now, if the Son holds pre-eminence over all intelligent nature, and if all the angels of God worship him, how much more should we reverence his teachings, and bow to his supreme authority! And if we should neglect either, how can we escape the fearful consequences?

From this practical inference, the apostle passes over to the objection so naturally recurring to the Hebrew mind: If the Messiah stands thus pre-eminent above all created intelligence, how came he to the degradation of the manger, the cross, and the tomb? How is it possible to reconcile such contradictory states? If he be the Son of God, and Lord of the universe, why hangs he on a tree? If God were his Father, wherefore did he permit the painful, humiliating, and contemptuous treatment of his only begotten and well beloved? Physical evils have their root in moral causes; could such sorrow and anguish, as he endured, be without a cause? How can such extremes be brought together without impeaching the love, the wisdom, and the justice of God?

To this the apostle presents the testimony of acknowledged Scripture. The eighth Psalm is universally allowed to refer to the Messiah. This the Hebrews maintained, and here is proof that the Son must be, *for a little time, lessened in comparison of the angels, in order that he may suffer death for every child of God.* The humiliation of Christ is not a bald fact, detached from his moral and legal relations; not a mere arbitrary freak in the Divine government; not an outburst of popular phrenzy outside of the Divine economy; not a spontaneity, having neither antecedent nor consequent. On the contrary, it is a part of the Divine plan of universal government; which plan embraces eternity and all its contents, minute and magnificent. It is a link in the endless chain of causes and effects, by which Jehovah

"Hangs creation like a precious gem,
Though little, on the footstool of his throne."

The mystery of the Word made flesh loses its paradoxical character the moment its legal relations are understood. Should it appear that, for an adequate reason, the Lord of glory bowed the heavens, and came down, and veiled his divinity in human flesh; should ends be answered, by this amazing transaction, in the moral government of the universe, meet and worthy of the Governor, then our amazement must cease, all that is paradoxical must pass away, the harmony of the divine attributes be displayed, and God stand justified, in all his acts, before the intelligent universe. And this is our position, "For it became him, for whom are all things, and by whom are all things, in bringing many sons unto glory, to make the Captain of their salvation perfect through sufferings."

An act, or work, is said to *become* a person, when it is such as people of good taste would generally expect from his known character and condition. It implies suitableness, propriety, and consistency; and pre-supposes a usual order of things. A dress is *becoming* when its texture, material, colour, and form, are such as is ordinarily found on persons of the same rank, in such circumstances. Gorgeous attire were unbecoming at a funeral; good works, Paul tells us, are the modest apparel "which *becometh* women professing godliness."

"For whom are all things," marks the final cause —on account of whom—for the manifestation of whose glory. "By whom are all things;" this covers the work of creation and government—by whom the universe was made, and by whom it is sustained, directed, and controlled. The phrase, "bringing many sons unto glory," has reference to the Captain of Salvation, as the object of the action described in the expression, "to make perfect through sufferings;" this last means, to complete, to finish up—as on the cross He said, "it is *finished*"—completed, brought to a close—all the bitter ingredients of the cup are exhausted.

"Bringing many sons unto glory," is delivering men from degradation, shame, and sin, and conducting them to holiness, and happiness, and heaven. The term "Captain" is descriptive, also, of the work; it means a leader in the way—one who goes before, and directs, guides, and draws others onward in the same way. "These follow the Lamb whithersoever he goeth."

The doctrine of our text then is, that *the great work of man's salvation, by the sufferings of Christ, is consistent with the character of God, as the Creator, Governor, and Proprietor of the universe.*

In the discussion of this subject we must consider,

I. *The work to be performed*—bringing many sons unto glory.

II. *The means of accomplishing this work*—the sufferings of Christ.

III. *The consistency of these two combined, with God's character* as Creator, Governor, and Proprietor of the universe.

I. The work—bringing many sons unto glory.

They are at a distance from glory. All mankind are by nature in a degraded and ruined condition—those who are to be brought unto glory equally with others; and a rescue from this is implied.

This degraded state involves condemnation under the law; and of course the first movement towards leading them to heavenly glory, is their deliverance from condemnation. Until such deliverance is effected, they cannot take the first step in the way to glory. How this can be effected we shall see in its proper place.

But again, the state of heavenly glory is unattainable except as the reward of holy obedience. Life and eternal joy are positive blessings, and can be conferred only in consequence of positive compliance of the divine law—"if thou wilt have life, keep the commandments." These two pre-requisites regard the legal relations of those who shall be brought unto glory; other parts of the work regard their moral qualities.

The spiritually dead man cannot walk in the way of life. These sons must be made alive before they can follow the Captain of their salvation. "Ye must be born again." Renovation to spiritual life must take place.

No unbelieving and impenitent man can see God's face in peace. "He that believeth not the Son shall not see life, but the wrath of God abideth on him." "Except ye repent, ye shall all likewise perish." True faith and sincere repentance belong to this work.

The state of glory is a state of purity; into it nothing unclean can enter. Be ye holy, for I am holy. Without holiness no man shall see the Lord. These sons must be sanctified before they can enter the gates of glory.

Heaven is the home of active benevolence. "God is love, and he that dwelleth in love, dwelleth in God, and God in him." But the heart of man is naturally at enmity against God; it is not subject to the law of God, neither indeed can be. This work involves, therefore, the slaying of the enmity, and the shedding abroad, in the heart, of this heavenly love.

The entire persons of these sons are to be brought unto glory; not the souls only, but also the bodies. This work, then, includes the resurrection of the bodies, and their entire transformation into the likeness of his glorious body. "Beloved, now are we the sons of God, and it doth not yet appear what we shall be, but we know that when he shall appear we shall be like him, for we shall see him as he is."

II. *The means of accomplishing this work*—the sufferings of the Captain of their salvation.

When the law has pronounced its sentence there is no evasion; it must be executed. Justice is an essential attribute of God; his law can pronounce none but a just sentence, and all the holiness of his character is pledged to its execution. "Though hand join in hand, the wicked shall not go unpunished." If Jesus has pledged himself to bring many sons unto glory, he has therein pledged the removal from them of the sentence of condemnation, which can be effected only by enduring it. "Die, he or justice must." There is no other method of breaking the yoke of bondage, and letting the captives sold under sin go free. That this method is practicable, the Scriptures abundantly testify. In verse 14, it is very explicitly stated, as the object of the incarnation, "that through death he might destroy him that had the power of death, that is, the devil; and deliver them who, through fear of death, were all their lifetime subject to bondage." So in chapter ix. 15—"That by means of death, they which are called might receive the promise of eternal inheritance." " Who his own self bare our sins in his own body on the tree, that we, being dead to sins, should live unto righteousness; by whose stripes ye were healed." 1 Peter ii. 24. "All we, like sheep, have gone astray; we have turned every one to his own way; and the Lord hath laid on him the iniquity of us all." Isa. liii. 6. So throughout the typical sacrifices of the old law, this is the leading thought—the death of Christ, our passover, procures exemption to us from death. No language of man, no symbol, no figure of speech, can ever be devised to express this master idea more clearly, fully, or forcibly. The sons who are to be brought into glory are condemned and ruined; their leader in the way of life must and does place himself under their sentence, and meet the penal claims of God's justice. For this reason he must become incarnate. "Forasmuch as the children are partakers of flesh and blood" (of humanity) "he also himself likewise took part of the same."

This doctrine is not incidentally taught, not occasionally to be met with in the Bible, but it is pre-eminently *the* doctrine of the book. It is all pervading; it is the alpha and the omega. Take it out of the Bible, and it is no longer the book of God; strike it out of the system, and the sun is gone—darkness reigns. Annihilate the law of gravitation, and the material universe is a chaos; annihilate the doctrine of atonement, and the moral universe is a chaos. "Other foundation can no man lay."

But we have seen many other items in the work; many other stones are necessary to the building besides the foundation; therefore, the relative position of this doctrine of atonement has much to do in enhancing its importance. The foundation stone in an edifice may be rough, unsightly, and buried beneath the earth; it may have less labour bestowed upon it than others, but in importance it is inferior to none. This, however, may not be owing to its intrinsic properties, but to its relative position. Without it the house cannot stand; all the other stones must fall; or rather, could not rise into an edifice at all. So the atonement is indispensable as a pre-requisite to all the other doctrines of salvation. But for this, the doctrine of justification through the righteousness, that is, the active obedience, of Christ imputed to the sinner, and received by faith alone, must remain a cold and dead abstraction. No man can be justified by the perfect righteousness of the Son of God, and by consequence receive life eternal, whilst he abides under condemnation, and so in death. He cannot be both condemned and justified, dead and alive, at the same time. Eternal life can be given as the reward of obedience only; the obedience of Christ in our nature. This, and this alone, entitles the believer to life; but before he can possibly receive and enjoy it, he must be delivered from condemnation imposing death. He must be pardoned; and pardon, that is, the lifting up and removing of his sentence of death from him, can be effected only by Christ's suffering under the law for him. When Christ takes away sin by the sacrifice of himself; when he unites the sinner to himself by faith, and applies to him the blood bought pardon, then the merit of his positive righteousness becomes actually available; the sinner puts on the spotless wedding garment, and stands justified and complete in him. This relative position of the two doctrines of atonement, and of justification proper, is referred to by our apostle, in Rom. iii. 24: "Being justified freely by his grace, through the redemption that is in Christ Jesus"—the redemption, the releasing, by paying the proper price. Death is the *medium* through which his righteousness becomes actually efficient to our justification.

Now, as with this, so it is with all other parts of the work under consideration. Still, it will be kept in mind, that these two, *atonement* by Christ's death, and *righteousness* by his obedience, regard man's legal relations; the other parts enumerated regard his moral character; and yet they stand in the same order of subsequence to the former. Of course, I speak not of order as to time, but as to nature. Could we, however, mark time here, it would most probably be found, that what I have called the natural, and might perhaps more correctly call the logical order, was also the order of actual succession as to time. But as this is only partly practicable, it is not necessary to affirm it here.

Thus regeneration is dependent on the atonement of Christ, because the mission of the Holy Spirit, who alone can change the heart and new create the soul, is dependent upon the Saviour's intercession; and all his power, as our advocate with the Father, springs from the perfection of his work whilst on earth. Had not he finished this work; had not he been made perfect through sufferings, he could not have risen from the dead, nor ascended to glory, nor appeared as our advocate, nor sent the Spirit into the soul for regeneration and conversion. This chain of relations Peter uses in his pentecostal address, and with it he binds the yoke of Christ upon the necks of three thousand of the former servants of Satan. This same chain the Saviour throws around his hearers at the first sacramental supper, where his longest recorded address was delivered. "It is expedient for you that I go away; for if I go not away, the Comforter will not come unto you; but if I depart, I will send him unto you." John xvi. 7. The entire work of the Holy Ghost, then, in the regeneration, conversion, faith, repentance, holy living, love, joy, peace, of the sons of God, unto their entire sanctification and glorification, is dependent upon the finished atonement of the gracious Mediator. So, also, is the final and grand act of raising them from the dead, and presenting them before the presence of the Father's glory. "If Christ be not risen, then is our preaching vain, and your faith is also vain;" but "if we believe that Jesus died and rose again, even so them also which sleep in Jesus shall God bring with him." But for the perfection of his sufferings, he could not rise from the dead and ascend to his glory, much less lead his many sons thither. How inconceivably important is this finishing operation! How transcendently glorious are the issues from death! What hopes cluster around the cross of Calvary!

These, all these, must pass away, and black despair for ever brood upon the human spirit, unless he drink the bitter cup, and cry "it is finished!"

III. We proceed now to the main topic of our text—*The consistency of accomplishing this work by these means, with Jehovah's character as Creator, Governor, and Proprietor of the universe.*

The salvation of lost man is a display of divine love under a peculiar form—that called mercy; the extension of the highest favours to persons the most undeserving. It is the outgoing of goodness, and, if viewed alone, must command universal admiration, and call forth praise from all, and gratitude unbounded from the favoured race. As to its consistency with God's benevolent character, there can be no question. If Jehovah were all love, all goodness, all benevolence, we have in this work its counterpart. But he hath not so revealed himself to us, either in his works or in his word. Other attributes belong to his nature. Justice and judgment are the habitation of his throne, whilst mercy and truth go before him. His providence teaches the same lesson. Evils innumerable are visited upon men in this world, and a dread surmise springs up in the mind, unaided even by a revelation, that the present are not all the evils man may possibly endure at the hand of his offended and insulted Creator. But this idea is no longer vague and undetermined when we open the sacred volume. Here it shines forth with terrible clearness; all doubt passes away; God is holy, just, and true; he will punish crime; he will vindicate the claims of justice.

Two views divide mankind on this subject. One theory assumes as its basis, the principle of infinite benevolence: God is good, benevolent, and merciful. This is the controlling attribute of his nature; indeed, they virtually deny him any other, and say there is no such attribute as justice *essential* to his nature; it is a *contingency* in the Creator. He may exercise justice, or he may omit its exercise; he may punish crime, or he may omit its punishment. Vindictive justice belongs not to God. It is blasphemy, in the opinion of these men, to represent God as angry; as a vindictive Being, marking sins as they occur, and pouring his wrath sooner or later upon the culprit. This, in their estimation, makes him malevolent and revengeful. But such philosophers have closed the Bible, and shut one of reason's eyes. They forget that it is written, "Though hand join in hand, the wicked shall not go unpunished." "The wages of sin is death." "God is angry with the wicked every day." "The Lord will not hold him guiltless who taketh his name in vain." To this class of men, more benevolent than God, he addresses a severe rebuke—"Thou thoughtest that I was altogether such an one as thyself; but I will reprove thee, and set them in order before thine eyes. Now consider this, ye that forget God, lest I tear you in pieces, and there be none to deliver."

They also close the eye of reason, and therefore see not that justice is as necessary an attribute in the government of God as in that of man. As man cannot exist without justice, as society would instantly run into utter chaos and ruin, so is this glorious attribute indispensable in the Divine government; and God has exhausted human language in order to enforce a due apprehension of this idea upon the human understanding. But still there are multitudes who will not believe it, even upon the innumerable testimonies written in God's holy Word. But their unbelief does not make the testimonies void; nor shall their unbelief last for ever, for "the Lord trieth the righteous, but the wicked, and him that loveth violence, his soul hateth. Upon the wicked he shall rain snares, fire, and brimstone, and an horrible tempest; this shall be the portion of their cup." Psa. xi. 5, 6. "And these shall go away into everlasting punishment, prepared for the devil and his angels." Matt. xxv. 46. 41, God is a *just* God, and a Saviour. Justice is an attribute essential to his being; love or goodness is so also; but mercy, which is the flowing forth of love toward transgressors, is a contingency. It is not necessary to the being of God, that he extend his boundless goodness to any particular class of sinful beings, or to all sinners. But if he in sovereignty do so extend it, his justice must be satisfied; its claims must be met. The question before us is not, whether the salvation of men is consistent with the Divine character; on this there is no dispute; but whether the accomplishment of this work, *by the sufferings of Christ*, be consistent. Does the exposure of the only Beloved to shame, and ignominy, and death, comport with the dignity of the supreme Governor? Assuming the scriptural facts, that God did send his Son into the world, expressly that he might obey and die under the curse of the law for lost men; that God did put into the hands of the Captain of Salvation the bitter cup of Divine wrath, and when he cried and prayed that it might pass, if possible, the Father did not remove it; that it pleased the Lord to bruise him; to make his soul an offering for sin—this undeniable scripture doctrine, this suffering of Jesus, by express appointment of God the Father, is this consistent? Can it be reconciled with his character as Creator, Governor, Proprietor of all things? The affirmation is Paul's assertion, and the proof now demands our attention.

1. It became him as Creator. The character of the maker is seen in the thing made. As long as men reason from cause to effect; as long as like causes produce like effects, will they judge of the tree by its fruits. It is on this principle that history

teaches. From a man's actions we infer his character. This, too, is the productive principle of all the inductive sciences. We note things as they appear, classify them, and infer the laws of nature from her works. This standard of judgment is safe; and, therefore, it is universally relied on. Our business, then, is to view the work of salvation in the method here contemplated, and then to inquire whether the attributes, or powers, or qualities displayed therein, are such as become the Creator, God. And we see, first, the highest manifestation of justice: he would not spare even his own Son.

Again, truth shines forth in connection with justice, as it is a fulfilment of the Divine declaration, that sin should be punished.

And, again, love is conspicuous: God so loved the world that he gave his only begotten Son to die for the lost.

Again, mercy to rebels, a modification of love, is pre-eminent. Here we have such an exhibition of Divine perfections as cannot be found in any other work of the Creator. We merely name them now, as in a moment they will come up in another relation.

2dly. Under the administration of a perfect government, suffering bespeaks previous wrong-doing. Painful endurance must have its origin in transgression of law. No moral being can be made to endure physical calamity, but in consequence of moral evil. This truth is assumed as an element in morals. All men acknowledge it—feel it, as it were, and instantly, upon seeing a person suffer peculiar calamity, begin to seek for its moral cause. "Who did sin, this man or his parents?" "No doubt this man is a murderer, whom, though he hath escaped the sea, yet vengeance (justice) suffereth not to live." The only error, in reasoning here, is the not keeping in mind the sin of nature; original sin, as the general cause of all calamity, and in supposing that God's government, like man's, was always specific, and every particular calamity was a precise infliction for some particular sin. But the general idea is the same, which lies at the foundation of all moral government. "The soul that sinneth, it shall die;" "the wages of sin is death;" "sin shall not go unpunished."

Sufferings do fall sometimes upon persons who have not themselves, individually, transgressed the law. God, in his providence, does visit the iniquities of fathers upon their children. Did not Israel groan under calamities unutterable, for the sin of David in numbering the tribes? Is it any thing new for the fearful scourge of war to fall upon a whole people for the sins of their rulers? Have not thousands of millions of widowed mothers and fatherless children, been crushed under calamities too dreadful to endure, to gratify the pride of kings, and maintain the figment of their blood-stained honour?

But all these cases involve the fact of some pre-existent relation; some connection between the parties affected, in consequence of which the calamities were brought about. In many cases we are unable to understand the reasons of the connection, and perceive how the results necessarily follow. But this, by no means, disproves such connection as justifies the Divine government. Human ignorance is not an adequate condemnation of Divine justice. It may be right that the children suffer in consequence of the father's crimes, though we may not be able to explain it. Yea, we must admit it, or charge God foolishly, which is to turn atheist. When the Psalmist saw the wicked prospering, he could not reason out the case, and was tempted to deny God's just administration, until he went to the sanctuary, and learned from revelation the doctrine of a future judgment. So must we admit the facts of providence, and fall back upon the revealed explanation, that he does visit the iniquities of the fathers upon the children, of the rulers upon the people.

Now, whilst we maintain the personal, spotless purity of the divine Redeemer, we must find some way to account for the fact of his sufferings, without charging the universal Governor foolishly. There must be a reason for his laying upon him the iniquities of us all. Such connection between Christ and his people does exist, as renders it right and proper, and every way befitting the attributes of the Divine character, to visit the Captain of Salvation with the perfection of sufferings. All the difficulties of the case vanish before the light of the glorious truth, that God, in eternity, appointed the Son as a covenant head of his people; a surety who voluntarily guaranteed their deliverance from death and introduction to eternal glory, by meeting all the requirements of law on their account. The Scriptures accordingly assure us, that believers were chosen in him before the foundation of the world; that he became the surety of a better testament;

that he freely offered himself as the head of his body, the Church. "Lo, I come to do thy will; O God I take delight." Now it is this covenant relationship, voluntarily entered into by the glorious Mediator, which constitutes the just reason why the Father laid on him the sins of a ruined world, and why, in the fullness of time, he endured the unutterable anguish of the curse for crimes that we had done. These countless heavy woes fell on him, as the necessary and legal consequences of his suretyship.

Here we have the principle, and the only principle, by which we can "justify the ways of God to men." This covenant of grace, which no created intellect could have devised, which no human wisdom could have discovered, which could originate only in the bosom of everlasting love, and find its way to created minds only by supernatural revelation—this everlasting covenant, ordered in all things and sure—this alone solves the mystery, and makes known *how* God can be just, and yet the justifier of the sinner that believes in Jesus. On the cross of Calvary justice and mercy meet together, righteousness and peace, the righteousness of God and the peace of man, embrace each other. When Jesus said, "It is finished," the sword of God's justice was bathed in heaven; the command, "Awake, O sword, against my Shepherd," was fulfilled, and yet no injustice is done. This blow is no *injury* to the Shepherd, although he himself had *personally* done no evil, but always felt and acted out the principle, "My meat is to do the will of him that sent me, and to finish his work." Still, "it pleased the

Lord to bruise him." How *can* this be? Because Jesus, "his own self bare our sins in his own body on the tree." Now the position before us is, that this smiting and its effects, under these circumstances, are becoming in God, the universal Governor, for whom, and on whose account, all things were made.

That its effects are so, is manifest on its face, for the perfection of government consists in promoting the greatest good, and preventing the greatest evil; that is, in the perfect administration of justice. But this work of saving men secures to them the highest happiness, and for the longest duration, even for ever and ever.

Nor let it be objected, that he does not save all; some go away into everlasting punishment, for we have no question as to what he did not do; our question is whether the thing he did be consistent with good and wise government. And this we affirm with confidence. In saving men by blood no injustice is done to them, nor even to those whom he does not bring unto glory; they receive nothing at his hand against which they can complain; but, on the contrary, infinite blessings which they personally have not merited. Let it not be objected, again, in reference to this last, that giving what a man is not entitled to is not justice, any more than withholding what he is entitled to. This is true, but it is not *in*justice. It is not a matter against which complaint can lie as a wrong thing; no, not even from a third party, to whom similar benevolence is not extended. "Is thine eye evil, because I am good? may not I do what I will with mine own?" is the most reasonable reply of the Master to such objection.

Besides, the *benevolence* displayed in this salvation, does not, properly speaking, spring from governmental power, but from sovereign love. Pardon is not an act of governing power, but of sovereignty and benevolence.

The greatest evils are also prevented. Sons brought unto glory sin no more. Their deliverance from physical is not more perfect than from moral evil, and both are perpetual and eternal.

So the smiting of the Shepherd, under the circumstances, is proper; for the Shepherd stands, in the eye of the law, as the head of his body, the church—the sons brought into glory. He became their surety, and, by necessary consequence, their failure devolves upon him the whole legal responsibilities of their guarantee. From these he could not shrink. Justice demanded of him what she had a right to exact from his people. The law rightly held them responsible to death, and it rightly exacted death from him; so, conversely, he having met the rightful requisition, having died the death, has a rightful claim for their exemption from death.

This transaction is equally consistent and becoming the universal Proprietor, for whom are all things.

The final cause of the universe, is the glory of its Creator—"for thy pleasure they are and were created." "The chief end of man is to glorify God, and to enjoy him for ever." This being undeniable, the manifestation of mercy, heaven's darling attribute, promotes this end in a very high degree; yea, "glory to God in the highest, and on earth peace, good will to men." There is no higher attribute of Jehovah than his love, none holier than his justice; there are no two that to created reason seem more at variance. Man sins; the trembling culprit stands self-condemned, heaven-condemned, before his Judge; the arm of Almighty justice is raised; the terrible blow that must smite the wretched sinner down to an everlasting hell is just ready to descend: when lo! Love, divine love springs forward—"Father Almighty, forbear! On me let the stroke of thy vengeance fall: smite the Shepherd!" The fiery blade is seized, and its burning point turned in upon the bosom of the innocent victim. Love bleeds—the languid head droops: "It is finished"—the agony is over—the curse exhausted. Mercy rises from the tomb, a lovely form, a new attribute, heretofore unknown in the universe of God. Angelic messengers, now for the first time beholding in its fulness the glory of their God, escort the heaven-generated, but earth-born stranger to the realms of day. The song of salvation swells from myriads of golden harps, and all heaven is filled with the echo of the beloved name.

In conclusion, let us glance at the bearings of this stupendous fact in the Divine government upon the destinies of the moral universe.

It is the act confirmatory. The nail that fastened Christ to the cross, gave the rivet of unchangeability to government throughout all its departments, human and divine.

It is confirmatory, in that it exhibits to all the intelligent creation, the highest evidence it has ever had, perhaps the highest it can have, of the immutability of Divine justice, and so of the stability of the moral system. The government of God is not, as man's too often is, one of mere expediency; it is based on fixed and unalterable principles, and will remain the same for ever. Here and now, if ever, justice must relax. Had it been possible, this cup would have passed from the Saviour's lips without his drinking it: for never was such an appeal made by intelligent nature under suffering—"Oh my Father! if it be possible, let this cup pass from me." It did not pass; thereby giving confirmation, full and perfect, to the unchangeableness of justice.

We may therefore expect that human governments will be stable, regular, fixed, and efficient, in proportion to the people's knowledge and practice upon the great doctrine of atonement—of salvation by the sufferings of Christ. To this facts correspond. In what countries do we find the best governments, the most justice, the freest, and the purest, and the happiest people? What says history? What is the testimony of the present? One voice comes down to us through the long line of ages; one voice rises up from the world's whole surface—that voice directs us to Calvary. Where the doctrines of Christ and him crucified are most known, there are to be found the freest, and happiest, and best governed nations. "These have washed their robes and made them white in the blood of the Lamb. Therefore are they before the throne of God, and serve him day and night in his temple." How deep then the debt, and how solemn the obligation, of all free nations, to the true evangelical church of God! How happy the people who wear the yoke of Christ!

This confirmation extends to the lost portion of our sinful race, who go away into everlasting fire.

That justice unchangeable, which upholds the Divine throne, falls as a crushing weight upon all who aim at tearing down this throne, and grinds them to powder. They are sealed up in endless death; but the sufferings of Christ do not produce this. Will the justice, which yielded not even to his strong crying and tears, relax, in order to let go the rebel who, to all the sins of his life and nature, adds the crowning one of unbelief? Shall *he* escape who tramples under foot the Son of God, and puts him to an open shame, accounting his precious blood an unholy thing? Shall not double vengeance fall upon his soul? He puts away from himself, by a wilful and deliberate resistance, the only salvation which infinite love ever provided; how then can he be saved? He seals his own condemnation, and justice confirms the deed for ever.

Still more obvious is the confirmation of God's redeemed in the joys of eternal salvation. Perish they cannot, for justice immutable has no claim against them, and has proclaimed the fact in raising Jesus from the dead; and trumpet tongues of thousands of angels have heralded the glad tidings throughout the universe. His blood has washed away the guilt of all their sins, and procured a full pardon. His sufferings procured him admission to his throne of glory in the heavens, sent the Holy Spirit down, created their hearts anew, sanctified their entire soul and body, arrayed them in his own glorious righteousness, and filled all their soul with heavenly love. Thus redeemed, regenerated, justified, and sanctified, how can they be kept from glory?— Where is the power to reverse the sentence passed upon them, and turn them back to perdition? "Who shall lay any thing to the charge of God's elect? It is God that justifieth. Who is he that condemneth? It is Christ that died, yea rather, that is risen again." "Who shall separate us from the love of Christ?"

To fallen angels, the sufferings of Christ in the room of his people afford fearful evidence of the hopelessness of their case. If God spared not his own Son, if justice could not relax to save him, how shall it abate its demands to save them? This may account for the deep interest Satan and his demons felt in Christ's mission and work; their eagerness to know whether this Jesus was the Messiah, and whether he could be diverted from his purpose to satisfy justice, by his death; and for all their machinations to thwart his plans for leading his sons to glory.

Is Jesus a confirming head of moral influences to the holy angels and the entire universe? By confirming head is, of course, meant, not that he redeemed angels, but that his sufferings stood in such relations to the Divine government, and to them under it, as to put an end to their probation, and place them beyond the possibility for ever of falling, as Diabolus and the demons fell. Until the resurrection of Christ, the conception is, that the holy angels were in a probationary or trial state, liable individually to sin, as Satan did, as Adam did, and perish under God's wrath. But after he had finished his work, and ascended to glory, that state ceased, and the Divine power and protection henceforth secures them for ever, as it does the saints redeemed;

so that they can go no more out, and are subject no more to the dread possibility of sinning, but rest in the ineffable felicity of a full assurance of life eternal.

To the affirmative of this question my mind strongly preponderates, and for the folllowing reasons:

The language of the text seems to imply it. "It became Him for whom are all things." In this precise relation, as *universal Proprietor* and *Governor*, there was a suitableness and propriety in putting the cup into his hands. But where is the ground of this propriety, if the other parts of the universe are uninfluenced by it? How could they be uninterested in the glory of their Governor? But if they are to be both influenced and interested, it is difficult to see any other way, than that this glorious transaction confirms the Divine government and them in the blessedness of its protection.

Again, this idea corresponds with the interest felt by the holy angels in the concerns of Christ and his Church. "Are they not all ministering spirits, sent forth to minister unto them who shall be heirs of salvation?" Do not they watch over the camp of Israel for good, and combat the legions of hell? Did not they herald the advent of their Lord Creator as our Lord Redeemer? Did they not guard his steps from the manger to the cross? Did they not cluster in embattled phalanx there, marking with intensest interest the agony in which he died? Did they not, on wings of light, bear the glad tidings of his resurrection to the regions of immortal day? Did they not now, and for the first time, learn from the Church below the manifold wisdom of God, and understand those things into which they had long desired to look? Let it, then, be supposed that these heavenly hosts were, till this hour, on probation, and not assured that Satan might not yet prevail, and they fall and perish; but that now confirmation came, and their destiny is for ever safe. Oh! what a moment of joy to them! With what glad emotions they hail the rising of the Sun of Righteousness! The mystery of redemption is unveiled, and the mystery of confirmation thrills through the boundless universe!

My third reason for favouring this idea, is found in its own magnificence. It seems to me the brightest ray which shines from this Sun of Righteousness. It enhances the riches of his mercy, and magnifies the glory of his cross. "Our earth's aceldama—this field of blood"—becomes the battle-ground on which is decided the fate of the universe. The groans of Gethsemane, and the agonies of the cross, establish the throne of Jehovah Jesus, and put into his nail-pierced hand the sceptre of dominion over the entire realm of nature, and all the creatures of God worship him. Surely "it became Him, for whom are all things, and by whom are all things, in bringing many sons unto glory, to make the Captain of their salvation perfect through sufferings."

EFFICIENCY OF CHRISTIAN PRINCIPLE.

BY

THOS. SMYTH, D. D.

PASTOR OF THE SECOND PRESBYTERIAN CHURCH, CHARLESTON, S. C.

Neither yield ye your members as instruments of unrighteousness unto sin: but yield yourselves unto God, as those that are alive from the dead, and your members as instruments of righteousness unto God. For sin shall not have dominion over you: for ye are not under the law, but under grace.—ROMANS vi. 13, 14.

THE first thing which demands our attention, in unfolding the meaning of this passage of the Word of God, (which is so pregnant with meaning that we must pass by any introductory observations,) is the duty which is here laid down as binding upon all men. This duty, to which we are all summoned by the authority of this inspired and divinely commissioned ambassador from the courts of heaven, is expressed both affirmatively and negatively. We are admonished what that is which we are required to do, and also what that is from which we should abstain.

It is commanded that we shall not yield our members as instruments of unrighteousness unto sin. The word translated "yield," means to give up to the use and control of another. "Your members," include not only the organs of the body, but also the powers, faculties, and capacities of the mind, and is used as a periphrasis for *yourselves,* that is, the whole man, as composed of a living body and a reasonable soul. These members we are not to yield as instruments unto sin. Sin is here personified as a monarch, ruler, or guide, and we are forbidden to allow to sin, in any of these capacities, the use or control of our mental or physical powers. When so employed, they are perverted, abused to a purpose contrary to their original design, and alienated from that service wherein they ought to be employed. If they are so devoted, voluntarily, and by our own choice, we are guilty of robbery, treachery, unfaithfulness, and disobedience, since we are stewards of these heavenly gifts, and responsible for their proper and intended use to the righteous Judge of all. Thus to yield them, therefore, as servants to sin, is a crime of inexcusable turpitude, for which we shall be held justly responsible at the bar of heaven. On the other hand, does sin lay siege to our hearts, and by the open assaults and fiery darts of grievous temptations, or by the secret wiles of more insinuating artifices, seek to gain possession of our citadel, and reduce us to a state of subjection and of vassalage? then are we to regard him as an usurper and a rebel, as without any right or title to such authority, and as one to whom on no conditions, and under no possible extremity, are we permitted to render our obeisance. Whatsoever may be the severity of his threatenings; whatsoever the strength and power with which he storms our hearts, and to whatever straits we may be brought by his long protracted warfare, yet at the peril of our soul's salvation let us not yield unto him. He that so yields becomes the servant of sin, the captive of Satan, and the enemy of God.

It is our duty, therefore, as subjects of the moral government of God; as having been created, preserved, and redeemed by him, and as being under his absolute control, to "yield ourselves unto God"—that is, to give ourselves up to his service and control. "And yield your members as instruments of righteousness unto God;" that is, yield yourselves in all your powers and faculties, whether of mind or of body, that they may be employed in God's service, and to his honour and glory. Now it is here evidently implied, as it is throughout the whole Word of God, that men are at present in such a lapsed and ruined condition as to be alienated from the service and love of God, and enthralled by the love and dominion of sin. Such is the disposition of mankind universally, that they listen with a ready ear to the voice of the tempter, and are incredulous to the forewarning of Jehovah. They bow willingly to the yoke of sin and Satan, hard and ignominious though it be, and they openly and blasphemously declare by their *practical* enunciations, which speak louder than any words, "As for God we will not have him to reign over us. We love the wages of unrighteousness, and after sin we will go."

It is also here as plainly taught us, that however this may be the determination of mankind, and however unanimous they may be in thus casting off the yoke and authority of God—that, nevertheless, they are still under his government, under untransferrable obligation to obey him, and amenable to that law whose wrath is revealed from heaven, not only against all *unrighteousness*, of whatever character and degree, but also against the *ungodliness* of all men, of whatever name, rank or station.

It is further and very clearly taught that, however men may be now guilty, and held justly accountable for the endurance of that penalty in which, by one man's disobedience, we are all involved; however they may have ratified that sin by their own voluntary choice of a course of like disobedience; and however habituated they may have become to the service of iniquity, they are not one whit the less under obligation, or less bound to render unto God a full and perfect obedience. By the very fact that God has permitted them to live, given to them the exercise of a free agency, and presented to them motives for such obedience, they are imperatively required, by every consideration of justice, to render unto God, and to his service, those powers and faculties with which he has endowed them. These powers are in no sense theirs, and cannot, therefore, without robbery, be withdrawn from the superintending care and claims of him by whom they were originally given, and by whom they are constantly sustained.

God has placed in the breast of every man a will, to which is given authority and power to govern and direct the movements of the inner man. By this the passions, affections, and desires move and exercise their being, and without its consenting fiat no rational act can be performed. Now, in the present corrupt state of human nature, this will has been seduced into the service of sin, and withdrawn from all natural allegiance to the dominion of heaven.

God, however, does not release from subjection this will, which he alone could either give or maintain. He, therefore, enters his demand in the conscience of every human being; and, calling heaven and earth to witness, he solemnly forbids that homage which the sinful heart of man renders to the god of this world, on the peril of everlasting death; while he encourages its devotion to himself and his service by the promise of everlasting life. And it is of God's infinite mercy that any such demand is made to that which is in itself of no account to him, and of which he has been so unworthily despoiled. It is because of God's unspeakable mercy we are spared at all, borne with in any patience, or permitted the opportunity of returning to our allegiance to him. And that we should be invited thus to submit our wills to him, and to devote ourselves to his glorious service, by those motives which are presented in the gospel of his Son, this truly is a mystery of love, whose height, and depth, whose length and breadth, is beyond our comprehension.

You will observe, too, how the exhortation requires not that we should, in this life, be absolutely free from sin as a law or principle within us, which would be impossible. The evil tendency, or law of our members, remains even in regenerated men, and is still ready to war against their renewed nature. This *tendency* we are not required, therefore, utterly to destroy, which it were impossible, while in this body of sin and death, that we should; but *voluntarily* to submit to this inward propensity, or to yield ourselves to its suggestions, so as to do its will, this is forbidden, and this we may not do. On the contrary, to be resolutely determined not to submit to this law of concupiscence or sin, but, contrariwise, to follow out, at every cost, the dictates of the law of holiness; this is what we are under obligation to perform at once and without delay, with full knowledge of what is required of us; with serious consideration; with a determinate judgment; with liberty of spirit, having disengaged ourselves from all other masters; with a belief in and acceptance of the Lord Jesus Christ, and of God in him as our only Lord, Sovereign, and Master; with all humility, joy, and gladness; and with the entire surrender of all that we are and have to his guidance and direction. This is that duty to which we are each called by all that is winning in mercy, and by all that is fearful in that wrath which burneth even to the lowest hell.

This duty is ours as fully as if we retained all man's original power and inclination to discharge it. It is plainly and absolutely commanded. And it is by simply believing that in doing what God has thus warranted and required, God will as certainly "work in us both to will and to do;" it is by thus casting ourselves before his footstool, in the entire surrender of ourselves to him in Christ Jesus, and trusting to Christ's righteousness and meritorious intercession, that every sinner has been, or ever will be, made able and willing to "yield himself unto God, and his members as instruments of righteousness unto him."

But this brings us, in the second place, to the consideration of the *principle* upon which this *duty* is here made to rest. This, also, is expressed both negatively and affirmatively. We are exhorted and required to devote ourselves to God, and to withdraw all allegiance from the service of the world, by the assurance that we are "alive from the dead." Herein is contained the principle upon which, as the only true and living root, the apostle would graft the duty of obedience. We are called upon to make this self-dedication unto God, not that we may thereby *obtain* life, but as those for whom that life has already been obtained; not that we may *merit* life, but as those upon whom it has already been most graciously conferred; not that, by any sacrifice on our part, it may be wrought out, but as those for whom it has been already purchased by the precious blood of Christ. The principle of the apostle is, therefore, diametrically opposite to the principle of legalism in all its forms. It is at direct variance with all the prescriptions by which men, in their arrogant pretensions to wisdom, would secure this heavenly blessing. "Yield yourselves unto God," *they* would tell us "that, by such a holy devotedness, ye may commend yourselves to God, and thus secure the blessings of life and salvation at his hands. Enter, therefore, upon this way of formal and ceremonial purification, since, without holiness, it is impossible that you can ever see God." Such would be the exhortation of those who build their hopes upon a righteousness within them, and not upon a righteousness without and beyond them, and who thus seek to be justified for their own doings, and not for the work and merit of "the Lord our righteousness."

But how widely different is the prescription of this

divine apostle. He inspirits us to this act of a self-devoting sacrifice, not so much by the prospect of what may in future be gained by it, as by the thought of what has been already achieved on our behalf; not so much by the hope of conciliating the divine clemency, as by the glorious assurance that God has been already reconciled. "As those who are" already "alive from the dead," and to whom there is held forth the promise of an ascension to glory, even to that glory with which Christ has been glorified, are we here urged to "yield ourselves to God."

There is a peculiar force and expressiveness in this declaration, which plucks up by the very roots all dependence, for the production of holiness, upon the ability or self-righteousness of the creature. "As in Adam all died, so in Christ shall all" the redeemed "be made alive;" "for as by one man's disobedience many were made sinners, so by the obedience of one shall many be made righteous." By sinning in the first Adam, as our public head and representative, we were all constituted sinners, and are treated by the divine Lawgiver as guilty in his sight, "and so death hath passed upon all men, for that all have sinned." Thus were we, and our entire race, under sentence of death, and bound over to the endurance of this dread penalty. And the righteousness of such a sentence we have all attested by the fact, that out of the universal race of man, there has not yet been found "one righteous, no, not one; all having gone out of the way, each in his own way" of sin and folly. But by becoming united to the second Adam, the Lord from heaven, the head and representative of the whole family of the redeemed, we are constituted righteous through the merit of his righteousness, which is imputed to us, and are treated by God accordingly. "There is, therefore," we are assured, "now no condemnation to them that are in Christ Jesus." Death hath no dominion over them. The law has no demands against them. For since death has been endured by their Surety on their behalf, and since the law has been magnified and satisfied for them, they can walk forth in all the freedom of deliverance, and rejoice in "the glorious liberty wherewith Christ hath made them free."

This, then, is one view of this all powerful motive, by which the apostle urges us to an entire devotion to God. Inasmuch as all the claims of that law, which you had broken, have been fully met, and the uttermost of its denounced penalty has been borne; since He who thus suffered for you still lives to intercede on your behalf; and since this whole plan of salvation was of God's devising, and has been completed unto God's well pleasing; as those, who are thus redeemed from the threatened penalty of death, and who are thus made legally entitled to the sentence of divine approval, "yield yourselves unto God," "who is now in Christ Jesus reconciling the world unto himself." Instead, therefore, of urging us to holiness, by the motive of thereby meriting the Divine favour, we are urged to it by the very fact, that thereby we can merit no favour, that propitiation having been already secured by the mediation of the Son of God; and instead of inviting to the pursuit of holiness, that we may thus open up a way of access unto God, it is by the very plea that such a way has been already made plain and obvious, that we are encouraged to approach. It is no longer, therefore, argues the apostle, impossible for you thus to yield yourselves as sinners unto God, seeing that every let and hindrance has been removed; that an "ATONEMENT" has been made, and that God is now "just, and yet the justifier of the ungodly." The doctrine of salvation is thus adapted by the God of nature to the mightiest principle of nature—"for we are saved by hope." We are begotten by the Gospel to the blessed hope of an immortal life. We are certified that the battle has been fought and the victory won, and that now there is announced to us, through Him who was mighty to save, that Gospel which bringeth good tidings of great joy, even "peace on earth, and good will to men."

But, while in this argument of the apostle, there is an appeal made to the principle of hope, the most potent affection of our nature, this argument is also addressed to the principle of gratitude, which is perhaps one of the most pure, pleasant, and disinterested of those affections by which the heart of man is actuated. "Yield yourselves unto God as those that are dead." By the very fact, that you who *were* dead; dead in law, dead by the utterance against you of heaven's righteous sentence of everlasting death; dead to all hope of any possible deliverance; by the thought that you "are *now* alive;" and by the infinite mercy of God in Christ delivered from that condition of despairing wretchedness—"yield yourselves unto God." Withhold not that soul from God, which had been brought under the sentence of eternal death by its apostacy from him, and which has now been re-purchased from the hands of eternal justice; "not with corruptible things, such as silver and gold," but by the endurance, in our stead, by God's only begotten Son, of all this deserved misery.

Sin is here, as I said, likened to some cruel and despotic monarch, who, after he has seduced poor and deluded souls into his service, by the pleasures which he affords them for a season, then gluts his bloody and ferocious spirit, by putting them to fierce and endless torments. "The wages of sin is death." We are now in the position of those who, by the interposition of another, have been rescued from the grasp of this destroyer; and we are, therefore, called upon to yield ourselves henceforth unto His service, by whom we have been redeemed, and by whom alone we can be preserved, and not again to yield ourselves to one from whose determined vengeance we were so mercifully and so wonderfully preserved. Let us take the recorded instance of that princely father, whose own son was found to be the first violator of a law, the penalty of whose infraction was the loss of both eyes. In the yearnings of paternal love, and yet as governed by the mastering principle of sovereign equity, he desires to maintain justice, and yet exercise compassion. The prince, therefore, humbles himself, though innocent of the crime, to a substituted endurance of one half of the denounced penalty, and was deprived, on behalf of his guilty son, of one of his own eyes. Now, were that son again actuated with a desire, whose indulgence would incur the vengeance of the law, how ought he to be dissuaded from such a suicidal act, by the affecting remembrance, that he was now freed from the full endurance of that penalty, which he had in part suffered, through the satisfaction rendered to the law by the suffering and loss of another? And how would his heart be made to relent, by the recollection that he who did so interpose on his behalf, was no other than his own offended father?

Now just such, though immeasurably stronger, is the appeal here made to us. We were condemned, not to the loss of our eyes merely, but to the loss of life itself; not to the loss of our bodily life merely, but to the loss of our spiritual and eternal life also, involving, as this necessarily does, the misery of eternal death. We "were dead in trespasses and sins," and "already condemned." And we may imagine, that having actually endured the bitter curse of death, we are again alive, through the miraculous and all merciful agency of the divine Redeemer. As those, therefore, who have been thus restored to life; as those whose death is not again required to meet the claims of a violated law; as those for whose deliverance salvation has been wrought out by none other than the very power against which we had so grievously offended; we are persuaded not again to bring ourselves into bondage to sin and Satan, but to throw ourselves upon the mercy of Him "who hath loved us, and given himself for us," and who was made a curse for us, being put to death in the flesh, that we, through his death, might have everlasting life.

Nor is this all that is contained within the compass of this heavenly principle. It makes its appeal not only to *hope*, which is the strongest, and to *gratitude*, which is the loveliest principle of our nature, but also to *the assured certainty of success*, which must leave us inexcusable for our disobedience. "As those who are alive from the dead." Not merely does this teach us, that by the meritorious sacrifice and atoning death of the Lord Jesus Christ are we alive *legally*, the sentence of the law having been endured by another. Not merely does it teach us that, being thus alive, we are bound gratefully to live unto Him who thus died for us, and by whom, also, we may be completely redeemed; but it teaches us, also, that if we will only believe on this Lord and Saviour Jesus Christ, as thus able, and willing, and mighty to save us, yea, "even to the uttermost," and though we be the "very chief of sinners," there is in him an omnific virtue by which we shall as certainly be made alive *spiritually*. We shall be made "alive unto God" as we have hitherto been alive only to sin. We shall be so wrought upon by the power of that Spirit, whose divine agency Christ has secured for us, by virtue of the everlasting covenant, that we shall become, as it were, "new creatures in Christ Jesus," "being born again" by a new and celestial birth. If any man will thus cast himself, in a believing acceptance of him, upon Christ Jesus, "he is a new creature," for "though he were dead he shall be made alive," even for evermore. Christ Jesus is thus our head, not only *legally*, but also *vitally*. He is the source, not only of justification from the guilt of sin, but of sanctification also from the power of sin. He has not only wrought out a work of grace *for* us, he also accomplishes a work of grace *within* us. He opens the heart. He sends into it his quickening spirit. He imparts to the soul spiritual energy and life.

He, therefore, in whom we are to believe, has power also to enable and dispose our hearts to believe upon him. He, to whom we are to yield ourselves, is able also to make us willing for such a consecration; and he, to whose service we are to be given, is also ready to fit and prepare us for all its requisitions, and to "give us power to become the sons of God."

Are you, then, now disabled by sin, and far gone from original righteousness? Christ, who raised up the dead by his mighty power, is also able to quicken your souls, and to make them alive unto God. Are you under the dominion of sin, and bound down hand and foot by its iron fetters? Only yield yourselves to Christ, and those chains shall burst asunder, and fall from around you as did the cerements of the grave from around the renovated Lazarus, or as did the fetters from the freed limbs of the imprisoned apostles. He who speaks the word gives the power. He who commands also inspires. He who bids the dead come forth, breathes into him the breath of life, and empowers him to walk forth in newness of life. He who requires you to yield yourselves unto him, is able also to assure you of your success, for "sin shall not have dominion over us."

And are you under a debt of obligation to God's holy and righteous law, which you are incompetent to satisfy, and exposed to its vengeance, which you dare not confront? Nay, but my fellow-sinner, "you are not under the law, but under grace."

Yours is a dispensation of mercy, and not of justice. Yours is the offer of a free purchase and gratuitous pardon; and the law itself rejoices, since "mercy and truth have in Christ Jesus met together, righteousness and peace have embraced each other."

Neither is yours "the spirit of bondage, that you should again fear," but the spirit of freedom and of love, that you should draw near in confidence, and even boldness. The law, as your creditor, has no demand; for, in the obedience of Christ, the debt has been more than liquidated.

If, then, there is any power in *hope* to inspire and animate the human breast; if there is any thing in *gratitude* to call forth its tenderest sensibilities; if there is aught in *the assurance of success* to inspirit to noble daring; if these motives are powerful, and the objects to which they lead invaluable, then surely there is in this argument of the apostle the law of evangelical holiness, and all the strength of divine principle. And hence may you perceive the ignorance and fatuity of vain and conceited men, who charge the doctrine of a free, unlimited, and gratuitous mercy, with the consequences of licentiousness in practice, and weakness in motive, or who fear to proclaim to men, in all its fullness, "the glorious gospel of the blessed God." The spirit of the Christian is free and not constrained. It is spontaneous, and not forced. It is filial, and not slavish. It is cordial, and not formal. It is liberty, and not law. It is love, and not fear.

The condemnation wherewith the finally impenitent sinner shall be everlastingly condemned will be, not that he could not discover the knowledge of the

Most High, but that he would not come to the light, lest his deeds should be reproved; not that he would not come unto God by his own power, which he could not do, but that he would not come unto God by Christ, who is "the way, the truth, and the life;" not that he did not make himself whole when he was diseased, or alive when he was dead, or righteous when he was sinful, or holy when he was polluted, but that he would not come unto that blessed Saviour, who, as a physician, is able to restore him; who, as almighty to save, can even quicken souls which are spiritually dead, and who of God is made unto every one that believeth wisdom, and righteousness, and sanctification, and complete redemption.

Just, then, as inexcusable is the obstinate and self-destroyed sinner, as is the man who, when sick, refuses to send for a physician, or to receive his medicine when offered. Yes, just as everlastingly self-condemned will you be, my impenitent reader, who now in this, the day of thy merciful visitation, putteth away from thee the things that belong to thy peace. Only continue in thy present course, and soon it will be said of thee, "but now they are for ever hidden from thine eyes, for thou hast destroyed thyself." "Because thou sayest I am rich, and increased with goods, and have need of nothing; and knowest not that thou art wretched, and miserable, and poor, and blind, and naked: I counsel thee to buy of me gold tried in the fire, that thou mayest be rich; and white raiment, that thou mayest be clothed, and *that* the shame of thy nakedness do not appear; and anoint thine eyes with eye-salve, that thou mayest see." "Behold, I stand at the door, and knock: if any man hear my voice, and open the door, I will come in to him, and will sup with him, and he with me. To him that overcometh will I grant to sit with me in my throne, even as I also overcame, and am set down with my Father in his throne. He that hath an ear, let him hear what the Spirit saith unto the churches."

THE GOOD MAN.

BY
JOHN M'DOWELL, D. D,
PASTOR OF THE SPRING GARDEN PRESBYTERIAN CHURCH, PHILADELPHIA.

"He was a good man."—Acts xi. 24, first clause.

This was said of Barnabas. He was a Levite, of the country of Cyprus. Some suppose he was one of the seventy disciples, whom our Lord sent out to preach the Gospel; but of this we have no certain evidence. He introduced Paul to the apostles and disciples at Jerusalem, and assured them of his conversion. He was afterwards, for several years, the companion of Paul in his travels, and his fellow labourer in the gospel ministry; and he was with him, as a delegate from the Syrian churches to the famous Council at Jerusalem. There was finally a dissension between him and Paul, about taking Mark with them on a missionary tour, and they separated, and Barnabas went to Cyprus, and we hear no more of him.

At the time, in the history of Barnabas, when the testimony in the text was given of him, he was at Antioch, in Syria, whither he had been sent by the church of Jerusalem, on hearing of a special work of grace in that city. When Barnabas came to Antioch, "and had seen the grace of God, he was glad, and exhorted them all, that with purpose of heart they would cleave unto the Lord." Our text is given as a reason why he was glad at the prosperity of the religion he witnessed, and why he exhorted the new converts as he did; "for he was a good man." The term *good* here expresses the whole religious character of the real Christian. In this sense the term will be understood in the ensuing discourse, the object of which will be

To give the *character* of the *good man,* or real *Christian,* and

1. The good man has had his *heart changed.* No person, however amiable in the sight of men his natural temper may be, has naturally a heart that is good in the sight of God, or in the sense in which the word is applied to men in the Scriptures. In his natural state every person is "dead in trespasses and sins." Eph. ii. 1. He "receiveth not the things of the Spirit of God, for they are foolishness unto him; neither can he know them." 1 Cor. ii. 14. He is carnal, for "that which is born of the flesh is flesh," or carnal. John iii. 6. And "the carnal mind is enmity against God, for it is not subject to the law of God, neither indeed can be." Rom. viii. 7. Such, according to the Word of God, is the native character of all men, and such was once the character of every one who is now a good man.

But, by the special operations of the Holy Spirit, the naturally corrupt heart of him who is now a good man has been changed. He has been "renewed in knowledge, after the image of Him that created him." Col. iii. 10. And "after God," or after his image, he has been "created in righteousness and true holiness." Eph. iv. 24. He has had imparted to him, by the Holy Spirit, a temper of conformity to the image and will of God. This change every good man or true Christian has experienced; for we read, "Except a man be born again he cannot see the kingdom of God. Except a man be born of water, and of the Spirit, he cannot enter into the kingdom of God. Marvel not that I said unto thee, Ye must be born again." John iii. 3, 5, 7. "If any man be in Christ, he is a new creature; old things have passed away; behold, all things are become new." 2 Cor. v. 17. The time and manner of this change may be different in different persons, and in some it may be more marked than in others; but the change itself every good man, without exception, has experienced; and in vain do any lay claim to the character of a good man if they are strangers to regeneration.

2. The good man has *come to Christ by faith*, and has placed his reliance for pardon and acceptance with God solely on his merits. With Paul, "knowing that a man is not justified by the works of the law, but by the faith of Jesus Christ, he has believed in Jesus Christ, that he might be justified by the faith of Christ, and not by the works of the law." Gal. ii. 16. Sensible of his sinfulness, guilt, and deserved condemnation, and that he has no righteousness of his own to merit forgiveness and acceptance with God, and approving of the way of salvation through Christ, he has renounced his own righteousness, and cordially accepted Christ as the Lord his righteousness; and on his merits alone he relies

for justification. Christ is the good man's all in the article of justification.

He is his all, too, in the article of sanctification. He feels that he is, of himself, unable to subdue his corruptions, and do his duty, and lead a life of holiness before God, and that Christ alone is the believer's life. He therefore relies on him, by his Spirit, to mortify sin within him; to impart, preserve, and quicken grace; to strengthen him to resist temptations, and do his duty; and to keep him, through faith, unto final salvation. He is sensible that without Christ he "can do nothing," and therefore he relies on him for every thing.

3. The good man is a *true penitent for sin.* He has been convinced of sin, and felt himself to be a sinner; he has been convinced of the odious and evil nature of sin, and of his desert of the wrath of God for his sins, and that God would be just in punishing him; he has sorrowed on account of his sins, been self-abased before God, and, with contrition of heart, made confession to him; and he has, with hatred of sin, turned from it unto God. This is repentance unto life, and every good man has exercised it; for our Saviour declared, "Except ye repent, ye shall all likewise perish." Luke xiii. 3. And the good man not only repented, when he first became pious, but he still repents. He is sensible that sin still cleaves to him, and dwells in him, and that his best services are marked with imperfection and sin. Sin is still odious and evil in his sight; he still feels that he deserves the wrath of God for his sins; he still mourns that he ever sinned against God, and still sins, and comes short of his

duty; and he still confesses his sins to God, and hates them more and more.

4. *The good man is, in general, correct in the articles of his faith.* It is an incorrect and dangerous sentiment, that it is a matter of indifference what a man believes if his life be good, for the Word of God requires us to believe the truth he has revealed, as well as do what he has commanded; and the doctrines of the gospel have such an intimate influence on the temper and practice, that it is very doubtful whether a man's life ever be really good, when his faith, in regard to the great doctrines of religion, is wrong. There are some doctrines which are fundamental in the Christian system! The belief of such doctrines is essential to the character of the good man. These doctrines are such as the following: the depravity and ruined state of man; salvation only through Christ; that he is a divine person, God equal with the Father; that he made atonement for sin, which is the only just foundation of a sinner's reconciliation with God; justification only by faith in him; regeneration and sanctification by the Holy Spirit; also a divine person, and the necessity of holiness of heart and life. These doctrines good men of all denominations believe, though they may differ on some points of less importance.

The good man, whatever name he may bear, takes the Scriptures implicitly as the rule of his faith. He does not set up his reason, or inclination, above the Word of God; he desires to know what the truth of God is, and as far as he knows, he believes what God has revealed; though he may not be able fully to explain or comprehend it, and though it may be contrary to his preconceived opinions, and humbling to his pride.

5. The good man *leads a holy life.* If the heart be good, the outward conduct will also be good. "A good man, out of the good treasury of the heart, bringeth forth good things." Matt. xii. 35. The good man faithfully endeavours to keep a conscience void of offence towards God and man; "he does justly, loves mercy, and walks humbly with God." Mic. vi. 8. And, "denying ungodliness and worldly lusts, he lives soberly, righteously, and godly in this present world." Titus ii. 12. He takes the Word of God implicitly as his rule of conduct; he reads and searches it, that he may know the will of his heavenly master; and he follows its directions, however self-denying and unfashionable they may be; whatever sacrifices they may require him to make, and to whatever opposition and trials they may expose him. He does not part with some sins while he retains others, but renounces all sin. Though a sin may have been to him as dear as a right hand, he cuts it off; or a right eye, he plucks it out. He does not desire to reconcile the service of God with that of Mammon, and endeavour to serve both; but the Lord is his only master. He gives him an undivided heart, and he makes every pursuit, even that of the world, subservient to his service. He faithfully endeavours to know his duty, and when he knows it, to perform it, whether it be to God, his fellow men, or himself.

In the performance of the *duties* which he owes more immediately to *God,* he engages habitually, and with delight in his worship. He reads and searches the Scriptures; he meditates upon them; "his delight is in the law of the Lord, and in his law doth he meditate day and night." Psa. i. 2. With David he can say, "I have loved the habitation of thy house, and the place where thine honour dwelleth." Psa. xxvi. 8. And he is statedly seen at the house of God, in the seasons of public worship. He is not willingly a half day worshipper on the Sabbath. The tabernacles of the Lord are amiable to him; and when he is necessarily kept from the house of God, he feels it to be a privation and affliction. He loves to meet with the people of God, for his worship, on other days beside the Sabbath; and when other duties will permit, he embraces the opportunity. He delights to renew his covenant with God at his table, and obey the command of his Saviour, "Do this in remembrance of me." He is not ashamed to own before the world, that he is a disciple of Christ; on the contrary, he glories in it. He loves the Sabbath; it is to him the best day in all the seven. He is not seen travelling on this sacred day, or riding, or walking for pleasure, or engaging in secular business, or spending its hours in idleness. The Sabbath is not a weariness to him, but he esteems it a "delight, the holy of the Lord, and honourable," and he remembers it to keep it holy.

He lives a life of prayer; and he prays, not merely because he feels it to be a duty, to which he is driven by conscience, but because he loves to pray. His affections are engaged in prayer, and he presents to his Heavenly Father the sincere and earnest desires of his heart; and when in prayer his affections are languid, and he does not meet his God, he is dissatisfied with himself, and mourns. He is daily in his closet engaged in secret prayer, at least morning and evening. Is he the head of a family? He is the priest in his own house; and there, with his collected family, he daily offers the morning and the evening sacrifice. Instead of allowing prayer to give way to worldly business, when they seem to interfere, he makes worldly business yield to prayer. It is with him a settled rule, that whatever is neglected, prayer must not be, in its stated seasons. Follow the good man to his daily occupations, and could you witness what passes in his heart, you would find his thoughts frequently going out after God, and fixing on divine things, and devout ejaculations ascending to heaven. In short, the good man engages with delight in all the ordinances of divine worship.

In the performance of the *duties* he owes his *fellow men*, the good man is equally faithful. In his conduct towards them he follows the rule laid down by his divine Master: "All things whatsoever ye would that men should do to you, do ye even so to them." Matt. vii. 12. He is strictly honest and just in all his dealings; and if he has any thing that belongs to another, when he discovers it he restores it, or makes restitution.

And he not only does justly, but he also loves and practices mercy. He has pity on the poor. According to the Word of God, "a good man showeth favour, and lendeth; he hath dispersed, he hath given to the poor." Psa. cxii. 5, 9. He feels also for the spiritual necessities and miseries of others, at home and abroad, and is ready, by his prayers, labours, and contributions, to do them spiritual good. He is a kind and obliging neighbour; he sympathizes with the distressed; he rejoices in the prosperity of others, and grieves at their adversity; "he rejoices with them that do rejoice, and weeps with them that weep." Rom. xii. 15.

He is tender of the good name of others; he is no slanderer nor tale-bearer; he "rejoiceth not in iniquity, but rejoiceth in the truth;" he bridles his tongue, and suffers it not to be used to the injury of others. When variances arise, between him and others, he readily becomes reconciled, and forgives them who have injured him. According to apostolic injunctions, "Laying aside all malice, and all guile, and hypocrisies, and envies, and all evil speakings," 1 Pet. ii. 1, he "puts on, as the elect of God, holy and beloved, bowels of mercies, kindness, humbleness of mind, meekness, long suffering, forbearing, and forgiving one another." Col. iii. 12, 13. The peace of God rules in his heart, and he even loves his enemies with a love of benevolence, desiring their good, and disposed to assist them when distressed or in need. According to the command of his divine Master, he "blesses them that curse him, does good to them that hate him, and prays for them which despitefully use and persecute him." Matt. v. 44.

He faithfully performs the duties of his stations and relations in life. Is he a magistrate, high or low? he discharges his official duties in the fear of God, and with impartiality according to law and justice. Is he a private citizen? he respects the laws of his country, and is subject to every ordinance of man which does not interfere with the rights of conscience for conscience sake. He "renders to all their dues, tribute to whom tribute is due, custom to whom custom, fear to whom fear, honour to whom honour." Rom. xiii. 7. Is he a husband? he loves his wife, and is not bitter against her. Col. iii. 19. Is the Christian a wife? she reverences her husband, Eph. v. 33, and submits herself unto him as is fit in the Lord. Col. iii. 18. Is the good man a parent? he loves his children, and trains them up in the way they should go. Is he a child? he honours and obeys his parents in the Lord. Is he a pastor? he loves the souls of his people, and watches for them as one who must give account, and labours diligently for their spiritual good. And is the good man one of the flock? he esteems his pastor "very highly in love for his work's sake."

With respect to *himself*, the good man denies himself sinful gratifications. He is sober, temperate, and chaste. He "keeps under his body, and brings it into subjection;" he "mortifies his members, which are upon the earth," and he "crucifies the flesh, with the affections and lusts;" he stands aloof from the fashionable vices of the world. You will not find the good man at the gaming table, in the ball room, or at the theatre. The Word of God directs him, "Whatsoever ye do, in word or deed, do all in the name of the Lord Jesus, giving thanks to God and the Father by him." Col. iii. 17. And, under the influence of this and similar instructions, he stands aloof from these places and amusements. He is "not conformed to this world, but transformed by the renewing of his mind;" he comes out from the people of the world, and is separate; he confesses himself a stranger and pilgrim on the earth, and that he desires a better country, even a heavenly. His conversation is in heaven, and his affections are there, set on things above, where Christ sitteth at the right hand of God. Such are the temper and conduct of the good man, as described in the Word of God.

It is true he is not a perfect man; for in many things he offends, and comes short of his duty, and his best services are imperfect. But this grieves him, and causes him to complain with the apostle Paul, "The good that I would I do not; but the evil which I would not, that I do. I find a law that when I would do good, evil is present with me. I see another law in my members, warring against the law of my mind, and bringing me into captivity to the law of sin, which is in my members. O wretched man that I am! who shall deliver me from the body of this death." Rom. vii. 19, &c. The good man is not satisfied, as some professors appear to be, with just so much religion as they think will gain them admission into heaven. He delights in the service of God, and he desires greater conformity to him, more zeal in his service, to glorify him more, and to enjoy more intimate communion with him. And he cannot rest satisfied with present attainments as long as he comes short of perfection in holiness, which will be as long as he continues in the body. He, therefore, with Paul, "forgetting those things which are behind, and reaching forth unto those things which are before, presses toward the mark for the prize of the high calling of God in Christ Jesus." Phil. iii. 13, 14.

Such is the character of the good man, as drawn by the unerring pen of inspiration.

Who of us possess this character? Each one ought to ask himself, is this my character? Are any ready to say, the description is too highly wrought? my character will not stand the test? In reply, I ask, is the description more highly wrought than the Word of God authorizes and requires? In most of the description, the language, and in a considerable part of it, the very words of Scripture have been used; and by the Scriptures we must be tried, and if our character does not correspond to the character of the good man as there drawn, in vain do we hope that we are the people of God.

Some who profess religion will probably, in view of this discourse, say, either the description which has been given of the good man is not correct, or we have deceived ourselves. It would not be strange if the latter part of this alternative were true, with respect to some professors; for, doubtless, many profess religion who are strangers to its reality. Our Lord said, "Strait is the gate and narrow is the way which leadeth unto life, and few there be that find it." Matt. vii. 14. He called his flock, to whom it is the "Father's good pleasure to give the kingdom," a "little flock." Luke xii. 32. And he declared that in the day of account, many will say to him, "Lord, Lord," claiming a relation to him as his people—to whom he will say, "I never knew you; depart from me, ye that work iniquity." Matt. vii. 23.

The Scriptures are complete and fixed. Nothing can be added to them or taken from them. Many desire, and endeavour to persuade themselves, that they are less strict than they appear to be, in their obvious meaning; or, at least, that their strict letter related only to primitive times—but this is a great and dangerous mistake. The way to heaven is the same now that it was in the time of the Scripture saints; and if we ever get to heaven, we must tread in the steps of those ancient worthies, who, through faith and patience, inherited the promises. We must come up to the scriptural standard of true piety, in its plain and obvious meaning. The Scriptures cannot be changed or relaxed, to come down to our desires or practice, as to the way to heaven. Let us make sure work in the great business of our salvation. The interests of our immortal souls are at stake, and to make a mistake in regard to such interests, would be inexpressibly dreadful.

The Word of God declares, that "the righteous are scarcely," or with difficulty, "saved"—and if this be so, "where," as the sacred writer adds, "shall the ungodly and the sinner appear?" If the good man alone can enter heaven—and it is so difficult, as we have seen, to be really a good man; and if many who profess to have this character, and manifest something of it, are deceived, and will fail at last—where shall those appear who have no pretensions to scriptural piety, manifest nothing of it, and care for none of these things? That they are in the way to perdition is as clear as a sunbeam. Let such be alarmed at their state, and while they are yet prisoners of hope be induced, without delay, to flee from the wrath to come; and to flee by faith to Christ, the only Saviour, and enter into the narrow way of life, in which the good man walks.

And let all who entertain a hope that they possess true religion, and are in the way to heaven, carefully and frequently examine themselves, and bring their character to the test of God's unerring word. And while they examine themselves, let them offer the prayer of the Psalmist, "Let me not be ashamed of my hope. Lord, search me, and try me, and see if there be any evil way in me, and lead me in the way everlasting." Amen.

THE HOUSE OF GOD.

BY

W. A. SCOTT, D. D.

PASTOR OF THE FIRST PRESBYTERIAN CHURCH, NEW ORLEANS, LA.

One *thing* have I desired of the LORD, that will I seek after; that I may dwell in the House of the LORD all the days of my life, to behold the beauty of the LORD, and to inquire in his temple.—PSALM xxvii. 4.

THE sentiment of the royal Psalmist in this verse, is one of devoted attachment to the service of God. Many are the passages of holy Scripture that express the great delight which the pious have found in the ordinances of the sanctuary. Those who have long been accustomed to the blessings of Christian worship, and those who, like Gallio, *care for none of these things,* may not readily appreciate the value of the Christian Church, neither in a temporal nor spiritual point of view. Because the *kingdom of God cometh not with observation,* they see it not at all. Because its heavenly influences are noiseless as the dew, men acknowledge them not, although every day enjoying them. It is our purpose to consider some of the ADVANTAGES WHICH THE HOUSE OF GOD CONFERS UPON SOCIETY.

THE HOUSE OF GOD IS THE FORERUNNER, ALLY, AND SUPPORTER OF THE BEST FORMS OF CIVILIZATION.

Civilization, whatever it is, in modern times owes its best estate to Christianity.* It is true that some ancient nations, as the Phœnicians, Egyptians, Greeks, Etrurians and Romans, attained to considerable eminence in refinement, in elegance of manners, and to honourable distinction in arts and arms without the Gospel. But it is also true that historians are agreed—*first*, that much of their knowledge, their philosophy, and of course their refinement, was handed down to them from their ancestors, that is, by tradition from the sons of Noah; from whom are descended the whole human race, and who were doubtless instructed in the religion of the Bible by their pious father. This opinion is supported by the analogy that is to be found in their respective systems of worship, of astronomy and of mythology, and by their own united testimony down to Aristotle—*that all knowledge was derived from tradition.* Hence, to become learned in ancient times, it was necessary to travel, not only because there were then no *printed* books, and but few MSS, and literary institutions were scarce, but chiefly that the traditions of all lands might be picked up. Their knowledge, and even their philosophy, was to be found in the songs of the Rhapsodists and the proverbs of their wise men. But, *secondly*, historians are agreed that even

---

* "*I know that the civilization of the age is derived from Christianity,* that the institutions of this country are instinct with the same spirit, and that it pervades the laws of the State, as it does the manners, and, I trust, the hearts of the people."—*Gov. Hammond, of South Carolina, in his letter of the 4th Nov. 1844, to the Israelites of Charleston.*

Phœnicia, Egypt and Greece, as also Persia and Rome, were not civilized without religion. Lord Woodhouselee expressly declares that Greece could not be civilized until the religion of the Titans was incorporated with that of the Aborigines.* It was not until the Pelasgi and the other tribes of Greece were taught to be *religious*, that laws were established among them. And *thirdly*, I ask any candid man whether the highest refinement ever known in Greece or Rome, even with all the light that glimmered upon them by tradition from the temple of the true God at Jerusalem, can be compared with that of the Gospel. I have not the time, nor is it necessary, for it has often been done by able hands, to draw a contrast between the morals of the purest systems of heathen ethics and the precepts of Christianity. But I leave it to the honesty and intelligence of any well read community to say whether Socrates is to be compared with Jesus Christ. Nay, Rousseau, Jefferson, and Paine himself, have already acknowledged that Christianity, in the sublimity of its doctrines, and the purity of its precepts, is immeasurably superior to any thing known to heathen philosophy. In a barbarous or savage state, passion predominates over reason, and lust over conscience. The *animal* is gratified at the expense of the *intellectual* nature of man. But when this order is reversed, when men are governed by an enlightened

---

* "It is universally allowed that from the period of those strangers settling among them, the Greeks assumed a new character, and exhibited in some respects the manners of a civilized nation. The dawnings of a national religion began to appear, for the Titans were a *religious* people."—*Tytler's Universal History*; vol. i. book i. chap. vi. p. 52.

conscience, then civilization in its best form exists. But no such a state as this is found without the Gospel. The missionaries sent to Greenland laboured *ten years* without success, in attempting to civilize its inhabitants without the Gospel. Then they exhibited, with all the eloquence of fervid feeling, the doctrine of a Saviour crucified, with an effect that more than realized their most sanguine expectations. The attention of the people was arrested, they received the *faith that purifies the heart, and works by love;* and this laid the foundation for civilization. Schools among our own Indians have always failed, except when they have been established under the influence of the Gospel.

It is the testimony of travellers and of missionaries to foreign lands, that savages cannot be civilized by systems of mere education. It is true religion, and true religion only, that changes the heart; and, until the heart is changed, there can be no real elevation of character, for out of the heart are the issues of life; and, until it is changed by the grace of God, it is the *hole of every foul spirit, and the cage of every unclean and hateful bird.* How can sweetness of manners mark the intercourse of society so long as ferocious passion is permitted to rage and brutify the human mind, and put out the light of truth, and hush the voice of conscience? Why has not infidelity supported missionaries in heathen lands? Why have infidels not civilized some island of the sea, or some spot of the globe? Why, if the Gospel is not necessary as the forerunner and ally of civilization? Let them point to a single spot of earth in Europe, Asia, Africa, or

America, or to a single island of sea or ocean that infidelity has civilized, refined, and blest. Let them point to a single family, neighbourhood, town or individual that has been made better, that has been educated, that has been made more useful and happy by infidelity. The infidels of England and the United States waited until Christian missionaries had partially civilized India, and then they sent thither their own books. The cross first civilized the poor Hindoo—taught him to read—then the infidel goes and endeavours to turn his reading to wormwood. Christianity opens the fountain of knowledge, then infidelity attempts to turn it all to poison. The only way to civilize and to refine, and to give permanent elevation to any community, is to give it the Gospel. Erect the pulpit, and around it schools and benevolent institutions will spring up, as the thousand lesser stars follow the evening star.

The accompaniments of the sanctuary are the living ministry, the preached gospel, the Sabbath, the ordinances of religion, and the blessings of education. Schools, acadamies, and colleges owe their very existence to the House of God. Ministers of religion are entrusted with the keys of the kingdom of knowledge, not to exercise despotism over the minds of men, but to impart truth for their redemption from ignorance and vice. As a class, the clergy have ever been the first great leaders in the work of education. Harvard University owes its foundation to the dying munificence of an humble minister of the Gospel, who landed on the shores of America, but to lay his bones in its dust.* The

* Everett's Orations.

great reform in our prisons, which has accomplished wonders of philanthropy and mercy, and made the penitentiaries of America the model of the penal institutions of the world, had its origin in the visit of a minister of the Gospel, with his Bible in his hand, to the convict's cell. The missionary enterprise, the glory of our age, is an offspring of the house of God. From the sanctuary the champions of truth have gone forth to the heathen, conquering and to conquer, beneath

"The great ensign of the Messiah
Aloft by angels borne, their sign
In heaven."———

A large portion of the literary institutions of the world are under the influence of the clergy. This is not strange. They are in fact, and by profession, the friends of knowledge and of intellectual improvement. Their religion is a system of light. *In it is no darkness at all.* It is their daily office to pour the light of mind and of the glorious Gospel upon the chaos of human intellect. Upon them, therefore, chiefly rests the responsibility of directing the education of youth. As a class, they create and circulate a larger portion of our literature than any other profession.* In judging of the literary excel-

* No disparagement of the other learned professions is intended here. There are learned and good men in all professions and in all denominations. There are literary men, and friends of general education, who are not even pious men. But, as a class of men, clergymen are the educators of our country. In nine cases out of ten, those that are eminent as teachers and as friends of education, who are not in the ministry, are the sons or the pupils of clergymen. It is too rarely the case that men qualified to be the

lence of the performances of clergymen, it ought to be remembered that they appear before the public much oftener, and with less time to prepare their discourses, than any other class of public speakers. Who but clergymen come before an intelligent audience two or three times a week, from year to year, with original discourses? and that, too, usually without any change of circumstances, without any relief from the arduous duties of pastoral charges, and without the rivalry of the bar, or the excitement of the halls of legislation. No one performance of any clergyman should be regarded as a test of his abilities, or of his literary attainments. It is a curious, but a truly philosophical fact, that the more a clergyman feeds his people with knowledge, the more they require of him. Sometimes, indeed, the people are like Pharaoh's *task masters; they require the full tale of bricks, without furnishing straw.* They require him to make great intellectual efforts every Sabbath, without allowing him either books to read, or time to study. After all due allowance is made for prosing sermons and quackery in the pulpit, the clergy as a profession, are men of mind, of intelligence, and learning. The ablest constitutional lawyer of America has recently pronounced their eulogy in the celebrated Girard case, and professor Vethak has given them and the learned professions their proper place in the productive capital of the nation. Their lips keep knowledge; works of cha-

instructors of youth, are willing to make the sacrifices required of the successful teacher. Learned men of the secular professions generally prefer the pleasures of literature, or the pursuits of wealth or ambition.

rity are their robes of state; mind is their empire; the pen is their sceptre; eternal truth is their throne.

The Gospel is not only the forerunner and ally of civilization, but its chief SUPPORTER.

Without the House of God, we shall go back to the skins, and acorns, and idols of our ancestors. Some two thousand years ago our forefathers were painted savages, wandering on the shores of the German ocean, drinking their beer out of human skulls, and worshipping Wodin and Thor. And what makes the Anglo Saxon of the nineteenth century to differ from the ancient Briton? The same that makes Christian nations differ from Heathen nations —that makes Tahiti *with* the Gospel, to differ from Tahiti *without* the Gospel. Christianity poured its light into the minds of Alfred and Charlemagne, and thence the civilization of Europe. The Bible has incorporated itself into the laws, languages, institutions, and philosophy of Christendom. Arts and sciences, jurisprudence, commerce, and national politics, owe their present advanced state to the Bible. Hume has ascribed the civil liberty of England to the Puritans. McIntosh says that the doctrine of JUSTIFICATION BY FAITH, the preaching of which by Luther produced the great reformation from Popery, lies at the foundation of all civil and religious liberty.* So emphatically is man's existence and happiness summed up in his religion, that the history of the religions of various nations is the history of their manners, literature, government and philoso-

* History of England, Henry VIII. ch. ix. "A principle which is the basis of all pure ethics, the cement of the eternal alliance between morality and religion," &c. p. 218.

phy. The *philosophy* of literature and of history is nothing more—can be nothing less—than the *philosophy* of the various systems of religious worship that have quickened and formed, or degraded and fettered the inhabitants of the world.

Without the House of God—without the Sabbath and a regular living ministry of the Word of God, we shall go back to heathenism. We cannot stand still. Motion is the law of our nature. The amount of knowledge does not seem at any time to be greatly augmented. It changes places, and passes from one generation to another, but does not seem to be greatly increased. Its progress is rather that of a door on hinges, backwards and forwards, now in the East, now in the West, and anon to the East. Territories once republican are now sunk into the most degraded despotism. Territories once traversed by the feet of the blessed Saviour and his Apostles, have run back to heathenism, and why? Because their CANDLESTICKS, in the language of Holy Writ, their Churches, have been removed out of their places. When the sanctuary declines, all that pertains to the ennobling of man declines. Pull down all our houses of worship, and let the church going bell utter no more hints of salvation through the Cross, and there will follow a train of litigations, and bankruptcies, and imprisonments, and frauds, and divorces, and murders, that no human power can control. A palpable darkness will come over the land, and gross darkness fall upon the people. Refinement will become sensuality—low and vulgar vices, clownishness of manners, coarseness of attire, and depravity of mind and morals, will complete the history. Separate civilization from the Gospel, and it will degenerate into heathenism. Separate institutions of learning and benevolence from the higher institutions of religion, and they will perish, sure as the frosts of autumn strip the forests of their foliage. Religion, science, and benevolence, are inseparably connected with the sanctuary.

II. THE HOUSE OF GOD INCREASES THE VALUE OF ALL USEFUL PROPERTY. This may be a novel proposition, but it does not follow that it is either fanciful or incapable of proof. It is a proposition sustained by the preceding, thus: civilization is necessary to give property its greatest value: the Gospel is the forerunner, pre-requisite, ally, and supporter of civilization: ergo, &c. The proposition is not only capable of demonstration, but is sustained by numerous facts. Time allows, however, of reference to but a few. Men are so prone to think of religion not at all, or to think of it as a mere abstraction, a thing altogether spiritual, and as having to do altogether with the next world, that they forget its influence upon the present. They remember not the words of an Apostle who has told us that *godliness with contentment is great gain, having the promise of the life that now is, and of that which is to come.* Men, too, are so apt to regard what they give to the support of religious institutions, as either thrown away or bestowed in charity, that they do not seem to consider for a moment that for the value of their property they are greatly indebted to the Bible. This, however, is a proposition so clearly established by facts, that the dullest apprehension must admit it when it is properly considered. Let any one acquainted with the history of the Jews reflect, and see if property was not worth more when David and Solomon reigned in Jerusalem, than during the reign of the unprincipled Ahab. The reason is obvious enough. In the reign of David and Solomon, religious institutions were honoured, and moral influence restrained the depravity of men, so that their rights, persons, and property were held sacred.— While in the reign of Ahab, a false religion was substituted for the true, and thus moral restraint was generally removed from the public mind. The vineyard of Naboth was not worth half so much under Ahab, as when Solomon was on the throne of Israel. Ahab was a wicked, avaricious, and cruel prince; under his administration every thing was in confusion, uncertainty, and peril. Solomon feared God, and his reign was just, and good, and prosperous. What was the value of Lot's house in Sodom, though it was, perhaps, built of the most costly materials, decorated with all the art, and furnished with all the elegancies of his age, yet subject to the invasion of a most depraved and licentious community, compared with the humble tent of Abraham under the oak in the plains of Mamre. Lot's neighbours were not under the influence of religion. Abraham's people were. *A sense of insecurity depreciates the value of property.* Thus in the time of war, when our coasts are ravaged, our cities plundered, our houses burned, and our fields laid waste, real estate falls far below its intrinsic value. During the invasion of Louisiana in 1814–15, land and houses were worth scarcely a tithe of what they were after the treaty of peace. In France, during the Reign of Terror, property sunk far below its ordinary value. And why was this? Because during the reign of terror, there was no security afforded by the government to life and property. And there was no security to life and property, because all religious institutions had been annihilated, and infidelity, cruel and licentious, had been set up in their stead, and as a necessary consequence, religious restraints were taken from the minds of the people. Men *fearing* not God, *regarded* not their fellow men. Not being *devout* towards God, they were not *just* and *merciful* towards their neighbours, nor did the public mind become settled, and property and life secure, till the re-establishment of the forms of religion, and of law. Let a false religion be substituted among us for the true, let rampant and licentious infidelity prevail, let all the hallowed influences of the sanctuary be withdrawn from off the public mind, and how much would your houses and lands decline in value! Take away all the restraints of our religious institutions, and what stability would remain? Who would be willing to risk his life and property in a community void of all moral restraints?

It is said that the intrinsic value of the soil of Turkey is greater than that of America; and yet the poorest acre of these United States is worth more than five of the richest land in Turkey. And why? because here you are protected in your rights by a vigorous conscience in the body politic; while in Turkey, you are constantly exposed to lawless rapacity, your property liable to be confiscated at any moment, and you yourself to perish by the hand of violence. Remove the House of God and its institutions from the United States, and we shall become as ferocious as the Turk. It is admitted that the Mahommedan faith has destroyed the agriculture of Persia; and Chardin thinks that if the Turks were to inhabit that country, it would soon be more impoverished than it is. Persia was once renowned for its fertility; but EVEN THE TEMPORAL PROSPERITY OF A NATION DEPENDS UPON THE PRINCIPLES OF ITS RELIGION.*

It is a remarkable fact, that nowhere, except where Christianity prevails, do we find those partnerships in trade and commerce, so indispensable to give property its greatest value. Travellers and missionaries inform us, that in pagan countries there are no associations for commerce and trade, for exchange, for banking, and for benevolent purposes. To use the language of another: "Why cannot heathens, as well as Christians, combine their wealth, so as to give it greater value, by giving it greater power of accumulation? It is because their religion, or rather the want of true religion, forbids the exercise of mutual confidence, creating universal distrust, and making every man an *iceberg* to his neighbour. Hence the reason why their resources are crippled, and the public mind is stagnant. But let the Christian Pulpit be planted there, and the truth, as it is in Jesus, pervade the hearts and minds of the people, and the now dead mass would at once exhibit signs of life, and put on such an aspect of enterprise and prosperity as Heathenism never saw, and can never produce." So true is this connection, that a distinguished instructor was accustomed to say to his pupils, "Give me the *religion*

*Ancient History, Vol. III. p. 82.

of a country, and I will tell you all the rest;"—the kind of religion chiefly determines the language, literature and characteristics of the people—whether they are torpid or active—ignorant or enlightened—bond or free. An instance is cited in a discourse by the Rev. Mr. Clarke, of Stockbridge, Mass., which will illustrate the point in hand. I give it in his own words: "In one of the towns in a neighbouring county, the people voluntarily deprived themselves of a preached Gospel for several years, till the difference between them and the adjoining towns, in want of thrift and prosperity, became proverbial, and till they themselves were convinced, that, in forsaking the Pulpit, they had forsaken their own mercies. At length, they repaired their weather-beaten and almost ruined church, and settled a devoted minister of the Gospel, with an effect so marked on the enterprise of the people, that one of their most intelligent men remarked, but a few weeks since, that their farms had increased fifty per cent. in value, and that an entirely new aspect had been put on the dwellings, as well as on the spirit of the people."*

The proposition is, that the HOUSE OF GOD INCREASES THE VALUE OF USEFUL PROPERTY. The proof is thus: First, security of life and property is necessary to give property its highest value: moral restraints are necessary to give security to life and property: and moral restraints are produced and maintained only by the Gospel. And, secondly, it is in Christendom alone that trade and commerce are carried on with the enterprise of combined wealth and mutual confidence. Almost the only government known among

* Clarke, in National Preacher.

men without the Gospel is tyranny. The ability of heathen statesmen consists in knowing how to deceive others by hypocrisy, fraud, perfidy, and perjury. Where the House of God is not, there is no bond of union between man and man. True honour, humanity, justice and commercial enterprise are promoted by the principles of the Bible. The English government supports missions partly for the sake of extending her commerce. Even the vicinity of houses of Christian worship, in several well known instances in some of our largest cities, has greatly enhanced the value of property—first, because of the convenience of being near the House of the Lord, and secondly, because a church-going people are good tenants, and thirdly, because the influence of the House of God changes the character of the population in its neighbourhood. Corrupt, licentious, profane, Sabbath-breaking communities have become, through the preaching of the Gospel, decent, sober, intelligent, industrious, pious and well-to-do in the world.

III. THE HOUSE OF GOD IS NOT SO EXPENSIVE AS THE SYNAGOGUES OF SATAN. This is a plain proposition, and like the two preceding, it addresses itself to men's temporal interests. It is simply this:— That *vice costs more than virtue.* It costs more to support a drunkard than a sober man; more to sustain the licentious than the chaste; more to secure and convict a criminal than it would have cost to have prevented him from becoming a criminal by placing him under religious influence. Sabbath-breaking is an expensive vice. One Sabbath spent in idleness and dissipation—in neglecting the sanctuary, costs more than five days spent in the discharge of their appropriate duties. Which costs the most, to lounge at the corner of the streets, bet on elections, ride to the country, attend the military parade or the horse race on the Sabbath, drink at the Exchange, and then to the theatre at night, or to worship God in his Holy Temple? Which costs the most, livery stable bills, Sunday dinners, oyster suppers, opera tickets, masquerade balls and coffee house indulgences, or attendance upon the sanctuary? Which is best, to spend the Sabbath in idleness or in dissipation, and resume business Monday morning, with an empty purse, and languid spirits, and a heart aching under the remorse of conscience? or to lay aside business affairs at a proper hour Saturday evening, close the ledger and lock the desk, and shut the world up in the counting room, and relax the energies of the week in the social endearments of the family—

"The only bliss that has survived the fall?"

Rise early Sabbath morn, and begin the day with its appropriate duties, and then to the Sabbath school, to swim in the smiles and glad faces of earth's brightest similitudes of Heaven—*little children*—and then mingle with the people of God, who keep holy time, and send up the voice of supplication and the shout of praise to the Most High—and then melted, softened, awed, refined, better fitted for society and for social and civil duties, return home to the Sabbath collation—and Monday, with health repaired, spirits refreshed, and the bright sunshine of the soul, a good conscience, which is a "continual feast," begin the labours of the week? *I speak as unto wise men, judge ye.*

IV. THE HOUSE OF GOD WIELDS THE ONLY POWER TO REFORM THE HEARTS AND LIVES OF MEN. Christianity is the only preventive of crime. We are aware that we live in an age of excitement and of bold experiments. The spirit of the day is restless, innovating. We have numberless forced systems of economy, of politics, of morals and of education. One cries, lo here! another, lo there! Each cries out, *I have found it—I have found it*, and a long line of Esqrs., Genls., D. D's, L. L. D's, and learned professors echo the lying sound. But, in a few days, like their predecessors, they in their turn give place to seven other ill favoured and lean kine, that "eat up the fat fleshed and well flavoured." And, like the flies in the fable, each succeeding swarm of quacks, strolling lecturers and reckless innovators, is more greedy than the first—more impudent and more ignorant. But with all the nostrums which have in their turn been promulgated as certain specifics for all our civil and moral diseases—such as those efficacious Protean balsams, cordials, pills and sudorifics, which are infallible cures, (or if no cure, no pay,) for the hepatitis, consumption, fever, and gout, for old men, young men, maidens, and children—is it not true of us, as Pope said, turning from his doctor: "Alas! dear sir, I am dying every day of the most favourable symptoms."

Our state pharmacopolists, each one like a *scribe well instructed*, can tell why the currency was deranged, why commercial credit depreciated, and why the times are hard, and show the errors of all past administrations, and if the people would only put him and his party in power, he would turn the very stones into gold. On the one hand, some *savans* have asserted that nature has endowed all the tribes of the earth with precisely the same dispositions, and fitted them in their turn for the same sort of institutions, and that there is no reformation to be expected—no elevation to be hoped for. That all our inventions and discoveries in government and in science, are but the recovery of what we have lost—and that, in short, we are doomed to float about in eddies, and fly round in circles—but that there is no progress, no elevation, no redemption for our race.*

Others teach that crime is owing entirely to the vagueness of accident—that vice and virtue are essentially nothing but the result of chance—the "rouge et noir" of life; and consequently, there is no redemption from the bondage of vice, but to wait the "fortunate concurrence of fortuitous atoms."

Others say law is the sole cause of crime—that the very fact that there are laws, which are intended to debar men from crime, begets a disposition to violate them—*that by the law is the knowledge of sin;* that is to say, because there are balustrades around the pit, to keep men from falling into it, men will plunge into it for the mere pleasure of getting over the obstructions put in their way for their good. "The danger's self is lure alone," and that, consequently, the only way to prevent crime is to annul all the existing laws of society, remove all restraints, reduce all to a common chaos, to a community of *rights*, and of *wives*, and of *goods*. But the history

* M. Fournier de Dejon, author of the Phalansterian sect.

of mankind abundantly proves that man is the creature of laws; that no society can exist without laws, not even a community of robbers, they must have a common bond of union—a code of rules. Laws are essential to our individual and social existence, and if we have *no other*, we must submit to the dominion of passion; and then we should see again the bloody days of Caligula, and of Nero, and of Robespierre.

But again, others assert that all crime is the result of education, that men are vicious because they have been improperly instructed; and that, therefore, all that we have to do is to reform our system of education, for that education is competent to heal all our maladies, and to exhibit man

"Full orb'd in his round of rays complete."

This system is called the Hylopathian, or the Anaximandrian, from its author, Anaximander, one of the earliest Greek Atheists. He taught that education is the creator of all things; that all things, even life and understanding, are *educated out* of matter, and are to be considered as nothing more than the passions and affections of matter; that all life and understanding are the products of these qualified atoms, hot and cold, moist and dry. Anaxagoras taught, at a later period, the same system, with this exception: he held to an uncreated mind.[*] This system, in substance, has been frequently advanced, and has even now its warm advocates. But all these systems fail to give life to man's moral powers. They all fall short of reforming his heart and regulating his life. They do not give the true cause of

[*] Cudworth's Int. Sys. Vol. I. p. 41.

crime, and consequently they fail to afford any adequate remedy. They undertake to build without a foundation. *They daub with untempered mortar.* The spring-head of all crime is that black spot which the Arabs say is in every man's heart by nature, which is very little at first, but at last spreads all over him—original sin—corruption of nature—a heart deceitful above *all things,* and desperately wicked. And as is the heart, so also is the life. Out of the heart proceed evil *thoughts, adulteries, murders and seditions.* The heart is the fountain of influences. Out of it are the issues of life. The only effectual remedy for the disorders of society is to change the heart—to make the tree good, and then the fruit will be good. It can be proved most conclusively, but for the want of time the proof is here omitted, from the history of Prussia and France, that intelligence, mere education, does not prevent crime; "that knowledge is power" indeed, but that it may be power to do evil as well as good. The more intelligence, the more power to serve the passions and the appetites. Knowledge awakens new desires and developes new and strong passions, and must then of necessity become the instrument of their gratification.

The history of Italy in the dark ages proves this fact. Italy was then the centre of civilization, the only illumined spot on the globe, and Italy was then, also, the scene of the darkest crimes on the catalogue of the human race. The same may be truly said of England at this moment. The most enlightened and greatest nation under heaven; yet, considering her moral and religious institutions, without a question the most haughty, ambitious, and wicked nation on earth. Education, as it is used, is a savour of life unto life, or of death unto death. The sources of power and pleasure, of dignity and wealth, may also become the sources of crime and vice, degradation and poverty. We practically acknowledge this when we make laws to keep our servants in ignorance, lest they should be wise to do evil. The stream of civilization too nearly resembles that mysterious river, whose waves both fold the crocodile and carry the fertilizing loam to the same shore. Let an evangelical pulpit sanctify our literature, and education will be the handmaid and supporter of morals. An appeal to criminal statistics—to figures that cannot lie—shows most conclusively, that while mere science does not prevent crime, but rather increases misdemeanors and felons; that, on the other hand, religious knowledge, education on Christian principles, literature sanctified by the pulpit, does prevent crime. The experiment made by the Prussian Government—the history of Sabbath schools—the statistics of the United States and of Scotland, compared with England and Ireland, all show that RELIGIOUS KNOWLEDGE IS A PREVENTIVE OF CRIME.

There is no country on the face of the earth so much affected by the facts here alluded to as our own. In our government the people are the *sovereign*. They rule—they make our legislators and our rulers. Consequently, if we should have wise and virtuous statesmen, we must have wise and virtuous citizens. Let the Bible, through the pulpit, and the school-room, and the press, give tone to public sentiment, and we shall not have legislators, and senators, and public functionaries, that can profane the day and the name of God. Let public sentiment be purified and elevated, and our cities would be rid of those hundreds of high-ways to hell that are to be found along our streets, and at almost every corner. Let the influence of the pulpit be felt, and our land would have a Sabbath, and vice would be put to shame and confusion. The fearful responsibility of our national sins is to be resolved back upon the sovereign people. Why has not the United States, why has not England, produced a Handel, a Haydn, a Weber, or a Beethoven? Because the public have little taste for music. Their ear is only for the sound of the hammer and the thundering of the steam engine; while in Germany every man is a musician, and every family is an orchestra. Why did England produce, in the seventeenth century, her Walton, Castell, Usher, Selden, Lightfoot, and Pococke? Then England was pervaded with the spirit of biblical inquiry and theological investigation. Why has France produced La Place, La Land, and La Grange? France honours and rewards science. Her scholars are her peers. It is true that ever and anon a mighty spirit arises, who leads captivity captive—who inspires and leads the people; such were Luther, Calvin, Knox, Newton and others. They may be said to have created their own age—to have marked out their own era. Still, to some extent, even they were the embodyings forth of the people. The people gave the response when they called, or they had never been heard. Columbus, the bold and adventurous, was but the crucible in which the traditions and the floating knowledge of the public, its hopes and conjectures, were reduced to a form, and breathed into action. Very much the same may be said of Dante, Ariosto, and Milton; Bacon, Washington, and Napoleon.

To a very great extent, public men are the mirrors of the morals and knowledge of the great public, *the omnific people.* Why have we pettifoggers, quack doctors, and ignorant preachers? because the people not only tolerate, but patronize them. Tolerated they should be, not patronized. *Tolerated,* because we allow liberty of conscience, and declare life and the pursuit of happiness an inalienable right; but *patronized* they should not be, because thereby an evil is inflicted upon the body politic and moral, which no man has a right to do, do what he may with or to himself. And least of all, should an ignorant, unsound preacher, be countenanced. It is better to have ignorance at the bar, or in the senate, or in medicine, than in the pulpit. *Let me lose my property through the negligence, or ignorance, or unskilfulness of my attorney; let me be murdered by a quack, rather than that my soul perish, eternally perish, through the error, or ignorance, or unfaithfulness of my spiritual guide.*

"If the people are industrious and virtuous, their representatives will be men of like spirit. But if ignorance, licentiousness, and a disregard of all religious obligation prevail in the community, then reckless demagogues, and loud disunionists, and abandoned profligates, will sit in the sacred halls of legislation, and ambition, and self-aggrandizement, and love of power, will take the place of patriotism and public spirit, and an unshaken attachment to the best interests of the nation. In such a state of society, the elective franchise, which is the peculiar glory of America, will become one of its deadliest scourges."

In many other countries the government, by a standing army, by racks, dungeons and spies, and by disarming the people, preserves some kind of public order; but here the people govern themselves, and keep the peace, and go through the most exciting elections without bloodshed and without a police. And why? Because the people of this country are free, and are under the influence of the Bible. The power of the world to come has always exerted an extensive influence on the hearts of the people of this country. They fled from oppression to this wilderness with the Bible in their hand, for "freedom to worship God," and they have made it blossom as the garden of the Lord. The Huguenot and Pilgrim fathers brought the sanctuary to America, and hence its independence, and its prosperity, and its illimitable influence on the destinies of mankind.

V. PUBLIC SENTIMENT IS MAINLY FORMED BY THE INSTRUCTIONS OF THE HOUSE OF GOD.—However great the influence of public sentiment may be upon the institutions of other countries, in our country it is greater. *Our government is the people themselves.* Every citizen is a part, it may be an humble part, but still a visible, a living and accountable part of the sovereignty of the nation. Divine Providence has bound us together by the ties of family, of country, and of necessity. We are twined and interwoven into the great web of our political institutions, like the threads of flax or the locks of wool in a piece of linen or cloth. The beauty and strength of American institutions is, that the fine and the coarse threads are so wonderfully interwoven and twisted together, that it is impossible to part them without tearing the whole to pieces. One cannot distinguish between the threads of a piece of cloth, which are manufactured out of the wool of the lean, from those which are manufactured from the wool of the fat of the flock—no more can a distinction be made between the rich and the poor, learned and ignorant citizen in the *sovereignty* of our country. The great principles of republican representation, and the pure sovereignty of the people, are the inalienable, indivestible inheritance of every American. And what are the consequences? The consequences are fearfully momentous: namely, that our government and institutions are what public sentiment is. The vices and the virtues of every one form an essential part of our national character. The wickedness of one, the drunkenness of another; the atheism, infidelity, or profligacy of a third; the avarice, cruelty, and deceit of a fourth; the malice, knavery, and idleness of a fifth; the Sabbath breaking, neglect of family education, worship, and government of a sixth—all these make up the gross amount of our national character and guilt, just as a mountain is made up of sands, or as the great and mighty ocean is made up of drops of water. The purity of public sentiment is therefore the *pillar of cloud by day and the pillar of fire by night*, which alone can preserve the peace and glory of republican America. BY THIS ONLY SHALL SHE CONQUER. *This is her heaven de-*

scended banner. The good order, the intelligence, and the religious influence of the family is the bulwark and strong tower of our defence. Every instance of parental neglect, of ungoverned, disobedient, and wicked children, tends to draw down the curse of God upon our country. Every evil word, every blasphemous oath, every malicious thought, every violation of the holy Sabbath, every species of contempt to the Lord's house, and the institutions and ministers of the everlasting Gospel; every sin, secret or public, against God, is a sin against our country, and is high treason against the State. And on the other hand, every virtuous feeling, every victory over our baser appetites, every benevolent aspiration, every tear of contrition, every groan of repentance, every sacrifice of our will and wishes to the supremacy of law; every holy act, every prayer of faith from the humblest cottage—every such act adds another stone to the spiritual rampart, which for so many years has surrounded and defended us. *Righteousness exalteth a nation, but sin is a reproach to any people.*

The conscience of the body politic, and the maintenance of law, are but developments of public sentiment. The best laws are perverted, misapplied, or neglected, when public opinion is against them. The statutes of departed wisdom, and the legacies of sainted worth, are no better than dead letters, when not in favour with the omnific public.

But what law cannot do, public sentiment can. To the ungodly, public sentiment is law irresistible. The thief and the robber are bound by it. Surround them with purity of sentiment, and you make them honest; first, because no man can habitually do what all about him disapprove. The most depraved will be perfectly wretched, embosomed in a holy community. They would break from it as from a prison, and seek some mountain glade or wilderness cave, where they might associate with men of their own stamp. Man cannot live without the countenance and sympathy of his fellow man. And, secondly, because where public sentiment is correct, human laws will be executed. Let duelling be regarded by public opinion, as it is in fact, murder, and it will no longer be the mark of a gentleman and the badge of honour. Let suicide be marked with the universal horror and disgrace of public feeling, and men will no longer take their own lives. Let Sabbath breaking, and drunkenness, and vices which are so depraved they may not be named, receive the detestation, and united and overwhelming frown of all who love morality and religion, and they will be abandoned. And for the formation of a correct public opinion, there is no means so powerful as the House of God. Its influence operates not only upon those that attend the public preaching of the Word, moulding and sanctifying their principles, but it goes out into the crowd that never attend the sanctuary. For the men who hear the Gospel, bear out into society, and act out, in their deportment, its principles; and others catch the moralizing influence, and spread it wider and still wider over the surface of the community, till the whole mass is in some degree leavened. "Hence, that portion of society which stand aloof from the House of God, and perhaps gnash their teeth upon its holy solemnities, are blessed through its influence. It bears obliquely upon them; but it is mighty, like no other law they listen to. It gives them indirectly all their civil privileges, the peaceable possession of their rights, security of life, and exemption from midnight depredations, and from hourly oppressions. It sets a watch about them and places a guard over their goods and persons at the expense of others;"* a watch and guard, which they should be ashamed to let their fellow citizens sustain alone, but without which society would be a den of thieves.

VI. THE HOUSE OF GOD FURNISHES THE ONLY TRUE STANDARD OF MORALS.—Without a rule it is not known what is straight or what is crooked. Without some standard of excellence, from which there can be no appeal, it is not known what is right or what is wrong. The Bible is the only rule of life by which to form our creed, and regulate our private and public actions. *Conscience*, although it is not, as McIntosh asserts, "a human generation," is, nevertheless, very much the creature of education. Set up conscience as the infallible standard, and then it will be right to worship the Grand Lama—to immolate widows upon the funeral piles of their husbands, and to murder our children and our parents. Conscience may be educated to tolerate any thing. It may be reared so as to approve of the most monstrous and cruel rites of Paganism.

Public opinion, though worthy of consideration, is not a safe standard. It is wayward and blind, fickle and feeble.

* Tract No. 223 of the American Tract Society, p. 6.

The laws of the land are also defective. There are many virtues which they cannot enforce: such as gratitude, fidelity in friendship, charity, proper education of children, and the duties of piety, love to God supremely, and to our neighbour as ourselves. There are, on the other hand, many vices and crimes which the laws of the land and the magistrates cannot prevent; such as luxury, wasting, disrespect to parents, partiality in voting, betting on elections, secret fraud and peculation, and the such like. And besides, the laws of the land and the civil magistrates never reach the heart. They cannot ferret out the motives and secret purposes of the soul, nor can they change and purify the heart. And what is still more, how often are statutes dead letters? The laws are perverted, misapplied, or neglected. Either from ignorance or fear, negligence or partiality, the guilty escape, and the innocent are oppressed.

If, then, it is desirable that men should live by Gospel precepts, that they should love their country —*fear God and honour the magistrate;* that they should be *fervent in spirit, diligent in business, serving the Lord*—upright in all their dealings with their fellow men, and faithful in all their duties, let them be brought under the influence of an able, evangelical pulpit.

VII. The House of God is the only preventive from a false religion—the Bible is the only antidote of Polytheism.—Whenever the Jews left off the worship of Jehovah, they bowed down to idols. Men may and do change their forms of religion, but they cannot abandon all religions. To what extent some individuals may have succeeded in eradicating religious truth from their minds, it is not for us to determine; but all history, and our own observation, teaches that no nation can exist without some kind of religion. A nation of Atheists is no where to be found; nor can man exist without some religious sentiments, as long as he is in possession of his present faculties, *intellectual* and *moral*. Some kind of religion is as indispensable in order to meet the demands of his intellectual and moral nature, as food is to satisfy the cravings of his appetite. A man without some religious sentiments is just as much deformed and mutilated in his moral nature, as his physical would be without a limb or an eye, or as his intellect would be without the power of reason. The question, then, is not whether we shall have no religion at all, but whether we have a *true* or a *false* religion; whether we will have *Mahommedanism*, or *Judaism*, *Paganism* or *Christianity;* Mormonism or any other fanaticism, or the religion which is pure and undefiled in the sight of God the Father.

The religion of the Gospel is not only true and excellent, but it is recommended by *its economy*. SOME SYSTEM OF RELIGION WE WILL HAVE. It is infinitely important, then, that we should have the best. Here we must take it for granted, that you believe the religion of the Bible, which is the religion of Protestants, and is the religion of this great nation, to be the most excellent system known upon earth. The religion of the Bible is also the cheapest religion. Every religion has its priests and altars; Paganism has its thousands of altars and its array of priests to attend on every altar, and its thousand,

thousand victims. The appeal is made to your intelligence, to your knowledge of false religions from history and travellers, to show that they are more expensive than the true. Your reading will also remind you of the evils and expenses of religious establishments supported by the State. Time forbids to notice the struggles of the people of Europe under the patronage law and oppressive tithes, collected at the point of the bayonet, to support a dotard hierarchy, overgrown, corrupt and tyrannical. These are things which we know by the hearing of the ear, and they make our ears to tingle, but they are not parts or parcels of our own glorious history. *The people of the United States are not, and never can be, a tax-ridden people, because they are not, and by the power of truth and the ever-living God, they never shall be a king or priest-ridden people.*

But think you, beloved hearers, if one should sweep, as with the besom of destruction, all Christian temples from our land, that we should not have to erect infidel or heathen ones in their stead; think you that if you do not support the American Protestant evangelical pulpit, that you will escape from all pecuniary contributions to religious institutions? By no means.

"Where'er ye shed the honey, the buzzing flies will crowd;
Where'er ye fling the carrion, the raven's croak is loud;
Where'er down Tiber garbage floats, the greedy pike ye see"—

Wheresoever the carcass is, there will the birds of prey be gathered together.

Silence the Protestant pulpits of America, and the vultures of a corrupt hierarchy would fatten on the wealth of the land. Look at Mexico, with all the wealth of nature; poor and ignorant, torn and distracted, wretched indeed—because it has long, even from the beginning, been subject to a wicked, avaricious, blood thirsty priesthood. The same may be said of South America; blest with every climate and every product, from tropical fruits and birds "on starry wings," to the gold and diamonds of Brazil, and the plumage and furs of colder skies. Let the Anglo Saxon Protestant go to Mexico and South America, and introduce his laws, language and RELIGION, and they will become as the garden of the Lord.

Look at France sixty years ago. Popery, the established religion, with 400,000 ecclesiastics to clothe and feed, who were princes of luxury, rolling in every species of sumptuous living and high debauchery, consuming the labours of the people—and at Spain, superstitious, bloody, unhappy Spain, with 180,000 priests, and you may form some idea of what it would cost to support Popery. The religion of the Bible is not only the true religion, but it is the *cheapest*. It demands fewer ministers, and a simpler dress; requiring a far less expensive apparatus for worship; neither robes, nor' sceptres, nor mitres, nor crucifixes, nor gorgeous altars, nor pomp and splendid ceremonial; but a broken heart, a broken and a contrite spirit; a simple, pure formula, the word of God, and a ministry evangelical, of pure hearts and clean hands. *This is the religion of Jesus Christ.*

VIII. THE HOUSE OF GOD IS THE DEPOSITORY OF TRUTH.—The pulpit is the expositor and interpreter of the Bible, which is *truth itself.* If the Bible were but the ruins of ancient learning; the fragments of remote annals, it would be a venerable document: were it a fiction only, it would be a grand one; then how much more interesting and valuable as it is *truth*, ancient, eternal truth—truth that is indissolubly connected with our very existence and well-being here and hereafter.

There is in the human mind a native love for truth. It is agreeable to our natural constitution, or, as Lord Shaftsbury has somewhere expressed it, "Truth is so congenial to our minds that we love the very *shadow* of it." Hence, truth is much easier than falsehood, and hypocrisy itself is but the *homage of vice to virtue*. And, on the same principle, Horace, in his rules for the construction of an epic poem, advises that "fictions in poetry should resemble truth." Then, as the Bible is the word of God, and the pulpit is its authorized interpreter, how necessary is the pulpit to our present and eternal well-being. As the eye was formed for light, and the ear for sound, so the mind is constituted for the reception and enjoyment of truth. As the limbs of youth resist confinement, so the mind abhors darkness. The eyes of the soul are formed to gaze on the light of truth, and to revel in its *ever new* and yet unchanging beauties. Must not the heart be educated as well as the head? and what but the enlightening, saving and purifying truth of the Bible as the Holy Ghost presents it, can form man's heart to holiness? Is it not the pulpit that explains, defends and brings home to the conscience and the heart, the truths of Revelation? Is it not from the pulpit religious instruction is to be chiefly sought?

Then, if school houses, universities and state houses are worth the expense of their erection, how much more are temples to the living God?

The HOUSE OF GOD ever has been, and ever must be, the grand receptacle of light from heaven, whence it issues to restrain the passions and mould the manners of men, and repair the ruins of the apostacy. Where the House of God is not erected, false religions eat up the people like a pestilence. Falsehood, fraud and theft, and rapine and murder so prevail, that no man sees another in whom he places confidence. Domestic happiness and conjugal fidelity, and parental and filial regard, are things unknown, and for which many heathen languages have not even a name. And every where, where the Gospel is not, there prevails a government that rules with a sceptre of iron. The hardest despotism is rendered necessary by the absence of moral restraint. The Church is both the *light and salt of the earth.* It was the blessed Saviour's prayer for the heirs of salvation: "Sanctify them through thy truth." It is by the truth we are to be saved. And it is ordinarily by the truth from the lips of a living ministry, waiting on the courts of the Lord's House, that men are convicted of sin, and converted to God. "By the foolishness of preaching it pleases God to save them that believe." The subjects of divine grace are taken usually from those that are in the habit of attending Church, and hearing the truth preached from Sabbath to Sabbath. In revivals of religion, those families are generally the most blest who are Church-going families. And far the greatest proportion of youth who unite with the Church are such as have been baptised in infancy. The Lord is faithful in all his promises. "His mercy is from everlasting to everlasting upon them that fear him, and his righteousness unto children's children, to such as keep his covenant, and to those that remember his commandments to do them." Prostrate the sanctuary, and we shall have neither creed, nor covenant, nor communion, nor revival, nor liberty of conscience, nor toleration of opinion, nor Bible in our houses nor in our schools, nor the voice of supplication and praise; and our children would soon be without God, and without Christ, and without hope in the world.

FINALLY.—THE HOUSE OF GOD IS THE FOUNTAIN OF LIGHT, LIFE, AND JOY TO THE WORLD. It is the altar of prayer. It is the presence chamber of the Great King, "whose sceptre pardon gives." It is there His honour dwells, and there he hath recorded his name—A GOD THAT HEARETH PRAYER. Better give up every other privilege than to have no share in the prayers of God's people. "I would," says one, "be without the means of self-defence, without the protection of law, and without a shelter for my head at night, but should not dare to cut myself off from an interest in the prayers of the sanctuary. Let no shower or dew fall on my field, or breezes fan my habitation, or genial sun warm me; but let me not be excluded from the health beaming influence of the House of Prayer. I would do without a roof to cover my head, and have my lodging in the clefts of the rock; but I must go to the House of the Lord, and fix my dying grasp upon the horns of his altar." It is in the House of God that law and conscience speak out; that a future state of existence, and a day of judgment and final retribution are held up before the intellectual vision; that life and immortality are brought to light; that the Gospel of the free grace of the ever blessed God is preached, glad tidings of great joy to all people, *peace* on earth, and good will to men. The House of God instructs our ignorance, enlightens our understandings, corrects our judgments, renews our wills, and reforms our lives. It imparts knowledge to the poor, it gives the orphan a parent, the stranger a friend, the sailor a brother, the prisoner a companion, and the *young man from home* a guide. The Lord of the Sabbath and the God of the sanctuary hath said: " Come unto me all ye that labour and are heavy laden, and I will give you rest." In the House of God we learn how to live usefully and happily, and how to die gloriously. Here, parents and children, husbands and wives, masters and servants, magistrates and people, are taught their duties, and to enjoy their privileges. Here they are taught how to live so as to gain everlasting life in glory; how to live that they may meet again, after death, in the heavenly world, where there is no more sorrow, nor crying, nor pain, nor sin, nor separation, nor death. The House of God enlightens, soothes, comforts, cheers, elevates, sanctifies, and saves. It imparts salvation to the sin sick soul, and seals it with pardon an heir of grace. It hushes into a calm the tempest raised in the bosom by conscious guilt, for it proclaims THERE IS BALM IN GILEAD, THERE IS A PHYSICIAN THERE—THERE IS FORGIVENESS WITH GOD THAT HE MAY BE FEARED. THE

BLOOD OF HIS SON CLEANSETH US FROM ALL SIN. It melts the most obdurate into tenderness and contrition. It cheers the broken hearted, and brings the tear of gladness into eyes swollen with grief. It maintains serenity under calamities that drive the worldling mad. It reconciles the sufferer to his cross, and raises songs of praise from lips quivering with agony. It teaches the fading eye to brighten at the sweet promises of Jesus, and brings a foretaste of heaven down to the "chamber where the good man meets his fate."

> "Jesus can make a dying bed
> Feel soft as downy pillows are."

BLESSED IS THE PEOPLE THAT KNOW THE JOYFUL SOUND: THEY SHALL WALK, O LORD, IN THE LIGHT OF THY COUNTENANCE.

BLESSED IS THE NATION WHOSE GOD IS THE LORD. BLESSED BE THE LORD FOR EVERMORE AMEN AND AMEN.

PERPETUITY OF THE CHURCH.

BY

J. C. LORD, D. D.

PASTOR OF THE CENTRAL PRESBYTERIAN CHURCH, BUFFALO, N. Y.

Wherefore we receiving a kingdom that cannot be moved, let us have grace whereby we may serve God acceptably, with reverence and godly fear.—HEB. xii. 28.

WHAT kingdom is this which *cannot* be moved? What kingdom is that which *has not been moved*, and shall not be for ever? Where is the law of absolute permanency manifested? Where are the everlasting foundations that never shall be shaken? Shall we turn to the kingdom of nature for an example, expecting to find unchangeableness there? Upon a careful examination, a state of facts will be discerned at war with the commonly received opinions of the permanency and fixedness of the course of nature. If we go back a few centuries in our investigations, we find that extraordinary interruptions and changes have marked the history of this kingdom, since God created the heavens and the earth, the proofs of which are graven in the rocks by the finger of the great Architect; the memorials of which are as numerous as the heights of the earth, and the depths of the sea. Our globe has been shaken by convulsions, which have overwhelmed existing orders of life; which have thrust the mountains skyward, and hollowed out the profound depths where are gathered the waters of the ocean. The chaotic state which preceded the present order of things, when the earth was without form and void, has left every where visible and indubitable marks of its existence. The ancient forms of life have passed away, and new ones have been created to supply their places. The economy of existence, in this world, has been changed more than once; and the present order of things reposes on the wrecks of pre-existent and extinguished forms of life. The ruins of primitive forests, of a diverse order or species from those which now exist, constitute the beds of coal from which we draw inexhaustible supplies of fuel. The metals we use were melted in furnaces in the interior of the earth, and injected in veins through the masses of igneous rocks, broken by a power which shattered the crust of the globe, and upheaved the mountains, whose scattered debris constitute the soils which now produce the precious fruits of the earth. The attrition and decomposition of substances forced out of the bosom of the planet, and distributed by the alternate action of cold and heat, by the agency of fire, air, and water, constitutes the basis of all vegetable production, and the support of the present kingdom of life. The roots of the present economy draw their sustenance from the graves of its predecessors. We build not only *upon*, but *with* the tombs of extinct orders of life; more than this, the regularity and uniformity of the present order of things is the result of a previous designed irregularity and disorder, which prepared the globe for the support of its present inhabitants. Mountains and valleys are the ridges of ancient volcanoes, which drove the plowshare of apparent ruin through the crust of the earth, only to prepare the way for man, and the orders of life with which it pleased God to surround him. The ancient vegetable kingdom was buried as a deposit for his use; before this, in the era of fire which preceded all forms of life, the metals were fabricated, and then deposited, or rather driven, near the surface by volcanic action, for the same wise and benevolent purpose. All the primitive systems have passed away, having performed their office by furnishing the means of support to that which was to succeed them.

The scriptural chronology commences with the creation of man, after a brief intimation of a pre-existing amorphous condition of the earth; and it is conceded that geological phenomena do not indicate a longer time than six thousand years for the present order or kingdom of life. The Bible no where limits the length of that period during which the planet was in an imperfect and forming condition; nor are we told how long the Spirit of God was moving upon the face of the waters, preparatory to the last six day's work of creation. But without dwelling further on this interesting theme, may we not presume that enough has been said to show that the kingdom of nature has none of the permanency spoken of in the text? It has been revolutionized;

it has been shifted from foundation to foundation; it has been moved from its earlier conditions; it has been without all life under the dominion of fire; it was inhabited for a time only by the inferior forms of existence, which sport in the waters, or by gigantic lizards, which haunted the marshes among ferns sixty feet high; it has experienced numerous interruptions destructive of the earlier organisms, which have been succeeded by new *acts* and new *forms* of creation.

The present economy under which we live is continued now by no necessity of nature, and abides in an orderly way, only because God "upholdeth all things" by the same word of power by which he called order and form, and life and light, out of darkness and death, out of emptiness and nothingness. It is the sure word of promise that perpetuates the kingdom of nature during the appointed time, for God said to Noah, when he came out of the ark, "While the earth remaineth summer and winter, seed time and harvest, cold and heat, and day and night shall not cease."

But as this kingdom of nature has been moved by the concurrent testimony of science and religion, so there is the same evidence that it is destined to new revolutions and changes. The promise to Noah implies the end of the present economy; "while the earth remaineth," that is, during the appointed period of its present state, "seed time and harvest shall not fail."

The apostle Peter, in his second epistle, declares that "the heavens shall pass away with a great noise, the elements melt with fervent heat; the earth also, and the works that are therein shall be burned." He announces that "all these things shall be dissolved;" "nevertheless," continues the apostle, "we, according to his promise, look for a new heavens and a new earth, wherein dwelleth righteousness." It appears to be the meaning of the inspired writer, that the present economy, its order, its laws, its atmosphere, its forms of matter, and life shall be dissolved; not annihilated, but reduced by fire to the same rudiments out of which God before educed the first creations. "We look," he says, "for a new heavens and a new earth," implying, we think, a *new* and *higher* organism, to be fashioned out of the old materials, because he adds, "wherein dwelleth righteousness." How strikingly analagous is this declaration of the final consummation of the divine plan, in the new heavens and the new earth, with the physical history of the planet, at first a globe of fire, upon which was superinduced, at length, an inferior economy of life, followed by new kingdoms, advancing in importance, increasing in beauty and glory, until man appears made in the image of God. But this condition, impaired by the apostacy and defaced by sin, must give way at length to a "new heavens and a new earth, wherein dwelleth righteousness." That the globe has once been a mass of fire, proves that it may again become so; and as God has superinduced new and more perfect creations upon the destruction of the older organisms, have we not here a confirmation of the divine word, which promises a new heavens and a new earth at last, perfect in righteousness—an immovable kingdom?

But there is proof in the present arrangement of our globe, that the kingdom of life that now subsists upon it must be dissolved. Is it not manifest that our economy is to wax old, and at last vanish away, or be changed into what the apostle calls a new heavens and a new earth? Consider, for a moment, what renders the world habitable. Are not the mountains and the valleys of our planet, its rivers and seas, essential to the healthy condition of its atmosphere, no less than to the productiveness of its soil, and its eligibility, in numerous respects, as an abode of man, and the circle of life of which he is the head? Now, it is philosophically and strictly true, that a time must come, however remote the period, when the earth, by the operation of known laws, will cease to be a suitable habitation for our race. The newly cut and sharply defined caverns of the ocean, made by the convulsions which preceded the existing economy, are slowly filling up, and must in time cease to fulfill their office. A single river, like the Ganges or the Mississippi, would, in a period which can be ascertained and stated in figures, discharge a continent into the sea. Every mountain on the globe, by an observable process, must in time be precipitated, until at last a dreary and stagnant level, exposed to the incursions of the sea, would characterise all its continents and islands. The earth grows old, like a decaying edifice, and by the operation of known physical causes must at length become uninhabitable—a worn out and broken dwelling, requiring the return of another chaos, a new fracture of its flattened crust, new convulsions destructive of all life, to heave up new mountains and hollow out fresh cavities, and then a new creation to people the new world. So then the kingdom of nature is not the kingdom spoken of in the text, which cannot be moved, for this kingdom has been moved, and shall again be; which is taught also by these words of the apostle in the context, "whose voice then shook the earth, but now he hath promised, saying, yet *once more* I shake not the earth only, but also heaven; and the words *once more* signifieth the *removing* of those things that are shaken as of things that are made, that those things which cannot be shaken may remain; wherefore we, receiving a kingdom that cannot be moved, let us have grace whereby we may serve God acceptably with reverence and godly fear."

The apostle here contrasts the visible things of the Hebrew economy, and with them all temporal and material forms which are to be shaken, with a kingdom which, he informs us, cannot be moved.

Where, then, are we to look for this kingdom? Is it among the kingdoms of the world? Let history answer; let us listen to the voices from the sepulchres of empires; let us mark the wrecks of kingdoms that lie scattered on the shores of time. Where are the first, and perhaps the grandest of monarchies among men, of the days of the giants of old, men of renown, who filled the earth with violence? Where are the antediluvian kingdoms, to which the first sixteen centuries gave birth, when men lived a thousand years, and had time to perfect their knowledge, to complete their plans, to make durable their monuments, and, if it were possible with temporal things, to lay immovable foundations? They are utterly finished, their memorials have perished from among men; all record of them is lost, save only the brief narration in Genesis of their guilt and their doom. The last great catastrophe in nature was ordained for their judgment, for God saw that the earth was filled with violence, and that all flesh had corrupted his way, and opened the windows of heaven, and broke up the foundations of the great deep, and swept away the debased populations who had filled the earth with blood and the heavens with indignation. The sea roars over the broken monuments of the antediluvian kingdoms which perished beneath its waves. Over the chasm of forty centuries the wail of the primitive generations comes echoing upon our ears like the noise of many waters. "He uttered his voice, the kingdoms were moved, the earth trembled; thou coverest with the deep as with a garment; the waters rose above the mountains, at thy rebuke they fled, at the voice of thy thunder they hasted away."

Was there no kingdom that survived that general doom? Mark you yon vessel upon that wild waste of waters, that fathomless and shoreless sea, the sport of storms that sweep from the equator to the poles? Keeps she, amid the terrors of the deluge, such a charge? Bears she a kingdom there, preserved out of the universal destruction, and which shall never be moved? If so, no wave shall break her bulwarks; no yawning grave of billows shall enclose her priceless freight. Who sails with her shall come to land, though naught but a howling sea, and a leaden sky are now visible; though every element of destruction rage around her battered hull, like roaring lions, greedy for their prey.

Where is that post diluvian kingdom, whose seat of power was in the plain of Shinar, through which flows the ancient river Euphrates, once bearing upon its bosom the commerce of nations, the wealth of the world? Where is that capitol city that styled herself the Lady of Nations, the Queen of Kingdoms, to whom a hundred and twenty provinces, comprehending all languages and tongues, sent tribute, and before whom, as to a divinity, they rendered homage? Where is that gorgeous Babylon, whose golden towers shone ever in that cloudless climate, reflecting the sun by day, and the stars by night? Where is that glory of the Chaldean's excellency, whose circuit, for a swift rider, was the journey of a day; upon whose walls, higher than the commemoration columns of modern times, three chariots could drive abreast, fearless of the dizzy height, and sheer descent on either hand? Alas! there is no response. Babylon gives no sign, though the neighbouring Nineveh is rendering up her sculptured forms, her glorious specimens of art, concealed for centuries, to the curious eyes of a generation, wise in its own conceit, but who from the Assyrian tombs might learn humility, if this were possible. But no man knows the precise site of Babylon; the Euphrates, which treacherously admitted Cyrus within its walls, spreads out her channel to conceal her crime, enwrapping in one dark morass the first and most magnificent of all the capitols of the world; and thus the royal word of prophecy, uttered before the glory of Chaldea had begun to diminish, is fulfilled; "And Babylon, the glory of kingdoms, the beauty of the Chaldean's excellency, shall be as when God overthrew Sodom and Gomorrah; it shall never be inhabited, neither shall it be dwelt in from generation to generation;

neither shall the Arabian pitch tent there; neither shall the shepherds make their fold there; but wild beasts of the desert shall be there. And their houses shall be full of doleful creatures, and owls shall dwell there, and satyrs shall dance there. And the wild beasts of the islands shall cry in their desolate houses, and dragons in their pleasant palaces, and her time is near to come, and her days shall not be prolonged." The kingdom was removed from Babylon with a destruction like that which overtook the cities of the plain, where the sluggish waters of the Dead Sea mark the place and the manner of the divine judgment. The site of the one is a noxious marsh, of the other a putrid sea, whose barren shores are watered by no dews from heaven. The wild Arab, himself the child of prophecy, avoids both as spots accursed of God, and pitches his tent neither by the sea of death, nor the marsh of the Euphrates, filled with doleful creatures.

What kingdoms of this world have not been moved, what political foundations have not been destroyed? The fate of Babylon and Rome, the *first and last* of the universal monarchies is the history of all the empires and kingdoms of this world. It is true a shrunken spectre yet haunts the banks of the Tiber with "the horns of a lamb but the voice of a dragon," claiming ghostly dominion over men, pretending to be the head of a kingdom that shall not be moved, exalting himself to the throne of God, nay, above all that is called God or worshipped, wearing upon his triple crown the words of blasphemy, changing times and laws, forbidding to marry, and commanding to abstain from meats; but he is a king of death among the dead, a ghoul amid the tombs, a galvanized corpse mimicking life in a sepulchre, a starving vampire amid the skeletons of nations, a throned shadow aping the old despotism that once set its heel upon kings. The scarlet mantled harlot of prophecy, drunk with the blood of saints, sits still upon the seven hills, with the prophetical name upon her forehead, seen in vision by the apostle John, "Mystery, Babylon the great;" but her strength is broken, the shuddering nations will no more drink from the golden cup of her abominations; she waits the day of her predicted doom. Rome is a city of dead men's bones, a tomb of giants haunted by pigmies. The kingdom spoken of in the text *is not there;* the spiritual tyranny that is enthroned in the place of God in the western church had its beginning and will have its end; it is an antichristian usurpation, whose days are numbered by the sure word of prophecy; the Pontiffs are destined to the same doom as the Cæsars. The fate of the empire will overtake the remorseless despotism which has ever imitated the splendour of Pagan Rome, and fashioned itself after the model of its government, and baptised its heathenish ritual with Christian names; which has travestied the example of the Lycaonians, who called Paul Jupiter and Barnabas Mercurius, by worshipping Jupiter under the name of Peter, and the demi-gods under the appellation of saints.

The souls of the martyrs, whose blood the Papacy has shed for the word of God and the testimony of Jesus, does still cry out from under the altar, saying, "How long, O Lord, holy and true dost thou not judge and avenge our blood on them that dwell in the earth?" and voices in heaven and earth respond, "Their judgment now of a long time lingereth not."

Where is the kingdom among men that has not been moved, from the golden head seen in Daniel's vision of the four great monarchies, to the feet of iron and clay? Have they not all been broken without hand and perished for ever? Are not the solemn words "passing away" engraven on all the monuments of modern civilization, on all the glory of the existing nations? What flaming portents of change and revolution come flashing across the Atlantic, visible in the new world; what rumors of oppression, usurpation and war are wafted on the winds; what wailing of the down trodden populations of Europe sweeps sighing over the ocean! Have they not found, from an exile on our own shores, a voice of surpassing eloquence, penetrating all hearts, filling all eyes with tears of compassion and sympathy? Like the restless waves the kingdoms of our own day are moved; they stagger to and fro like drunken men; they heave like the earth, which treasures in its bosom the fires of the volcano; as Samson, bound to the pillars of Dagon's house, shook its foundations in his death agony, so the populations of the world are writhing in their chains and shaking the ecclesiastical and political despotisms which crush them. Those scenes which were witnessed a few years since in Europe seem about to be repeated;

> When Death was riding grimly forth with Terror by his side,
> And blood stained war and pestilence, and famine hollow eyed.

And while the kingdoms of the old world are moved, is there no danger for us? Shall we presume upon our precocious infancy, upon our gigantic and vigorous youth, in our wide territory and rapidly advancing population, in our free institutions and glorious union of States? Is there not danger that we may forget our exposedness to this universal law of change? Have not clouds already arisen upon our horizon, which, though no bigger than a man's hand, have threatened the dissolution of the Republic, and darkened the hopes of political and religious liberty over the world? Have we not seen enough to teach us the mutability of national greatness, and to lead us to implore the Founder and Ruler of nations to preserve that which he has established, to save us from evil counsels, from ruinous divisions, that we may not perish as a people in our childhood, but may at least pass through the period ordinarily allotted to great empires, and that we may not madly hasten and anticipate that decline and decay which sooner or later fall upon the most fortunate kingdoms of this world?

But you have already anticipated the direct answer to the question, "where is this law of permanence? where is the unchangeable foundation of which the apostle speaks in the text? You know it is the kingdom of God, the church purchased by the blood of Christ, the people assured to him in the counsels of the eternal Trinity, and by the covenant of redemption. But a question still remains. Where is the attribute of permanency manifested? In what does this unchangeableness consist? There are various aspects under which the kingdom of Christ may be considered. In which does the declaration of the apostle find its verification? Let us briefly reply.

In order intelligibly to decide this inquiry, we must look for those things in the kingdom of Christ which exhibit the *unity* of the church; which have been the same in all generations, and which must continue the same to the end.

It will not be denied, by any called Christians, that this immovable kingdom has existed from the beginning; that the Church was founded in the family of Adam, and had its fundamental doctrine in the word which God uttered in the ears of our apostate progenitors, as they were driven forth from Eden, "the seed of the woman shall bruise the serpent's head;" that it had its first sacrament in the lamb offered by Abel as an expiation, symbolising the lamb of God slain in the divine purpose before the foundation of the world. What the external order of worship was in the antediluvian church we know not, but it is obvious that the apostle, in the text, has no reference to this, because he is contrasting the visibilities of the Hebrew economy, which were now passing away with that in the Church, which is ever unchangeable. "And this word," says the apostle, "signifieth the remaining of those that are shaken as of things that are made, that those things which cannot be shaken may remain, wherefore we, receiving a kingdom that cannot be moved, let us have grace whereby we may serve God acceptably, with reverence and with godly fear." As though he had said that which is external and visible in the Hebrew economy is shaken, and will pass away with all temporal things; what is immovable and unchangeable in the kingdom of God and of Christ, we receive in the dispensation of the Gospel, which is committed to us. The external order of the Church has ever partaken of the same law of change which we observe in the kingdoms of this world. There have been various dispensations, various external successions, and diverse forms of government in the kingdom of Christ. The Church has worshipped under different forms and administrations; she has had priesthoods and rituals, and she has been without them; she has had sacred localities to which her service has been confined, and where it has been prescribed. "Our fathers," said the woman of Samaria, "worshipped in this mountain, and ye say that in Jerusalem is the place where men ought to worship. Jesus saith unto her, Woman, believe me, the hour cometh when ye shall neither in this mountain, nor yet at Jerusalem, worship the Father." The Hebrew was shut up to the hill of Zion; the tribes went up to worship God at the sacred temple; there was the holy of holies; there was the Shekinah, the visible glory of the invisible king; there only could the sacrifice of the law be offered. Of that locality the Holy Ghost had uttered these words, "His foundation is the holy mountain; the Lord loveth the gates of Zion more than all the dwelling places of Jacob; glorious things are spoken of thee, O city of God; all my springs are in thee." But the true succession, the unchangeable priesthood, the one sacrifice that perfecteth for ever, was not in the temple service which passed away, because it was but a shadow of the substantial things in that kingdom that cannot be moved. The same faith that had been symbolised in the temple for centuries, preserved, as in a fortified city, by the Hebrew, to whom was committed the oracles of God, embalmed in his economy, defended like some forms of life in nature in the chrysalis state, until the appointed day of their enlargement, when they can spread their wings safely in the sun. The faith of Abel, and Enoch, and Noah, and Abraham, was now proclaimed in every valley and on every mountain. Christ crucified was set forth in every habitation, from the palace of Nero at Rome, to the hut of the savage Scythian in the northern wilderness. "The Church of God, which is in thy house," was the language of the apostles in their epistles to the brethren; the congregation of believers assembled for worship in dens and caves of the earth; the sacred symbols, of the most holy passion of our Lord, were exhibited in fields and forests, or wherever else the Christian minister and his flock could escape from the observation of their persecutors. The ensigns of the kingdom that cannot be moved went out from the temple and the ritual of the Hebrews, to be given to the breeze in every island, and continent, and sea.

Nor is ecclesiastical order in the house of God the element of permanency spoken of in the text. There can be no doubt of its value and importance in its place, but it is very certain that no visible priesthood, no one form of church government, no unbroken succession of ordinations or ordinances have constituted or manifested the unchangeableness of that kingdom that cannot be moved. There are many administrations, though but one Lord. The Church is represented by the apostle as having an unchangeable priesthood only in Christ, who abideth for ever; the *doctrines* of the Cross and not *the forms in which they are exhibited* remain, through successive dispensations, and survive them all, the same with the divine Authors "yesterday, to-day and for ever."

There is an analogy in civil governments which are ordained of God, in which we perceive a diversity of administrations, or rather a diversity of forms under which they may be and are administered. We have a right to our opinion as to which of these is preferable, but it is no where contended that government can have no valid existence except in a particular mode. We think the Scriptures clearly make the validity of statutes, and the recognition of the authority of the magistrate to consist, not in the *form* but in the *fact* of government, and this is agreeable to the principles of international law. States do not refuse to recognise each other because their governments are administered under different forms; it is only a condition of anarchy which is out of the pale of all national fellowship. "The powers that be," says the apostle, "are ordained of God," that is, *existing* powers or administrations, under whatever *diversities* they appear; the fact and not the form of government is that which is divinely ordained, and hence the former is universal and unchangeable, according to the purpose and will of the supreme Governor, while in respect to the latter there is no law of permanency, but rather one of change, accommodated to the wants, the progress and circumstances of particular nations, ages and races. Is there any evidence that a different principle prevails for the government of the church, or that God has prescribed an infallible order of external rituals, without which all faith and all penitence are vain? Has the Most High bound his Church to any thing more than the fact of government, upon the general principles found in the New Testament, since the day that the shadows of the Hebrew economy gave place to the light and liberty of the gospel dispensation? While we endeavour to approximate as nearly as possible to what appears to us to have been the order of the apostles and the primitive Church, have we a right to refuse *to all others* the Christian name; to say with the Jews, "The temple of the Lord are we," or to exclude from the pale of the visible kingdom of God and from our Christian charity, those who cast out devils in the name of Christ, though they follow not with us? That charity has its boundaries we freely concede, but we do not believe that they are to be found in mere questions of church order, for these are not the immutable foundations of the kingdom of Christ. Wherever the fundamental doctrines of the gospel are denied, there is no basis for fellowship, and to form one in such a case is betraying the Master into the hands of his enemies. "If there come any to you," says the apostle John, "and bring not this doctrine, receive him not into your house, neither bid him God speed; he that abideth not in the doctrine of Christ hath not God, and every spirit that confesseth not that Jesus Christ has come in the flesh is not of God; he is antichrist that denieth the Father and the Son, and whosoever denieth the Son the same hath not the Father." The doctrines of the divinity, incarnation and sacrifice of Christ, of the divinity and office of the Holy Spirit, and his work of conviction, regeneration and sanctification, of salvation by grace without the deeds of the law and of eternal judgment, are fundamental in the gospel scheme, and if rejected compel us to refuse fellowship with those who deny them.

That is a true Church which maintains what has been common in all the dispensations of the kingdom of Christ—the doctrine of redemption by the sacrifice of the Son of God, and the symbol or sacrament of it as found in all the economies of the Church. The first revelation of the truth was in the garden; its symbol or sacrament, which is the visible sign and expression of it, was in the sacrifices common to all the dispensations of the Church until the coming of Christ, when the Lord's supper took its place, pointing back to the cross, or to a perfected work, as the former had prefigured it before its consummation. Upon this view that congregation of worshippers who profess the common doctrine, and exhibit the common sacrament, which has been maintained in the kingdom of God in all ages, dispensations and changes, is a true Church of Christ, and to be recognised as such by all believers, whatever external differences of order, ritual or government may distinguish them.

But there is another aspect in which this subject may be presented, another sense in which the immutability, and, consequently, the real visibility and unity of the church may be apprehended. The kingdom of grace, as established in the soul of every believer, called according to the purpose of God, is one that is *immovable;* and that this is principally intended in the text, may be argued from the form of the expression, "we receiving a kingdom that cannot be moved," for we *come* to what is *external* and *ritual in* the church; *we receive* what is *renewing* and *sanctifying;* we *come* by a public profession to the city of the living God; *we receive* by divine grace "the kingdom of heaven within us."

The kingdom of grace is that principle of holiness which is imparted to, and sustained in, the soul by the Holy Ghost. It is practically manifest and visible to men in a cordial reception of divine truth, and in practical obedience to the commandments. It is known by its unity of faith and character in all ages and dispensations. Here is the abiding unity of the Church from the family of Adam to the present day, and to the existing company of believers, by whatever name called; here is the "holy generation, the royal priesthood, the peculiar people," whose succession is visible not merely from the apostles, and for the last two thousand years, but for sixty centuries, and from Abel and Enoch, from Noah and Abraham. As the book of Genesis and the gospel of Mathew, as the revelation of Job and that of John, contain the same doctrine, so there is a succession of men, from the apostacy to the present time, receiving the same faith, practising the same godliness, and exhibiting the same sacrament. Here is the remnant after the election of grace, here the *true Israel*, for what is real and fundamental in Christian experience is real and fundamental in the visibility of the Church, and constitutes that TRUE UNITY which binds together all true believers from the beginning to the end of the world.

But, more particularly, let us inquire why this kingdom of grace cannot be moved.

1. Because it is a spiritual kingdom set up in the soul itself, which does not partake of the changeable character of temporal foundations. "The things that are seen are temporal," even in the Church of God; but the things which are unseen are eternal. The visible and external dispensations of the Church have each in turn been shaken and moved, and shall be; its rituals and ordinances, its government and sacraments, have their appointed day, and must at last disappear, when time is swallowed up in eternity, and death in victory; but the kingdom of grace, set up in the soul, abides for ever. The heavens shall pass away, the elements shall melt with fervent heat, all visible things and forms shall wax old, and, as worn out vestures, shall be folded up, but this kingdom, like its Author, shall not fail, and of its years there shall be no end.

This kingdom shall not be moved for another reason. It originated in the purpose of God, and is maintained by his power. It can never die out of the world, because the Father hath given a seed to the Son in all generations; because, in the covenant of redemption, the heathen are promised to him for his inheritance, and the uttermost parts of the earth for a possession. The Church for this has survived all changes, outlived all persecutions, and, with immortal youth, walks among the graves of false philosophies, of decayed superstitions, purifying the polluted atmosphere, and pointing the heirs of sin and death to an inheritance incorruptible and undefiled, eternal in the heavens. So, in the soul, if the kingdom of grace be set up, it cannot be moved; for it is the Spirit that quickeneth, it is Christ that died, yea rather that is risen again, who ever liveth to make intercession for us, so that neither death, nor life, nor angels, nor principalities, nor powers, nor things present, nor things to come, nor heighth, nor depth, nor any other creature, shall be able to separate us from the love of God, which is in Christ Jesus our Lord."

This kingdom cannot be moved because it is that on account of which all others exist. God perpetuates the race, and ordains governments and exercises a universal providence over the evil and the good, for the reason that he has a people which he will take out of all nations and races. For this the wicked live, because in their generations are numbered the elect; for this empires are founded, and flourish and fall; for this the tares and the wheat grow together till the harvest; for this "the heathen are permitted to rage and the people to imagine a vain thing," until the day when all nations shall hear the voice of him that sitteth in the heavens, saying, "Yet have I set my king upon my holy hill of Zion, and I will give him the uttermost parts of the earth for his possession." All temporal kingdoms are but scaffolding for the building of God; all revolutions tend to accomplish his designs. Wars break down the barriers which prevent the progress of the gospel; migrations for gold are caravans to carry the Bible and the missionary of the Cross to the dark places of the earth. *God and the Church are the explanation of history,* without which it is a dark unreadable enigma.

This kingdom of grace is immovable, because its author and head, its prophet, priest and king, is divine, co-equal and co-eternal with the Father and the Holy Ghost. The eternity and immutability of his nature attaches itself to the church purchased by his blood; because he lives and reigns, his people shall live and reign with him. The two natures of the God-man mediator may be said to symbolise the two aspects under which his church may be viewed; in one we see the weakness and changeableness of finite things, in the external order of his visible kingdom, in its exposedness to corruptness, declensions and heresies; in its various dispensations and changing rituals; in the other, we see the law of absolute permanency in the one faith and the one sacrament preserved in all generations. So in the individual Christian, the weakness of a finite nature and its remaining corruptions are ever in noticeable contrast with the power of that divine life in the souls of believers, which is the working of the Holy Spirit, who is able to keep them from falling, as the Son in his own righteousness is able to present them faultless and spotless before the presence of the Father with exceeding joy.

Finally, do you inquire how can a congregation of professed worshippers know that they belong to this immovable kingdom; how can the individual satisfy himself whether he be of the household of faith to whom pertain the promises? The answer is easy; upon the principles we have suggested, the congregation have only to ascertain whether they have the faith and the sacrament that has characterised the true Church in all her dispensations; for this they must search the Scriptures, and seek to know the voice of the Holy Spirit speaking in them, the only infallible guide to truth and judge of controversies.

There is no view of the subject which can furnish so solid a ground of satisfaction to the individual as the one we have suggested. Whether he has received this kingdom, is upon the basis presented, a matter of consciousness; it is not a matter of investigation, of endless genealogies, full of difficulties which perplex even the learned, but a question of fact in the believer's personal experience. Is the kingdom of God within him? Is the love of God shed abroad in his heart by the Holy Ghost? Are the fruits of the Spirit manifested in his life? Are the truths of the gospel dear to him? Does he cleave to Christ and his imputed righteousness as the sole ground of his justification? Are the doctrines which exalt God and stain the pride of human glory precious to his soul? Has he some foretaste of heaven in the religious emotions, the gratitude and praise that are kindred in his bosom? Has he received the same spiritual baptism with holy men of old, and does he find the revelation of his own conflict with the world, the flesh, and the devil, in the inspired record of their trials and their experience? Is not here the only reasonable and satisfactory assurance of eternal life? Is not all else of the nature of formalism or rationalism vague, uncertain and unsatisfactory? I speak to wise men, judge ye!

SEEING THINGS INVISIBLE.

BY

J. H. JONES, D. D.

PASTOR OF THE SIXTH PRESBYTERIAN CHURCH, PHILADELPHIA.

We look not at the things which are seen, but at the things which are not seen.—2 Cor. iv. 18.

AND this furnishes a key to the changed conduct and life of Paul after his conversion. His sundering of personal, social, and domestic ties; his voluntary renunciation of so many things that were gain to him—wealth, distinction, and honour—for the sake of Christ. However appalling to others the prospect before him—disgrace, poverty, extreme bodily peril, and probable martyrdom—yet none of these things moved him. There were other things, and greater far than these, by which he was influenced, and which had a substantial presence, though invisible to the eye of sense. Those grand and awful realities of the unseen world that were hidden from others were visible to him. Hence the apostle acted as if the Judge of quick and dead, to whom he was to give account, was ever present to counsel, direct, and overawe him. But what is here asserted by the author of our text concerning himself, is verified in the life of all who are governed by his principles. While the things that present the predominant motives of their conduct are not seen, they act as if they were habitually before them, as really as are the objects of sense, which so much affect the conduct of others. This is the truth on which it is proposed to enlarge in this discourse, and use for our practical advantage.

The thought here is complex, and may be expressed in the two following propositions:

I. That the things which furnish the most cogent motives to a religious life are invisible, but

II. That the consistent believer lives habitually as if he saw them.

The former of these propositions, it is well known, has been urged by the sceptical as a serious objection to our religion, viz: that its motives are, to such an extent, derived from things unseen, and not from objects best suited to affect us in our present condition; that its rewards and punishments are, in the main, prospective, and look to a future state, and not the present. The same has been said of its doctrines generally, that they are abstruse and incomprehensible. What a dense and impenetrable mist of darkness hangs over the grave! Death, we are taught, is but the beginning of an endless life; that it is not the end of consciousness, but a physical change merely—a separation of the mortal from the immortal part of man for a season only, when they are to be reunited in a state of eternal retribution. But how little of this is warranted by what we see? Even the Saviour, who is represented as the only hope of the guilty, is also concealed; and God *no man hath seen nor can see.* He dwelleth *in light which no man can approach unto,* and why is this? Why should that sort of truth, on whose practical influence depends the eternal welfare of the soul, be so hidden from our senses? Why not indulge us occasionally with the sight of a resurrection—a favour which it is so easy for God to grant? Why not permit the reappearing of a departed acquaintance or relative, to tell us about the invisible world? Why could not Paul, or Augustine, Luther, Baxter, Watts, or some other distinguished saint, come back to the earth for a time, as Moses and Elias did for the special instruction of Peter and John? What a confirmation of our faith if we might be permitted to see them!

The objection implied in these and similar queries would be reasonable, if the evidence of sense were the only sort that is satisfactory and conclusive; or were the main obstacles to a practical belief of the truth to be found in the mind, and capable of being dislodged by argument, and not in the heart beyond the reach of any appeals merely to the reason; or had not the impotency of ocular demonstration been exposed by repeated cases of restoration to life, and in none more signal than the example of Lazarus. But the influence of vision was tried, and its inefficiency shown, under both the Old Testament and the New. The Saviour tested its power in the case to which I have just referred, and had he opened the door of the unseen world a hundred times, and evoked Abraham, Isaac, Jacob, and scores of departed Hebrews from the unseen world, it could have proved no more concerning a future state of existence than was witnessed in thus recalling the spirit of one of the family at Bethany. The Jews, who saw this resurrection, were just as sceptical afterwards as they had been before. Nor would your heart, reader, nor mine, be more impressed by the sight of apparitions from the other world than theirs were. It is equally true concerning us, that if we hear not Moses, the prophets and apostles, neither will we be persuaded, though one rose from the dead.

It is a mistake, therefore, to assert that the motives of religion are so inoperative, because they are drawn from things *not seen* or remote. On the other hand, it could easily be shown that our knowledge, even of sensible objects, is rather presumptive than real, and that our senses are continually leading us into error. Indeed, the terms of what we call *science* are rather symbols of what we do not know, than exponents of what we do know. There is much that is mysterious and inexplicable in matter, motion, electricity, life, &c., as well as in original sin, the Trinity, or regeneration. The technical definitions of philosophy would seem to be invented to conceal her ignorance; and we are just as unacquainted with the real nature or essence of things that we see, taste and feel, as we are with *the invisible things of God.* It is well known that Dr. Berkeley, bishop of Cloyne, disproved the existence of matter in opposition to the testimony of the senses, and not by quibble and sophistical reasoning, but, as Reid says, by taking up the principles laid down by Descartes, Malebranche, and Locke, and carrying them out to their legitimate conclusions.

It is the boast of those who reject the supernatural and unseen in religion, that we have a competent guide and instructor in reason; but the history of the inquiries which philosophers have instituted into the powers and laws of the mind, is suited to impress us far more deeply with the imperfection of our faculties than their greatness.

It is now the nineteenth century of progress in human philosophy since the advent; ample time, we should say, for arriving at definite conclusions on the most familiar subjects, as, for example, the problem of our own nature, the number, the office, and the laws of our several faculties. We should naturally suppose it to be easier to gain a knowledge of these than of the elements and laws of the material world. And yet there is no question, among the metaphysicians of the day, more absolutely unsettled than this. Some of them tell us that "God is the only cause in the universe, and that we are but the subjects or organs of effects which he immediately produces. Others, that we are real and responsible agents. Some teach that creatures are a part of God; others, that God is but the aggregate of his creatures; and others again, that we are wholly material, mind, soul, and body, and that we perish at death; most, however, that we have a spiritual and immaterial, as well as corporeal nature. Some maintain that none of our perceptions and thoughts are any thing more than sensations; others that we have ideas of immaterial things, as well as of those that are discerned by the senses. Some that we indeed have conceptions of God, but are without any proofs of their truth; others that we are capable of a real knowledge of him. Many contend that we put forth our choice under the impulse of blind power, and others that we exert our volitions for reasons of which we are conscious."

Here then, are no less than twelve proposed solutions of this problem of our nature, which appears to be just as open to debate now as it ever was. We might turn, then, upon the boaster of the sufficiency of reason and inquire, Why is this? Why is knowledge derived through the senses or by study so uncertain and unsatisfying? Why are things tangible and visible so deceptive, that we need only love and follow them with all our heart to be involved in certain ruin? Though they inspire us with the highest hopes, they fulfil none of their promises. They never make us happier in this world, nor fit us to be happy in the world to come. What other explanation can be given of this perplexing fact than that which is furnished by the volume of Revelation? Here we learn that *the whole creation groans* and sympathizes in the lapsed and unhappy condition of man. That the "things seen" are in their very nature uncertain, unsatisfying and fallacious, and that those which are real and worthy of our love and confidence are invisible. And while they who look only at the former will be disappointed and lost, those will be infallibly happy as well as safe who look at the latter, and who rely on that higher good which lies beyond and without the scope of mortal vision. To those who have not made the trial, this may seem impracticable, but it is just the reverse with those who have made it, and who, like the apostle Paul, judge from experiment

Of these there has always been a "little flock" in the world, from Abel and Enoch downwards, and the day is fast approaching when their number will be greatly increased.

Having offered these few hints concerning the former, and the power of those motives which are drawn from things invisible, I proceed to notice the other truth inculcated by the apostle, that

II. The consistent believer lives habitually as if he saw them. He "looks not at the things that are seen, but at those which are not seen." That wonderful faculty, by which a man is enabled to realize the paradox of seeing the things that are invisible, is called faith. And because both classes to which I refer, they who look at the visible as well as those who look at the things not seen, lay claim to this faith, the Scriptures discriminate. In the nomenclature of theology the faith of the one is called speculative, and the other an evangelical faith; a difference founded not on the comparative amount of their intellect, advantages of education, standing in society, or extent even of their religious knowledge, but solely on the different state of their hearts.

The things unseen, though commended to the mind with the cogency of moral demonstration, are repelled by the one, because they are distasteful. The mind assents to the truth of them as things that are proved, but they are not obeyed because they are rejected by the heart, just as a patient often admits the excellency of a medical prescription, which he will not follow because it is nauseous. This is the faith of one class of believers. In the case of the other, these invisible things receive at once the approbation of the mind and the heart. By the influence of the Spirit their heart has been so prepared, that its affections and tastes are brought into conformity with those invisible realities of the spiritual world, which are now made to influence their conduct. Hence their view of the unseen things, by faith, is not only more accurate, but it is more operative than are any discoveries of reason, or even of sense.

It is more accurate. Indeed, as it is the province of reason to correct the errors of sense, it is the prerogative of faith to correct the mistakes of reason. If we look upwards and survey the heavens, the planet Venus appears to the eye as diminutive as the blaze of a candle. This is an error of sense, which reason corrects by having discovered that it is nearly the size of our earth, and the cause of its seeming so little is its distance. So the rejecter of Christianity is equally deceived by his reason in his estimate of Jesus Christ, and the cause is the same—his immense moral distance. "This mistaken man accounts the Saviour and his glory a smaller matter than his own gain, honour or pleasure; for these are near to him, and he counts them bigger, yea, and far more valuable than they really are." But they who, like our apostle, can look at things that are not seen by others, and by help of the telescope of faith can see the remote glories of Christ in their proper dimensions, regard the coveted pleasures and honours of the world as dross; they are but a taper, when compared with the light of the sun.

It is well known, moreover, that constant sight produces familiarity, so that the effect of objects seen grows less. It is not so with faith; this becomes stronger by continuance, and the more frequently we dwell upon any object by faith the more we feel its power; a familiar fact, which suggests another answer to the objection against Revelation, already noticed, founded on the want of sensible evidence. We see that faith is better adapted to bring the sublime truths of the gospel home to the soul, and make them to be felt at once, and more permanently, than if they were apprehended by reason only, or sense.

Reason, says Pascal, acts so tardily, and on the ground of so many different views and principles, which she requires to have always before her, that she is continually becoming drowsy and inert, or going actively astray for want of seeing the whole case at once. It were well, then, after our reason has ascertained what is truth, to endeavour to feel it, and to associate our faith with the affections of the heart. For *with the heart man believeth unto* righteousness. "The heart has its *reasons*, of which reason knows nothing. We find this in a thousand instances. It is the heart which feels God, and not the reasoning powers; and this is faith made perfect; God realized by feeling in the heart."

BUT THIS VIEW OF INVISIBLE THINGS BY FAITH IS MORE OPERATIVE.—The unseen heaven is constantly before such a believer as his home, and the place of his everlasting rest. The unseen hell is before him, not as a figment of the Christian school, nor a frightful invention of pagan mythology, but a reality, to be escaped for his life, as Lot fled from the fire and brimstone that were bursting on Sodom. The law of God is before him; it was invisible once, like the angel with his sword in the path of Balaam, or, like Saul of Tarsus, he was alive without it; but the scales have fallen from his eyes also, and he sees it plainly now. His faith renders the truths of Revelation all palpable and real. As the apostle so emphatically defines this grace, *it is the substance of things hoped for, the evidence of things not seen.*

Such, then, is the characteristic difference between the two classes of believers to which I have referred. How they are divided, or what the ratio of real to nominal or speculative believers, who but the Searcher of hearts can tell? But if only they belong to the former who evince their faith in the unseen realities of religion by their lives, the number is very small compared with the multitudes who are known as religious professors. Where is the man who lives as if he felt the eye of the invisible and rein-trying God to be continually upon him? Who is he that obeys the precepts of the law as if the omniscient Author were always present, to bestow its gracious rewards or enforce its penalties? And if you look abroad, from the Church to the world, how are we impressed with the abounding practical atheism?

Who is the Almighty, say the multitude by their conduct, *that we should serve him, and what profit should we have if we pray unto him?* To them he is only a Deity in theory, an article of a creed, a metaphysical abstraction, a God afar off, and not at hand. But how soon must this epicurean dreaming be over, and the curtain fall which separates the seen from the invisible? It may seem remote to many of you at the same time that it is fearfully near. A slip of your foot, a mistake of your apothecary, a cold, a fever, an attack of epidemic disease, or some arrow from the ten thousand which fill the Almighty's quiver, may lay some of us low even before another week, and reveal the retributions of eternity. Happy, healthful, and sanguine as you now are, so short a time as this, may bring you to the bar of this unseen but disregarded and dishonoured God. Nor are these things any more distant and unreal, because so many live as if they were at an infinite remove; because they are little more heeded than if they were the mere epic fictions of a Virgil or Dante, and not the inspirations of God. It was amazing effrontery in Jehoikim to treat the message of Jeremiah with so much contempt, in spite of the expostulations of Elnathan, Delaiah, and Gemariah. But his despising of the prophecy did not rescue this infatuated prince from being made a captive, put to death, and having his body cast into a common sewer, like the unburied carcass of an ass. His coolly taking the prophet's roll, cutting it with a penknife, and casting it into the fire, did not prevent its fulfilment. And however the gay and the worldly may disregard the inspired roll of warnings, expostulations, and promises which are addressed to them, the time is coming when they will all be verified. Heaven and earth shall pass away, but His word shall not pass away. The distinction between a life of Christian virtue, and a life of sin, which so many will not see now, they will be compelled to see and acknowledge when they begin to feel its results. And, in view of such humiliating facts in human experience and conduct, who, that reflects and feels their import, can doubt man's need of supernatural aid? He is not an alien and a wanderer from God, because his true condition has not been revealed to him. He does not reject the Saviour because he does not hear him preached, and even listen with assent to the recital of his advent, life, and death, as the substitute and friend of the guilty; but with all this persuasion of the mind and conscience, like some spectators at the resurrection of Lazarus, the truth does not reach his heart. The real beauty and excellency of the Saviour are invisible, nor are any teachings of the pulpit and pen sufficient to make them known. There is an obstacle to knowledge here, which man has neither the desire nor the power to remove.

Imagine a garden of exquisite beauty, and adorned with every plant, fruit and flower that money and taste can collect, with fountains and rivulets to enhance its varied attractions. Suppose that you meet a stranger here, who, with an eye to all appearance healthful, passes along without bestowing the least attention upon a single object. In your bursts of ecstatic delight, as you look at this or that beautiful parterre, so blooming and fragrant, he is silent, returning only a vacant gaze. Surely, you would say, this stranger is blind; he cannot see as I see, or what I see; and, upon inquiry, you find your conjecture to be correct; this man has eyes that see not. What you perceive and enjoy is invisible to him, and something more is needed than you can impart by your taste and botanical knowledge to make him share in your enjoyment. The case supposed is easily interpreted: *the natural man receiveth not the things of the Spirit of God, for they are foolishness unto him; neither can he know them, because they are spiritually discerned.* Some time ago, a young man of gay and dissipated habits, on returning from a meeting of kindred spirits, at a late hour of the night, discovered on his table a printed sheet, left there he knew not by whom; he was a despiser of tracts, and scarcely less of those who distributed them; but, wearied and exhausted, and yet, unsatisfied as he was with the pleasures of the evening, he was in a mood for any thing that would occupy his thoughts. This little sheet proved to be a messenger of God; his mind had been well instructed in the truths of religion before, but they had never reached his heart; the night was spent in a state of deep and overwhelming conviction, but morning came at length, and with it the beams of the sun of righteousness; he left his chamber, he knew not what, so changed were his feelings and views of every thing; he looked upwards, and "the heavens declared the glory of God." He never saw it there before; he looked abroad, and every object, and every stream, plant, flower, tree, bird and beast, reflected the same. The Bible was new and full of God, especially as manifested in Christ.

> When God revealed his gracious name,
> And changed his mournful state,
> The rapture seemed a pleasing dream,
> The grace appeared so great.

The whole creation was teeming with beauties, thrown over them by the hand of God, and, though hidden before, they were visible now. And can you tell me, reader, why? The heavens were not changed, nor the earth, nor the objects that cover it; these were all the same, but the change was in himself. And does any one inquire in what respect? How were his eyes opened? He was a trophy of the Spirit; the man was born again; old things had passed away, and all things had become new. Are there not some among the readers of his story who need the same change? Do you know that this life giving Spirit is promised to all who seek his influences? And what is so ineffably important as that you should know or practically feel the teaching of the Saviour to the Jewish ruler, *except a man be born again he cannot see the kingdom of God.*

CHRIST, THE LIFE OF HIS PEOPLE.

A DISCOURSE

TO ILLUSTRATE THE NATURE OF THE DIVINE LIFE; AND ITS DEVELOPMENT IN OUR SPIRITUAL, OUR MORTAL, AND OUR ETERNAL BEING.

BY

ROBERT J. BRECKINRIDGE, D. D., L. L. D.

PASTOR OF THE FIRST PRESBYTERIAN CHURCH, LEXINGTON, KY., AND SUPERINTENDENT OF PUBLIC INSTRUCTION FOR THE COMMONWEALTH OF KENTUCKY.

Christ, who is our life.—COL. iii. 4.

THE grand point of view in which we should habitually contemplate the Scriptures, is as a divine revelation of the only mode in which lost sinners can be saved. As a history of much that has happened in this world of ours, the enduring importance of its statements results from their setting before us the method in which this salvation is brought to light, and applied practically to men. As a spiritual system, unfolding and enforcing a most peculiar view of the unseen world, and our relations to it, its living power is derived from the bearing of its doctrines upon our eternal destiny, as depraved creatures to whom divine mercy is offered in a particular way. As a code of morals suited to direct the conscience, and to regulate the life of such beings as we are, it is the connection of its precepts with the doctrines which constitute its spiritual system, and the dependence of both upon its great proposal of salvation for sinners, which invests its rules of duty with so much majesty, and gives such sublime force to the idea of duty itself. As a source of support, of consolation, of peace, and of joy, in such a world as this, and in such a course as our pilgrimage through it must needs be, it can avail us nothing, except as we receive its precepts, and accept its doctrines, and believe its statements, as one and the other bear directly upon the grand conception of the Gospel—salvation for lost sinners. Every thing short of this is little better than trifling with our own souls. Every thing inconsistent with this is little else than handling the word of God deceitfully.

Whatever men may imagine concerning other portions of the contents of God's Word, it is past all doubt that the portion which relates to the person, the work, and the glory of the Lord Jesus, must be invested with divine power, or must be absolutely useless in the matter of our salvation. That part of the Scriptures is a glorious revelation, or it is a most empty imposture. Let us proudly conceive what may suit our vain and foolish hearts, about the history, the morality, nay, even the religion of the Bible, using the word religion in its largest sense, and persuade ourselves, if we will, that all these things are level to our unaided faculties, and that no divine wisdom, nor any divine power, is manifested in them. The moment we come upon the conception of the Son of God incarnate to save sinners, and begin to expatiate amidst any of the multiplied and overwhelming exhibitions which are made, throughout the Scriptures, of this vast conception, we find ourselves carried at once, into a region where, at every step, we must recognise the guidance and the presence of God, or we must nerve ourselves before the most daring of all human impostures, invested with more than all human force and grace, and all available to no end. There is not one solitary point connected with the person, the work, or the glory of Jesus Christ—nothing that touches his humiliation or exaltation—that is involved in his prophetic, his priestly, or his kingly office—that concerns his incarnation, his sacrifice, or his resurrection—that fits him to be the Redeemer of God's elect, or exhibits his work of redemption—that relates to his eternal being or his eternal reign; there is absolutely nothing, in the presence of which human nature can stand and say, I know this to be true, or, I know this to be effectual in the manner, and for the end proposed! God must utter it, God must propound it, or it must be uttered and propounded alike in mockery of God and man—an audacious braving of the majesty of heaven—a ferocious trifling with the sorrows and the hopes of earth—a fiendish aggravation of the woes of hell!

The alternative we take is the one which gives us peace and reconciles us to God. They who like can take the other, and reap its fruits. Taking that alternative, we must bear in mind its fundamental condition as a question to be settled at the bar of human reason, namely, that this whole doctrine of Christ, and of the salvation offered to us through him, is a matter of pure and absolute revelation. It is God who has spoken, it is God who propounds it to us; we accept, in its simplicity and its fulness, every word which has proceeded out of the mouth of God; and we attest our sincerity herein by sitting down at the feet of Jesus, to learn of him, and by resting our souls upon him. We must remember, also, the second great condition, which in the very nature of the case controls the whole question, namely, that all these utterances of God, all that he propounds concerning his only begotten Son, are matters connected, more or less, directly with the salvation of lost sinners, and that herein lies the sum total of our interest in it all. Thus full of the sense of God's presence in his Word; thus alive to the awful interest with which that Word is invested for us—there is no part of it in which we may not find some manifestation of that infinite grace in which all of it is conceived, and we shall see, with joyful surprise, how directly and how continually this recovery of our souls is its burden and its theme. Amongst ten thousand other passages, my text is all alive with this precious Saviour, and this great salvation. To him as our life, and to the nature of the life we enjoy in him, in our spiritual, our mortal, and our eternal being, the apostle, in this passage, directs our thoughts. Such is, therefore, the subject of our present meditations.

Amongst the things expressly revealed to us, concerning the origin and destiny of our race, are these which follow, namely, that the Lord Jesus Christ is the only and the absolute Creator of the entire physical universe, and every part of it; that he is the author of all that we call _life_, the bestower of every thing that we understand by conscious existence, throughout the universe; and that every form, and every grade of what we mean by *intelligence*, from the lowest manifestation of it, in any living thing, up to its most exalted exhibition in his presence around God's throne, is an emanation and a gift from him. (John i. 1—14.) By the entrance of sin, first into heaven, and then upon the earth, this universal frame of nature has fallen under God's curse; and every creature that possesses conscious existence, and every being endowed with intelligence—each in proportion to its own degree, and its own connection and dependence with fallen angels and fallen men—has lost its primeval estate, and fallen under the divine wrath. (Gen. iii. 14—19; Rom. v. 12—21, and viii. 20—23; Jude 6.)

The wages of sin is death; (Rom. vi. 23.) This is the comprehensive, the unalterable necessity which pervades the universe, and which God has announced to us as the simple and universal result of the administration of divine justice against sinners. They who sin must die; transgression leads directly to death; in the nature of the case, and without any exception, and by the eternal ordination of God, when lust hath conceived it bringeth forth sin, and sin, when it is finished, bringeth forth death, (James i. 15.) This terrible and universal penalty of sin is set before us in the Scriptures in a threefold light. 1. In a point of view purely moral; namely, the separation of our whole man, in this life, from the likeness and favour of God—which is spiritual death. 2. In a point of view purely physical; namely, the separation of our souls and bodies from each other—which is temporal death. 3. In a point of view resulting from a certain combination of both the preceding; namely, the ruin of our souls and bodies in hell for ever—which is the second death. (Ephesians ii. 1—3; Ecclesiastes xii. 7; Matt. xxv. 41; Rev. xx. 14.) To each one of these conditions, as fully comprehended in the penalty of death denounced against sin, every sinner of the human race is exposed. He is liable to have the sentence of death executed upon him, in every one of these aspects, in exact proportion, as to the measure of its relative severity, as comparing the case of one sinner with another, to the demerit of his offences. As a sinner, he already lies under the condemnation, and only awaits the full execution of the entire sentence, because God does not desire him to perish, but would rather he should turn and live. Under each aspect of the penalty denounced against him for his sins, is involved all the sorrows and all the anguish which the very vilest can ever incur or endure; and he may so run to the most terrible excess of riot, that the depth of his pollution and spiritual death, the anguish and degradation of his physical existence, and the temporal death which will close it, and the eternal agonies of his soul and body in hell, when the second death shall swallow him up for ever—may make any sinner, who now least expects it, a monument of eternal horror. As sinners, we are actually, to every moral intent, dead in trespasses and in sins; as sinners, we are actually dying daily, as to every physical intent; as sinners, we have not yet incurred the irreversible sentence of the second death, simply because our souls and our bodies are not yet separated by the stroke of temporal death. To add to all the terrors of such a condition, it is absolutely remediless by all human means; nay, even according to any human conception; and the interposition of God himself is liable to conditions resulting from his own glorious being, and from the very nature of his relations to his fallen creatures, which appal human reason, and crush the wildest human hopes. We have not only incurred this death—we have not only deserved it—but our destiny is cast under a divine administration, in which there is an absolute necessity for that which is deserved to be done; an unalterable determination to inflict that which is incurred.

Thus are we undone; thus are we sold under sin; thus are we shut up under the law. All behind us is shame; all within us and around us is darkness; all before us is terror. And now it is, through all this gloom, and above all this despair, that heavenly accents fall upon our trembling hearts: "Come unto me, all ye that labour and are heavy laden, and I will give you rest!" And then the majestic utterance, before which hell and the grave tremble, bursts over our troubled souls: "He that believeth in me, though he were dead, yet shall he live; and whosoever liveth and believeth in me, shall never die!" And then the sublime and consoling appeal, at once to our reason and our faith: "The first man, Adam, was made a living soul; he was of the earth, earthy; as is the earthy, such are they also that are earthy: and ye have borne the image of the earthy. But the last Adam was made a quickening spirit; he is the

Lord from heaven; as is the heavenly, such are they also that are heavenly; and ye shall also bear the image of the heavenly." (Matt. xi. 28; John xi. 25, 26; 1 Cor. xv. 45—9). "Behold the new and living way! He who knew no sin hath been made sin for us, that we might be made the righteousness of God in him. Jesus Christ hath abolished death, and hath brought life and immortality to light through the gospel." (2 Cor. v. 21; 2 Tim. i. 10.)

Now, then, standing in the very centre of the plan of salvation, we are prepared, as we look in all directions through the unsearchable riches of God's grace, to appreciate with clearness the sense in which Christ is our life. And knowing that all that was lost through the first Adam is more than recovered through the last, and that where sin hath abounded and reigned unto death, grace shall much more abound and reign through righteousness unto eternal life, by Jesus Christ our Lord, we may, with a firm hand, take up and unravel the thread of our sad destiny as sinners; and, as we retrace the points of our condemnation unto death, develope that life of our souls, of our bodies, and of both united to all eternity, which, though we be dead, is hid with Christ in God.

And, *First*, of Christ, as the life of our souls.—If you would either see or enter into the kingdom of God—if you would comprehend or possess the divine life—you must be born again. This is the simplest, the most elemental principle of spiritual religion. Do not marvel at it, said Christ to Nicodemus, for it is the first and the clearest part of all that portion of the mystery of Christ which is developed in this world; and the comprehension and reception of this earthly part lie at the foundation of our ability to comprehend and to possess all its heavenly parts. Do you not perceive? You are dead in sin: but God so loved the world that he gave his only begotten Son, that whosoever believeth in him should not perish, but have everlasting life. As Moses lifted up the serpent in the wilderness, that all who looked upon it might live, so is the Son of Man lifted up, a sacrifice for sin, that a divine Saviour, crucified for us, might become the specific object of that saving faith by which, being united to him, we obtain eternal life. For, by our union with him, he bears our sins in his own body on the tree, and offers up to divine justice a full satisfaction for them all. Now, then, can God be just and justify those who believe in Jesus Christ. But still further—this offering up by Christ of himself for the redemption of his people hath wrought far deeper than any outward work, even for the pardon of sin. That which is spirit can be born only of the Spirit; and your spirit is dead, in the only sense in which a spirit can die; it is corrupt, depraved, alienated from God. The life inherited from the living soul, Adam, is utterly forfeited and polluted, and is incapable of being healed again any more for ever—infinitely incapable of re-creating itself. But there is a power adequate to this new creation; and there is, as has been already shown, a ground and a cause adequate to justify it. The eternal love of God is cause enough, and the infinite sacrifice of his Son Jesus Christ, is ground enough; and it is plain enough, that if we could live at all by reason of our connection with that first

Adam, who was only a living soul, we may also live a new and better life by reason of our connection with the last Adam, who is a life giving spirit. A spiritual power, sent down from heaven, is therefore expressly declared by Christ to be the efficient agency in our new creation; and this is true, without exception, concerning every one that is born again. Because God has loved us with an unchangeable love, Christ has redeemed us with his most precious blood; and the divine Spirit of life covenanted in that blood, and purchased by it, sets us free from the power of sin and death, opens our eyes, and turns us from darkness to light, and from the power of Satan unto God, that we may receive forgiveness of sins and inheritance amongst them which are sanctified by faith that is in Christ. As the wind bloweth where it listeth, so this free Spirit, sovereign as it is divine, cometh and goeth, not by mortal control; but so cometh and goeth as for ever to justify and honour Christ; for ever to condemn the world for its darkness and its evil deeds; for ever to comfort and bless all the children of the light and the truth; for ever to manifest his special presence while he abides, and leave ineffaceable proofs of his work when it is done. (John iii. 1—21.)

Verily—verily—is the reiterated assurance of Christ; marvel not—marvel not—his earnest command. Why should we doubt—why distrust God? This doctrine of a spiritual and supernatural regeneration is not only distinctly and continually asserted throughout the Scriptures, as the very foundation of the life of God in our souls, but it underlies every portion of God's dealings with the human race, both in time and eternity, as those dealings are explained to us in his holy Word. When we speak of the fall of man, we utter we know not what, unless we intend to signify that man has lost the image of God and needs to be restored to it. When we dilate on the whole work of Christ, in his estate of humiliation, we rob that tremendous dispensation of all its significance the moment we lose sight of the condition of man, as helpless and depraved, and the necessity of a divine intervention to save him from perdition. When we speak of the entire work of the Holy Ghost, we utter sheer nonsense, unless we mean that man needs, and that God has provided, in the agency of that Spirit, the effectual means of his moral renovation. When we think of God as the moral ruler and final judge of a race of sinners, we have no alternative but to admit the universal destruction of the whole race, or to admit the existence of some divine and efficacious mode of restoring a sinful soul to God. When we contemplate our race as rational creatures, having any souls at all, no matter how sinful those souls may be, it is the merest absurdity to speak of any regeneration for them that is not purely spiritual; and when we survey them as helpless creatures, morally helpless through their depravity, though still spiritual creatures, every thing short of supernatural aid is a mere trifling with their despair. Every part of the plan of salvation revealed in the Scriptures involves the idea of a supernatural and spiritual regeneration of the soul of man; and every fact upon which that glorious plan rests, and every issue to which it points, is contradicted and rendered nugatory the moment we reject the doctrine of the Holy Ghost in its divine fulness. And then, to crown all, and as if to set in the most awful light God's estimate of the necessity under which we lie, to perish if we are not born again, and of the clearness with which that necessity is revealed to men, he forewarns us that the sin against the Holy Ghost is one for whose pardon we need not pray, for it will never be forgiven! Yet, beyond all doubt, a low appreciation of the work of God's Spirit in the hearts of the children of men lies at the root of most of the heresies that now dishonour and deface the nominal Church of God, and is the cause of most of the deadness and unfruitfulness of the true followers of Christ. Belief in the efficacy of forms and ceremonies, confidence in the power of rites and ordinances, bigotted advocacy of errors and delusions, daring rejection of saving truths, growing indifference to instructive and pungent ministrations, aversion to strictness in doctrine and in life, mournful departures from simplicity and spirituality, shallow interpretations of God's word, increase of ostentation and laxity in all religious things, and wide spread restlessness, commotion, and love of carnal excitement in spiritual matters; all these, and how many other sorrowful proofs rise upon every side, to attest that the work of the Spirit is not cherished amongst men, and that Christ is not the life of their souls in that exalted sense which the Scriptures inculcate, and which other times have witnessed. It is the Spirit that quickeneth, the flesh profiteth nothing. (John vi. 43—65.)

Still, the life of God in the soul remains the fundamental necessity of every renewed heart, as it is the first and simplest element of practical Christianity; and in connection with the aspect of it presented in my text, there are several things further which ought to be briefly suggested, before I pass from this topic. You will note, in the first place, the peculiar turn of the apostle's thought. He does not content himself with saying, that we have a life derived from Christ, nor yet that Christ has bestowed on us a life essentially like his own; but he mounts to the loftiest height, and declares that Christ is himself our life! Christ is found in his people, the hope of glory. In receiving, accepting, and relying upon him, there is a lofty and hallowed sense in which they are nourished by him. I am, said he, the bread of life! (John vi. 48.) Beside all that Christ has uttered—and he spake as never man spake; beside all that he hath done for us—and he hath done more than it has entered into our hearts to conceive; there is Christ himself, the friend, the teacher, the master, the Saviour, the very life of our souls! Again: you are to remember that this abolishing of our spiritual death by Christ, and this regeneration of our souls by his Spirit, is the condition not only of all other and further mercies to be received through him, but, in part, constitutes our very capacity to enjoy any of them aright, and the chief of them at all. The carnal mind is enmity against God, for it is not subject to the law of God, neither indeed can be. Without form and without comeliness; or the chiefest amongst ten thousand, and altogether lovely; one or other of these two is the only view we can take of him. One is the view of a dead soul, hastening to perdition, and fit only for it. The other is the view of a living soul, renewed in the image of the invisible God, and meet to partake of the inheritance of the saints in light. Once more: you will bear in mind that the Lord has said, this spiritual regeneration is an earthly, in contradistinction to a heavenly, thing. It must occur, if it occurs at all, while you are in the flesh. The life of Jesus, if it is ever manifested in us, "must be made manifest in our body"—"in our mortal flesh." (2 Cor. iv. 10, 11.) Temporal death puts an end for ever, to every hope of impenitent men. From the instant that the soul and the body are separated, the expectation of the wicked shall perish. Whatsoever thy hand findeth to do, do with thy might; for there is no work, nor device, nor knowledge, nor wisdom, in the grave, whither thou goest. (Eccl. ix. 10.) Still further: you may rejoice in the divine assurance, that the gift of this new and imperishable life in Jesus Christ, draws after it every other blessing, and every other benefit of the covenant of grace, in so far as is needful to bring you off more than conquerors, through him that loved us. Many toils—many tears—fightings without—fears within—troubles on every hand—fierce temptations—fearful backslidings—the malice of hell—the plagues of your heart! It is no light thing to make such sinners angels of light. Nevertheless it can be done. It has been done. It will be done again. If when we were enemies we were reconciled to God by the death of his Son, much more being reconciled we shall be saved by his life! For I am persuaded that neither death, nor life, nor angels, nor principalities, nor powers, nor things present, nor things to come, nor height, nor depth, nor any other creature, shall be able to separate us from the love of God which is in Christ Jesus our Lord. (Rom. v. 10, and viii. 38, 39.) And finally: you may take continual comfort, and make continual progress in that new life into which you have been begotten by the Holy Ghost; more and more of the knowledge of God; a conformity unto him, greater and greater; an insight into his word, and into divine things, deeper and deeper; a love of Christ more and more fervent; a more rooted abhorrence of all sin; increasing joy in the Holy Ghost; compassion for sinners, tenderer every day; hardness borne as becomes a good soldier of the cross; the good fight of faith manfully waged; the cross borne aloft through our pilgrimage; Christ, and him crucified, more and more the life of our souls! For the Lord Jesus Christ, of whom the whole family in heaven and earth is named, doth grant, according to the riches of his glory, that you may be strengthened with might by his Spirit in the inner man; that Christ may dwell in your hearts by faith; that ye, being rooted and grounded in love, may be able to comprehend, with all saints, what is the breadth, and length, and depth, and height, and to know the love of Christ, which passeth knowledge, that ye may be filled with all the fulness of God. Therefore, unto him that is able to do exceeding abundantly above all that we ask or think, according to the power that worketh in us, unto him be glory in the Church, by Christ Jesus, throughout all ages, world without end. (Eph. iii. 16—21.)

Secondly—Of Christ as the life of our mortal nature. I remind you that the whole doctrine of Christ is matter of pure revelation. It is only from God himself that we can know what Christ is, and what Christ does. All this is not less true concerning every portion of Christ's work in us, and every part of our relations to him, than concerning the essential truths which relate to his own being, and to his relations to the Godhead, and to the whole universe, of which he is the central object.

Temporal death, as we call the separation of the human soul and body, is to the human race the direct result of the entrance of sin into the world. God not only forewarned Adam of a fact infinitely certain, in the nature of that dependence in which the whole creation stood, but denounced to him the ordained penalty of transgression, when he told him that in the day he should eat of the tree of the knowledge of good and evil, "dying he should die." From that moment he and all his race should endure the power, and incur the judgment of death in their bodies, as well as pollution in their souls; and starting from that point of deliberate rejection of God, dying they should die, man after man, and generation after generation, as long as the curse of a violated covenant, and the penalty of a broken law, worked together with the power of sin in the ruins of their fallen nature. And then, after the work of ruin was begun, and to prevent the immortal continuance of death itself upon the earth, "lest he put forth his hand and take also of the tree of life, and eat, and live for ever," the Lord God drove out the man from the garden of Eden, and placed a cherubim and a flaming sword to keep the way of the tree of life. (Gen. ii. 17, and iii. 22—24.) Expounding and enforcing these solemn truths, prophets and apostles have argued the whole matter with unusual fulness, and made it clear above most of the wonders of our being. By one man, even Adam, sin entered into the world, and death by sin; and so death passed upon all men, for that all have sinned. That offence was an act of deliberate disobedience; and that death which followed it, was not only a condemnation, but a judgment. And if we shall say that death reigned from Adam to Moses, that is, before the giving of the law, and that sin is not imputed when there is no law, and, therefore, death cannot be either the fruit or the penalty of sin; the divine answer is, that we have just perverted the facts and drawn an inference that is precisely opposite to the one which those facts imply. For as death *is* both the fruit and the penalty of sin, God being the judge, the reign of death, before the law was given, proves that there is a law deeper than that given by Moses, even that covenant of works, under whose curse we lie, and that law of our very being, created in the image of God, and that law of eternal order, and fitness, and truth, which is involved in the very being of God, and to which he has made the human conscience responsive; and that the violation of each one of these primeval laws is, in a proper sense, sin, and is imputed. Again, if we answer further, that death reigned, even from the beginning, over those who never sinned after the similitude of Adam's transgression; that is, over those who never wilfully transgressed the known law of God, and, therefore, this plainly shows that death is neither the fruit nor the penalty of sin, the divine response is, that herein we abuse ourselves by a false idea of sin, as before by a false idea of law; for the fundamental truth being, that death *is* the result of sin, simply, absolutely and universally, in the absence of known law and deliberate transgression, death proves the existence of that which is properly sin, and which God will impute; namely, sin in our very being, original and congenital with us, derived from the first parent of our race, as its natural and its covenanted head, in whom we fell. And again, if we now turn to attack the very nature of such an order of things, and urge that it cannot be after this fashion, because it involves that the sin of Adam should be imputed to his race; that through the offence of one man judgment should come upon all men to condemnation; that for one offence so terrible and universal ruin should occur; and that by the fall and death of one man death should pass upon all men; the divine answer is, that as before we deceived ourselves as to the nature of sin, and the nature of law, so here we delude ourselves about the nature of God's relations to his creatures, and attack the very foundations of divine grace. For the righteousness of Christ must be imputed to his people; the obedience and sacrifice of Christ must lie at the foundation of that free gift which came upon all men to justification of life; and by one man, even Jesus Christ, and by one sacrifice of himself, grace must reign through righteousness unto eternal life; or else, where sin has abounded it must continue to abound for ever, and where death has reigned it must continue to reign eternally. Rom. v. 12—21.

Taking their start from this point, the Scriptures develope the whole dispensation of man. For awhile he abides here on earth, his ordinary condition being that of an immortal but sinful soul united to a mortal and sinful body, and his best estate that of a partially sanctified soul united to that mortal and sinful body. His soul may be regenerated, and to a certain degree sanctified, while in union with the body; and this change, as has been shown, must occur during that union here below, or never occur at all. By and by he dies. His soul and his body are separated; the latter returning to the dust, as it was—the former to God who gave it. In their separated state, regenerated souls pass at death into the presence and fruition of God; and impenitent souls pass to a place of torment. Of the whole human race two men only, Enoch and Elijah, have as yet escaped the stroke of death; and at the second coming of Christ, his people who are then alive will also escape that stroke. (1 Cor. xv. 31; 1 Thess. iv. 15—17.) But that second coming of Christ will cut short this dispensation of man upon earth, and bring death itself to its second great arbitrement. The dead will arise. A resurrection of life—a resurrection of damnation. This is the end of temporal death. The souls and the bodies of men are united once more, and so united will undergo the final judgment. (1 Cor. xv.)

It is said of our divine Redeemer, that in order that he might be a merciful and faithful High Priest, it behooved him to be made like unto his brethren in all things. (Heb. ii. 17.) In every part, therefore, of this human dispensation, this resemblance exists to the utmost degree possible. He has taken a true human soul, and a true human body, into ineffable and eternal union with his divine nature. The man Jesus of Nazareth was as really a man as any man that ever was born of woman, though supernaturally made in the womb of the virgin Mary, and so not begotten under the covenant of works, and thus not polluted by original sin. He tabernacled amongst men—tempted in all points like as they are, and bearing all those temporal sorrows which the Scriptures embrace under the wide appellation of death—so far as that was possible to one free from sin. Being sinless, he was, so to speak, naturally free from temporal death, in its proper sense, whether as the fruit or the penalty of sin. Though he was crucified, yet it is also true that he laid down his life, of which there was no power in the universe that was able to rob him. (John x. 18.) Like his brethren, who are to be changed in a moment, in the twinkling of an eye, he was transfigured upon the mount. Like his brethren, who endure the stroke of death, he also gave up the ghost. Like his brethren, whose separate souls dwell with God, while their bodies sleep in the grave, his separate human soul was in the bosom of God, while his human body laid three days in the sepulchre. Like his brethren, who are to arise and shine, he first of all arose from the dead. And so we may not doubt that the parallel will complete itself utterly; and his brethren like him will yet walk the earth in their resurrection bodies, and then ascend like him in glory to the highest heavens! (Rev. xx. 4, 6, 15.)

Now, then, I may group together, as under the preceding head, several topics too essentially connected with the subject matter of my text, to be passed by even in the briefest exposition of the subject. And, first: you will perceive how absolutely our life depends on Christ, and how completely the whole scheme of the resurrection rests upon him and terminates in him. Since the fall, we are as essentially mortal as we are depraved. In him we not only live and move and have our being; by him and for him not only were all things created, and by him do all things consist; but, since by man came death, by man came also the resurrection of the dead; for as in Adam all die, even so in Christ shall all be made alive. (1 Cor. xv. 21, 22.) Except by the power of Christ, and for the sake of Christ, there is no reason why the human race, or any individual of it, should live for a single moment, or receive a single mercy while they live; or why, having died, they should rise again from the dead; just as there is no reason why any human being should be either regenerated or sanctified, except for the sake and by the work of Christ; for to this end Christ both died, and rose, and revived, that he might be the Lord both of the dead and living. (Rom. xiv. 9.) Again: It is very obvious from what has just been said, how fundamental to the whole theory of Christianity, and therefore to the whole destiny of man, is the fact of the resurrection of Christ himself. To establish this fact is one main end of all the Gospels; to illustrate its bearing is one capital object in all the discourses of the apostles and inspired evangelists that have come down to us; and to settle it in our hearts as a truth, at once infinitely certain and infinitely pregnant, is the aim of perhaps a larger portion of the New Testament Scriptures than is devoted to any other single point; for if Christ did not rise from the dead, then we shall never rise; then is our preaching vain, and your faith vain; then are the apostles false witnesses of God, and we are yet in our sins, and all they which are fallen asleep in Christ are perished. But if Christ, who is the image of the invisible God, and the first born of every creature, has risen from the dead and become the first fruits of them that slept, then it is certain that in him shall all be made alive, every man in his own order, and next after Christ himself they that are Christ's at his coming. (1 Cor. xv. 3—23.) Still further: though the union of the divine and human natures in the person of Christ, and his death and resurrection, establish the unalterable certainty of the utter destruction of temporal death and the resurrection of the whole human race, yet the resurrection of the righteous, and the resurrection of the wicked, will be infinitely diverse in their manner and in their results. It is of the bodies of men only that the Scriptures predicate the idea, and proclaim the fact, of a resurrection. Death and resurrection will produce on the bodies of the righteous a change so far analogous as is possible to the change wrought upon their souls by regeneration and sanctification; and they will in like manner produce upon the bodies of the wicked a change analogous to that produced in their souls, by the total and final withdrawal of the Holy Spirit from them, and their own complete and irreversible rejection of Christ and salvation.

There will be a resurrection of life and a resurrection of damnation. In the latter, the wicked will rise to shame and everlasting contempt; monuments of dishonour, of corruption and of the second death. In the former, the righteous will arise to incorruption, immortality and eternal glory; monuments of the grace of God and of the triumph of Christ over his last enemy. (Rev. xx. 4—15.) Once more: in the very nature of the whole case, as the Scriptures open it to us, the necessity of our enduring what we do, is clearly set forth. God has provided for us an immortal existence, not here, but in another and higher estate. For his own glory, and for our blessedness, the scheme of redemption is so arranged as to operate upon us partly while our souls and bodies are united, partly after they are separated, and partly after they are united again. In the first period of its operation, it proposes to do nothing directly for our mortal nature, beyond what is involved in the bearing of its provisions for our immortal part upon our mortal during its pilgrimage. Therefore we suffer, and weep, and die. Jesus himself suffered, and wept, and died. Yet even in these conditions the grace of God presses to the very limit of the possibility which his own glorious goodness and wisdom had established. Our sufferings are made the means of drawing us to Christ and perfecting us in holiness; our tears are wiped away as they flow, by the hand of God himself; all the struggles through which we pass give greater vigour to the life of God within us; when we come to die, our very death is precious in the sight of God, and the grave yields to us a glorious victory; and then comes the resurrection, to own and crown us heirs of light! (Psalms xxxvii; Rom. viii.) And, finally: from the beginning to the end of all, how completely is Christ our life; and how wonderfully is the foundation of all laid, and the surprising result brought about! In such a world as this, what would we be without a throne of grace to which we could flee? Amidst the afflictions and temptations of life, what are we without divine support? Under the burden of sin, and the doom of impending death, and the darkness of a fathomless eternity, whither can we turn without a Saviour? But who would ever have thought, with hearts full of enmity to God, of asking him to save us, by the sacrifice of his only begotten Son? Who would have conceived the idea of the incarnation, or, after it, that of redemption by the blood of Christ? Who would have imagined the stupendous concatenation of removing the sting of death by removing the virulence of sin; of getting rid of the guilt of sin by satisfying the law which denounced it; of silencing the law itself, by enduring its curse and penalty; of conquering death, which the law denounced, by entering into the consuming and pitiless grave? In such a case, such a plan, with such a result! Oh! the depth of the riches both of the wisdom and knowledge of God! Oh! the unsearchable riches of Christ! (1 Cor. xv. 54—58; Eph. iii. 8—21.)

Thirdly, of Christ as the life of our eternal being. The Scriptures hardly recognize what we ordinarily call life, as an estate worthy of that name. The pollution of our moral nature, the darkness of our rational faculties, and the perishing and suffering condition of our physical man, make up an estate not so much of life as of living death; the resurrection of the wicked is expressly distinguished from a resurrection of life, by being called a resurrection of damnation; and the final estate of the impenitent is denominated their second death—the doom of Satan, and of all who are deceived by him, of "the beast and the false prophet," and of all whose names are not found written in the Book of Life. (Rev. xx. 10—15.) God alone hath life in himself; and the Lord Jesus, claiming for himself this divine prerogative, and the right, at his own good pleasure, to bestow life upon others, expressly sets it forth as a proof of his own Godhead. Himself the way, the truth, and the life, it was his express errand upon earth to bestow eternal life upon as many as the Father had given him; and this, saith he, is life eternal, that they might know thee, the only true God, and Jesus Christ whom thou hast sent. (John v. 26, and xvii. 3.) I have already traced the operation of this incorruptible life in man, up to the period of the resurrection. It remains, under the present topic, to indicate briefly its after course.

God hath appointed a day, in the which he will judge the world in righteousness, by that man whom he hath ordained; whereof he hath given assurance unto all men, in that he hath raised him from the dead. (Acts xvii. 31.) This, you will observe, is the pith of the crushing argument why men ought to repent of their sins, addressed by the great apostle of the Gentiles to the Epicurean and Stoic philosophers in the Areopagus at Athens; the last men to hear, and the last place in which to utter such an appeal, unless there was that in it to which the human conscience responds, and on which the human reason may rest. Somewhat dilated the argument might run thus: You are sensible of your ill desert, and that you ought to be held accountable for it; the proper result of that state of mind is repentance; but this is the more urgent when you consider that your inward sense of ill desert and accountability is but the shadow of your impending destiny, for the true God has in fact appointed not only a time to judge you, but also the judge, even Jesus Christ, whom I preach unto you; and of these truths he has given you absolute assurance in the resurrection of Jesus, which resurrection not only I, and hundreds besides, still live to attest, but which the power of the divine truths I proclaim, and the power of the eternal Spirit accompanying those truths in your souls, which truths and which Spirit alike proceed from Christ, enforces with an intimate and divine demonstration. Probably not one of these sceptics and fatalists had ever, before he saw Paul, had any distinct idea of any single one of all the great elements of this universal and overwhelming argument, delivered that day on Mars' hill. Natural enough, therefore, was it that some mocked, and that others doubted; and most natural of all that the link they struck at in the argument was the one they knew least about, and on which all turned—the resurrection of the dead; for even they could see, and that on the first hearing, that if that were true, all the rest must needs follow. Howbeit, Dionysius the Areopagite, and certain men beside, and a woman named **Damaris**, and others with her, clave unto Paul and believed; God thus attesting that his servant had divine warrant for what he uttered. And therein, through eighteen centuries, down to this very hour, the proclamation of this impending judgment—of its divine demonstration—and of its eternal issues—has been the burden of the message of Christ's servants to a ruined world. To it we are now come.

Let us stand first in the midst of the just, that we may see how completely Christ, in this tremendous period of their being, is to every one of them eternal life. Here are the redeemed of every race—every age. Patriarchs, prophets, apostles, martyrs—all are there. They who had seen from afar the promised Messiah; they who had followed him as he went in and out upon earth, despised and rejected of men; they who had heard and believed, through all succeeding ages, the sound of him, as it went out through the whole world, not one of them is missing. The throng that had fought the good fight; the hosts that had passed through great tribulation; the multitudes who had sung the song of rejoicing, and the still greater multitudes who had wept all along the ascent of Zion; pilgrims who had counted their years by centuries; pilgrims whose days had been few and evil; pilgrims snatched from the evil to come, who had seen of earth only the valley of the shadow of death; multitudes—multitudes—thousand thousands—ten thousand times ten thousand! Here and there are scattered those who never tasted death; they had been changed in a moment at the coming of the Lord. The rest had been with Christ in glory, and their sleeping dust had heard the trump of God; and now they stand arrayed in glorious, spiritual bodies. Mortal has put on immortality; death is swallowed up in victory! And yet it is judgment, eternal judgment, to which they have come. And there are thrones, and dominions, and principalities, and powers, and heavenly hierarchies—all the exalted spirits of the upper world. And in the midst of all—enthroned in light that is inaccessible and full of glory—one like unto the Son of man—the Judge of quick and dead! Think of Pilate's bar—where he once stood and was condemned, and then see him seated on the throne of the universe, with all that universe contains of pure and good, waiting with adoring trust to hear his judgments. Think of his crown of thorns, and then behold the diadems which are cast down before him, in token of exulting love that will not be repressed! Think of the cruel mockings, the unpitied agony of Calvary, and then listen to the triumphant alleluias that arise around his throne, and, mounting with eternal melody, strain after strain, from countless millions, re-echo from the highest spheres, and swell beyond the farthest star! Alleluia! salvation, and glory, and honour, and power unto the Lord our God! Alleluia! King of Kings, and Lord of Lords! (Matt. xxv. 31; Rev. v. 9—13; xv. 3; xix. 1—16.)

Yes, it is a judgment, but a judgment of the just made perfect. Of the countless millions who have part in that resurrection of life, there is not one who has not been washed in the blood of the Lamb, and been made a king and a priest unto God. (Rev. i. 5—6.) It is not a judgment to ascertain whether they will be saved or not—for they are saved already; nor to ascertain whether they are worthy of eternal life—for every one of them has already received it at the hands of Christ. Most of them have been with him in glory; the rest were changed, and caught up to him, at his second coming. But still the Books are opened—that Book which is the rule of eternal judgment—God's blessed Word, which we have in our hands to-day; the Books of convincing testimony, in which is written the whole record of our lives; the Book, also, in which are set down the names of the redeemed—the Lamb's Book of Life! One by one the story of every saved sinner is traced. All the secrets of his heart are revealed—all the actions of his life are recounted—all the greatness of his ill desert established and confessed. But along with all this, the dealings of Christ with his soul— the commencement, the progress, the consummation, of the grace of God towards him—the life of God within him. And then his glorified Saviour, the God-man, proclaims, as King of Kings, the result he has reached as eternal Judge, and the precise method of that result in that individual case. Come, ye blessed of my father, inherit the kingdom prepared for you from the foundation of the world! Here is the mansion you are to inhabit for evermore; here is your seat at the marriage supper of the Lamb; here is the light with which you are to shine to all eternity; here is the service in which you are to be glorified for ever and ever! Enter into the joy of your Lord; inherit eternal life! And then new alleluias arise from all the armies of Heaven! And so another exhibition of God's method of grace and salvation, and renewed alleluias. And then another, and another, and another; onward, and onward, as the eternal cycles pass over a universe in which time no longer exists to be measured; until every manifestation of God's grace in every redeemed sinner shall be exhibited to all the angels of God, and to all the just made perfect; and until the fact and the method of salvation, in the case of every saved sinner, shall be judicially ascertained, and the position of each one in the heavenly hosts proclaimed from the throne of God, in the hearing of all worlds! Oh! what majesty to God; what blessedness to the redeemed; what glory with Christ their life in this first period of their eternal being, as they reign with him in the heavenly Jerusalem, and expatiate through a universe wherein he has made all things new! (Matt. xxv.; 2 Pet. iii.; Rev. xx.)

And where are the impenitent? David has told us long ago that sinners shall not stand in the congregation, nor the ungodly in the judgment of the righteous. (Psalm i. 5.) Christ himself has said, that when he comes in glory he will separate the blessed from the accursed, as a shepherd separates his sheep from his goats, and then will judge the righteous first, and afterwards doom the accursed. (Matt. xxv. 32.) We are abundantly informed that there is a first and a second resurrection; that there is an eternal order, both in the resurrection and the judgment, by which the triumphant acquittal of the redeemed precedes the doom of the wicked; and by which the rest of the dead live not again till the thousand years are fulfilled, during which those who have part in the first resurrection live and reign with Christ. (1 Cor. xv. 23. Rom. xx. 3—6.) And now, when the hour is come for the Lord Jesus to be revealed from heaven with his mighty angels in flaming fire, to take vengeance on them that know not God, and that obey not the Gospel of our Lord Jesus Christ, they shall be punished with everlasting destruction from the presence of the Lord, and from the glory of his power. (2 Thess. i. 7—8.) Now is the hour fully come for fire to come down from God out of heaven and destroy all the wicked; for hell to give up the dead that are in it; for Satan to be cast into the lake of fire; for death and hell to perish; for the enemies of God to be tormented day and night for ever and ever; for the second death to begin its interminable reign! (Rev. xx.) As we contemplate this scene of horror, and bear in mind that we have deserved to incur its eternal woe, and will escape it only because Christ is our life, we ought to have some foretaste of the thrill with which the hosts of God turn away from the abyss and shout hosannah to the Lamb!

There is another point. The Scriptures teach us, with abundant clearness, that although every part of the dispensation of God's grace has direct relation to the person, the work and the glory of Christ, yet Christ occupies, in many respects, a different position under each successive development of the whole plan of God's infinite mercy. During his personal ministry on earth, he occupied a position materially dissimilar to any he had ever occupied before; and so now, seated at the right hand of God, his position is widely different from what it had ever been before his infinite exaltation. In like manner, when the dispensation of grace, strictly so called, is ended by the second coming of Christ and the resurrection of the righteous, a new aspect of his work and his relation to his people manifests itself; and again another, in all that constitutes the judgment and acquittal of the righteous, and the doom of the wicked. After these things, what will follow? Let us hear what the Holy Ghost saith. In his great discourse on the day of Pentecost, under which three thousand souls believed, and in his second mighty exposition a little after, in the temple, under which five thousand men believed, the apostle Peter carries us far into these sublime events. The heavens must receive Jesus Christ, said he, *until* the times of the restitution of all things, which God hath spoken by the mouth of all his holy prophets since the world began; and he urged that great testimony of David: "The Lord said unto my Lord, sit thou on my right hand *until* I make thy foes thy footstool." (Acts ii. 34, and iii. 21.) That exaltation and that reign of Christ was not, therefore, the final dispensation; it was a dispensation and a reign *until* such a time and such events. I suppose the second coming of Christ, and the resurrection of the righteous dead, will develope what was wrapped up in that *until*. Again: in the revelation of Jesus Christ, amongst the infinite blessings and glories promised to those who shall come off conquerors, the crowning promise is: "To him that overcometh will I grant to sit with me in *my* throne, even as I also overcame and am set down with my Father on *his* throne." (Rev. iii. 21.) Here is a very broad distinction between the throne of the Father and that of the glorified Godman; and a very clear indication that, as yet, the latter had not been ascended; that *until* before spoken of stood between the two thrones; the whole period, namely, from the ascension of Jesus Christ till his second coming. Now, of those who have part in the first resurrection is it expressly written, that they lived and reigned with Christ a thousand years. (Rev. xx. 4, 5.) The Lord Jesus plainly said to his apostles, that when the Son of Man shall sit in the *throne of his glory,* ye also shall sit upon twelve thrones, judging the twelve tribes of Israel. (Matt. xix. 28.) And the apostle Paul, in his treatise on the resurrection, declares that the resurrection of Christ's people, at his second coming, will be followed by the reign of Christ *till* he has put all his enemies under his feet, and that the last enemy that shall be destroyed is death. (1 Cor. xv. 23, 25, 26.) Here, then, is another limitation, another *until;* and as we are told that death will be destroyed when Satan is cast into hell, and the wicked enter upon the second death, (Rev. xx. 10, 14,) this *until* is explained to us, and a new development of the dispensation of Christ intimated to commence after the doom of the wicked. There remains, therefore, after that, another development of the eternal life of the blessed; and the Scriptures briefly, but clearly, initiate us into the knowledge of it.

In the passage just cited from the first epistle to the Corinthians, this order is declared touching the sublime topic of which the apostle is treating. First, the resurrection of Christ himself; afterward, who can tell how long afterward? the second coming of Christ, and the resurrection of his people at that coming; then, when he shall have put down all rule, and all authority, and all power, and shall have destroyed death, *then*, after that reign of the saints with Christ, *cometh the end!* (1 Cor. xv. 23—26.) And then will Christ deliver up the kingdom to God, even the Father. (verse 24.) He will deliver up the kingdom to the Father, upon the Lamb's Book of Life, (Rev. xx. 15, and xxi. 27,) that glorious record containing a complete list of their names, and being of itself a perfect evidence of their redemption, their regeneration, their sanctification, their glorious resurrection, their acquittal in the day of judgment, their reign with Christ, and their right, through him, to inherit the eternal kingdom. And then shall the Son also himself be subject unto Him that put all things under him, that God may be all in all. (1 Cor. xv. 28.) And here made partakers of the divine nature—admitted to the immediate presence and full fruition of God—made perfectly blessed in the enjoyment of him—the Scriptures launch us upon this eternal and inconceivably glorious and exalted state of existence, and close the revelations of God! The dispensation of Jesus Christ, as the Redeemer of God's elect, has passed through all its wondrous phases; the kingdom, the power, and the glory, have all been illustrated and established; nothing remains that is not subject to him, except only He which did put all things under him (1 Cor. xv. 27); the end is fully reached, in that highest conception which mortals can have of it, that God is all in all! The human race, too, has passed through all its revealed phases; its existence upon earth; its existence after death; its existence after the resurrection; and its high service and enjoyment of God in glory to all eternity, is begun. In the broadest view it is possible for us to take of all Christ's work, and our own career and destiny, as well as in the most minute and circumstantial examination we can make of every particular part, both of one and the other, nothing is so clearly and so constantly obvious, as that Christ is our life in the whole, and in every part; the life of our spiritual nature, the life of our mortal being, the life of our immortal existence. This is the sublime and consoling truth we set out to elucidate by the testimony of God.

If we desire to live under the impression which this divine truth ought to create, and which this glorious destiny requires, we have only to listen to what the apostle has told us in connection with the words of my text, to discover what is required of us in that great endeavour. We ought, says he, to seek those things which are above, and set our affections on them, and not on things on the earth; remembering that we are dead, and that our life is hid with Christ in God. We ought to mortify our members which are upon the earth; for the lack of doing which, we are prone to fall into those sins, for the sake of which the wrath of God cometh on the children of disobedience, and in which we once lived ourselves. But now, seeing that we have put off the old man, with his deeds, and have put on the new man, which is renewed in knowledge, after the image of him that created him; we ought continually to shun all evil, and pursue all good; under the fixed and felt conviction, that to us Christ is all and in all. We ought, as the elect of God, who profess righteousness and who trust that God loves us, to put on bowels of mercies, kindness, humbleness of mind, meekness, long-suffering, forbearance, forgiveness; striving to imitate the Lord Christ, and crowning all with that charity which is the bond of perfectness. Thus may the peace of God reign in our grateful hearts; thus may the Word of Christ dwell in us richly in all wisdom; thus the power of the Lord Jesus may be shown forth in us; thus in all the relations which we sustain upon earth, may we adorn the doctrine we profess, and honour the Lord whom we adore. So may we be able, by God's grace, to make our way good out of this, a ruined world, and get safely, perhaps triumphantly, through the sin and death that reign in it. And when Christ, *who is our life*, shall appear, then may we also appear with him in glory. And when all the redeemed shall be presented faultless before God, and be delivered up upon the Lamb's Book of Life, then may we too inherit the kingdom, prepared from the foundation of the world, for all the blessed of the Father! Glorious hope, which maketh not ashamed!

FAITH AND SIGHT CONTRASTED.

BY

A. T. M'GILL, D. D.

PROFESSOR IN THE WESTERN THEOLOGICAL SEMINARY, ALLEGHANY, PENNA.

For we walk by faith, not by sight.—2 Cor. 5—7.

It is a singular fact, in the history of redemption, that the faculty in man, which deceived him to his ruin at the first, is never restored to perfect confidence this side of heaven. That faculty is sense, in the widest acceptation of the term, which we here extend to internal emotion as well as external perception. While, in the direction of ordinary life, the most simple and unerring of all evidence is that of the senses, in the great duty of dealing with God, in reference to the conduct, acceptance, and everlasting welfare of the soul, it is the most imperfect and fallacious of all reliances. Through this avenue sin entered, and God seems to have closed it indignantly against all further intercourse with him, while we continue in this evil tenement. As if it were some facile door, through which thieves and robbers once entered, and would still enter, to mar and spoil the house, the glorious Builder will have it opened no more, in spiritual communication with himself, until the whole building shall be taken down, and reconstructed on the model of a glorious immortality.

Through the senses it was that the tempter first invaded the soul; "when the woman saw that the tree was good for food, and that it was pleasant to the eyes, and a tree to be desired to make one wise, she took of the fruit thereof and did eat, and gave also to her husband with her, and he did eat." Now that eye, that ear, that touch, that taste, that sense of every kind is all disparaged in the remedial dealing of God; and faith is the eye, the ear, the touch, the taste, the one all engrossing faculty by which grace renovates and rules the soul. Religion and the senses are divorced. These are degraded to the rank of handmaiden; and never will the soul repose with confidence upon them more, until error and frailty shall have been for ever removed. The apostle intimates, in this connection, that we shall hereafter walk by sight. When appearances will no longer deceive us; when the highest good will be for ever present to the soul; when the senses will be gloriously transformed, and made perfect in heaven, we shall walk by what we do see and know. But, for the present, wherever there is spiritual life,

I. We walk by faith, and not by *carnal* sight.
II. We walk by faith, and not by *spiritual* sight.
III. We walk by faith, and not by *glorified* sight.

I. "All men have not faith." There is all the difference between those who have this grace, and those who have it not, that another sense would make in the range of man's power and enjoyment. How immeasurably wider the perceptions of a blind man, when suddenly admitted or restored to the window of the eye. Where he had groped along, and stumbled with faltering footsteps, a wide, and distant, and adorned horizon bursts upon his view. More extended, more enchanting, more important unspeakably, is the enlargement when God restores the eye of faith to the soul. It sees a guide, a chart, a destination, which the spiritually blind can never perceive. It spreads another hue on all it scans; inspires new emotions, new estimations, and animates to incomparably greater speed the career on which it enters the soul.

1. Sight regards only things which are seen; but faith, things which are not seen. (2 Cor. iv. 18.) It could not be otherwise with maimed and defective nature than to seek those things only which its powers are fitted to perceive. We may crowd assurances of divine realities upon the natural man, and compel his assent to the evidence that they are realities of momentous import, and yet he is no more actuated by them, in his conduct, than is the deaf man by all the harmonies of music. There may be a notional apprehension entertained with zeal. Men, from what they read in the Word of God, and what they see in the conduct of others, and what they love by the dint of habit, and what they fear by the force of conscience and superstition, may seem to walk at times as though divine realities were believed, when all the while it is but sight that actuates them. Every thing short of the faith, which fixes a clear, and calm, and steadfast, and *transforming* reliance on the Lord Jesus Christ, "whom, having not seen, we love; in whom, though now we see him not, yet believing, we rejoice with joy unspeak-

able and full of glory;" every thing short of the faith which "endures as seeing him who is invisible," is sight; which gathers all its motives and activity from what is visible and palpable.

2. Sight regards what is present, faith what is future. It is "the substance of things hoped for," as well as "the evidence of things not seen." It is its great peculiarity, not only to displace palpable things in their power on the heart, by things of purely fiducial realization, but to grasp these as they lie in futurity also. It is not only impossible that the natural man be influenced by what is unseen, more than what is seen and felt, but still more, that he be influenced by unseen realities, in anticipation, more than by what is in present and actual contact with his feelings and desires. Without true faith, to fill up the void with animating hopes of the future, religion, which sweeps from the soul its temporal gratifications, would be an agonizing emptiness—the most intolerable of all conditions. All men would forsake it, like Demas, through love of this present world. Sight is always spreading enchantment over the present scene. Fast as experience detects the mockery of one illusion, she spreads another and a fresh attraction, persuading the soul, in spite of its sober convictions, to live as though its inward thought were, "this house shall continue for ever, this dwelling place to all generations." But faith unmasks the charm, and however faintly done, holds the future with steady and constraining influence before us; all is disenchanted at her touch; the world is a wilderness; the soul is made to come up from it, leaning on none of its pleasures, repos-

ing on none of its confidences—leaning on "the beloved" alone. "But now they desire a better country, that is an heavenly; wherefore God is not ashamed to be called their God, for he hath prepared for them a city." While the companions of a believer, like the children of Reuben, are always choosing their inheritance on this side of Jordan, his eye is onward and over to Canaan itself. While one takes up with this, and another with that earthly portion, "God forbid that I should glory, save in the cross of the Lord Jesus Christ, by whom the world is crucified to me, and I unto the world."

3. Sight regards what is pleasant; faith what is good. It is pleasant to choose a broad and downward way through this rugged and inhospitable world; and to crowd the way with as large a company as possible, where we have so many mutual wants and dependencies—pleasant to incur the reproach or disfavour of no one in the journey, but go hand in hand with the multitude, who "measure themselves by themselves, and compare themselves among themselves." It is pleasant to avoid every high hill and threatening danger on the road; and to turn away backward, or wind circuitously onward, rather than encounter hardships and perils in the straightest course. But faith gives other counsel. "Enter in at the straight gate; for wide is the gate and broad is the way that leadeth to destruction, and many there be that go in thereat." "Be not conformed to this world." "The fear of man bringeth a snare; but whoso putteth his trust in the Lord shall be safe." "Cursed is the man that trusteth in man, and maketh flesh his arm, and whose heart

departeth from the Lord." " Woe to them that call evil good and good evil, that put darkness for light and light for darkness, bitter for sweet and sweet for bitter." Through every gilded pleasure, faith perceives the poison and the sting; through every kiss of kind profession, faith detects a dagger for the heart; through every green and flowery resting place, faith discerns bowels of burning lava underneath, ready to engulph the soul, and drown it in destruction and perdition. "Come," says sight, "I have decked my bed with coverings of tapestry, with carved works, with fine linen from Egypt; I have perfumed my bed with myrrh, aloes, and cinnamon;" and, "as a bird hasteth to the snare of the fowler, and knoweth not it is for his life," we would go after her, but for the guardian counsel of faith; "the dead are there, her guests are in the depths of hell." "Come with me from Lebanon, my spouse, with me from Lebanon; look from the top of Amena and Shenir, from the lions' dens, from the mountains of the leopards."

4. Sight recoils from present evil as eagerly as it embraces present good; while faith welcomes present evil as cordially as it rejects the present gilded good. "Therefore I take pleasure," says the apostle, "in infirmities, in reproaches, in necessities, in persecutions, in distresses, for Christ's sake; for when I am weak, then am I strong." Affliction, which sight considers heavy, too heavy for us to bear, faith considers "light;" affliction, which sight will reckon to be long as life, and for ever, faith considers to be but "for a small moment;" affliction, which sight and sense regard as deadly, baleful to

every fond hope of the future, faith discovers to work "a far more exceeding and eternal weight of glory." He hates me, says sense, and therefore chastises me; "whom the Lord loveth he chasteneth," says faith, "and scourgeth every son whom he receiveth." She is never ashamed or confounded, world without end. The darkest hour of night is to her the harbinger of brilliant morning. "When clouds and darkness are round about him," she sees that "righteousness and judgment are the habitation of his throne."

II. We walk by faith, and not by *spiritual* sight. Besides that carnal sight, which believers retain, to some extent, in common with other men, and which, although subdued by grace, and subordinated by the power of faith, is ever beclouding and enfeebling the exercise of this heavenly grace, there is in the renewed man a consciousness of spiritual life and power, which impels him to the duties and enjoyments of religious experience, in a manner that is clearly distinguishable from the controlling power of faith. This principle of walking is known by various names in theological parlance—the religion of feeling, sensible assurance, spiritual affection, &c. But, however delightful and animating this impulsion may be to the soul, it is not the great principle by which we walk; it is not the means of our daily strength and comfort in the service of God. Faith, as even distinguished from this sensible experience, constitutes the mainspring of all our present obedience and enjoyment.

Faith is duty—sight or sense of grace is privilege Duty is ever incumbent and invariable—privilege is, for the most part, occasional, and granted or withheld according to the sovereign pleasure of God. "Trust in the Lord at all times," says the Psalmist; "Who is among you that feareth the Lord, that obeyeth the voice of his servant, that walketh in darkness and hath no light, let him trust in the name of the Lord, and stay upon his God." All believers have faith in God; but all have not sensible joy in the light of his countenance. This, like every other privilege, is granted only where He sees it to be for our good. It would be of no benefit to some believers to enjoy full assurance in themselves, that they stand firm and safe in the everlasting covenant. Some servants of the world are such prodigals in living that their wages must be kept from them until the season of working is over; some children of God have so much pride and self-confidence besetting their spiritual life, that glimpses of sensible delight are withheld from them for a lifetime, in order to develope the most needful graces and give them appropriate culture. Mortification and self-abasement peculiarly befit their constitutional weakness, and every disclosure of divine love, which this weakness might readily pervert, must be in mercy withheld; so that the very same love of God which imparts to humble believers transporting demonstrations of covenanted favour, denies them to the proud through a long probation, which may be lasting as life. You are as safely held in the securities of the great salvation without one gleam of absolute assurance, through all the course of your pilgrimage, if faith be following hard after God, as if you could see and feel the certainty of this salvation at every step of your journey; although, indeed, a sad deprivation of heaven upon earth must be the loss of such a diversity in your spiritual lot.

Faith is direct—sense is reflex. It is only in the way of exercising faith—it is only after faith has journeyed onward for a distance, that we can look back and see that our pathway is certainly right and heavenward. They who would walk by a sight of grace in their hearts, and hesitate in the exercise of faith upon Christ, because they do not first feel and know that he is gracious, are about as reasonable as men who would try to know how far they have travelled towards their destination before they take a step in the journey. Faith is the hand which opens the fountain of every blessing; and long must a fountain flow into a broken cistern before it is full enough to reflect the image of Jesus from the calm surface of a bosom replenished with graces. Faith is precious seed, which contains the germ of sensible assurance as one of its fruits or developments; and while other fruits must be put forth, more or less, under all circumstances of the present life, here is one which we may expect only in soil peculiarly cultivated with the graces of humility and meekness. And for us to falter and hesitate in believing, because we do not already enjoy this sensible experience, is about as reasonable as to expect fruit before we have planted the germ, and to decline all ordinary fruits because we do not first enjoy one of rare and extraordinary production.

This sensible experience of grace in the heart is not necessary, even as an evidence that we do believe; the fruits exhibited in our life and conduct are such evidence. Be this all your concern—to prove your faith by your works, and be assured that joy in the Holy Ghost, "joy unspeakable and full of glory," will be vouchsafed, so far as it is needful, to help you on the way to heaven.

Faith gives more glory to God than does sensible delight. Thomas would not believe unless he saw the object of faith in every particular of sensible demonstration; and it was then said, with an emphasis for ever memorable: "Blessed are they who have not seen, and yet have believed." It gives God but little glory when we can trust him only as we trust our fellow men, on whom we must lean by the help of something beyond their simple words—when we cannot venture the soul upon a promise without some feeling that it will be fulfilled. Abraham was "strong in faith, giving glory to God," because, "against hope he believed in hope;" against all probabilities for the fulfilment of a promise, and even mountain impossibilities to the eye of sense, he reposed, with unshaken trust, upon the truth and faithfulness of God. This, indeed, is to honour his word. And until our faith is schooled in the art of clinging to the naked truth of Jehovah in his promise, without a ray of visible demonstration, within us or without us, it is not schooled enough for heaven.

Faith is uniform—sense is fluctuating. The Christian career is called a walk, a race, a fight; without discharge for a moment. If we travelled on shoes which are not "iron and brass" in durability—on wheels of agitation, which are ever and anon rolling off from us; or the ebbing and flowing of a tide, which tosses us to heaven to-day, and leaves us dragging on a rock to-morrow—could we ever make the destination sure? Must we not have a principle of progress that is uniform in acting, and always ready; that will pierce the heavens for light when they are embossed in thickest darkness, and make even the lightning flash of God's anger help along the way of duty when his face is hidden with impenetrable gloom?

Faith is indubitable—sense may deceive the soul with innumerable counterfeits. The object of faith is the Lord Jesus Christ—the warrant of faith is his true and faithful word; and while ever it holds this object, by the strength of this warrant, heaven and earth may fail, and your very existence prove a delusion before such a faith can fail or deceive the soul. But we know how miserably fallacious may be the religion of feeling, and how false a joy may pervade even the breast of a true believer. "Where is then the blessedness ye spake of?" may be the reproachful query, after many a season of mistaken delight. "My mountain stands strong, I shall never be moved," said the Psalmist, in a season of high feeling and emotion; but how quickly afterwards does he exclaim, "Thou didst hide thy face, and I was troubled."

Faith will triumph in death, when the religion of feeling may be all overwhelmed. When all the powers of darkness are summoned to their last efforts of hostility and rage; when fiery darts of doubt, disquietude, and fear, are hurled by a thousand practised arms of temptation; when our natural strength is all abated and sunk to the feeblest infancy; when memory itself has failed, and not one Bethel of happy communion, not one anointed pillar in the way, can be recalled for comfort, what shall be the refuge of the soul, or what its armour? What we see and feel of grace in the heart, or demonstration in the life which is now passing away? Ah, here may be the source of direst terror and dismay in that critical hour! What can it be, but that shield of heavenly temper with which alone we can now "quench the fiery darts of the wicked?" Faith only can make us fearless then; faith only can repulse the enemy and proclaim the victory. The rod and staff of the promise, grasped by a present faith in Jesus, can vanquish every evil in the valley and shadow of death. "My flesh and my heart faileth, but God is the strength of my heart, and my portion for ever."

III. But we advance to another contrast, between faith and sight, essentially different from any that we have noticed; when the scale is turned, and faith is dropped in vision; when the home is reached, and the talisman is laid by as necessary no more; when the battle is ended, and the "shield" is hung high in the temple of God, where we shall endure as pillars, "to go no more out." Here sight and sense cannot be trusted. Without faith they lead us to perdition; and even with faith in the heart, culturing and refining them with experience of grace, they cannot be trusted. But the day is coming when this miserable crazy tenement of folly and mistake shall stand a glorious and unerring medium, through which the soul will for ever drink blessedness at the fountain of life. Faith will then be superseded, as a principle of walking, and cease to shine as the star in heaven ceases when the sun is risen to meridian splendour; cease to flow in "the desire of our soul to his name, and the remembrance of him," as the majestic river ceases when its waters mingle with the ocean.

1. The object of faith is obscure and reflected; the object of sight will be direct and resplendent. Now "we see through a glass darkly." We see not the very person of the Saviour, but, as it were, his image reflected from a mirror; and we see not this image with a direct and simple eye, but, as it were, through many reflections in a telescope. The Word of God is not dark in itself; it contains as bright a manifestation of Jehovah Jesus as the present condition of humanity could bear. Subdued emotions, and mitigated transports, are all that mercy intends, for the frailty on which he looks from "behind our wall," and "through the lattice" of means and ordinances. But in the heavenly vision, "we shall see him as he is," admitted to his own immediate presence, for ever "to behold his glory."

Incomparably brighter is the revelation we enjoy than that of our fathers, under the cloud of Old Testament figures and shadows. In eager longing for our time, when "the day would break, and the shadows flee away," how did they rejoice to catch even a glimpse of Gospel resplendence. Their time was that of the shadow—ours is that of the image; between the shadow and the image there may be comparison, but between the image and the substantial and present reality, there can be none.

2. Faith's object is unseen at times; vision's ob-

ject will be for ever unclouded before us. Between the telescope and the mirror, the "star of Bethlehem" is often hidden from our sight. "My beloved had withdrawn himself and was gone." "Behold, I go forward, but he is not there; and backward, but I cannot perceive him; on the left hand where he doth work, but I cannot behold him; he hideth himself on the right hand, that I cannot see him." But there "we shall be ever with the Lord." "The Lord shall be to thee an everlasting light, and thy God thy glory." No darkness nor desertion can be there indeed, where there is "no need of the sun, neither of the moon to shine in it; but God doth lighten it, and the Lamb is the light thereof."

3. Faith itself is imperfect in its operations; vision will be perfect and complete. In the very nature of the thing there must be imperfection with the use of an instrument, whose materials are altogether imperfect. How much does the exercise of faith depend on the knowledge of God and of Christ; how much on the memory of his promises; how much on diligence in spiritual reflection and contemplation; and how deplorably defective are all these, in the present life of lapse and corruption! Add to these the interruption of the world and Satan. Even if the object of faith were ever before us, with steady twinkling, and without a cloud; if no film of error shaded the eye, nor tremor of weakness agitated the arm; and we could hold the glass of faith, in all its realizing power, unshaken by any inherent debility of our own; yet would the jostle of the world and the rage of hell turn, ever and anon, the telescope aside. But vision on high will be

sound and energetic in itself, rich and perfect in every material, and for ever sustained by surrounding influences there.

Witness the amazing acuteness and perfection of Stephen's vision, as he was just advancing to the portals of "the excellent glory." One beam of it burst through the canopy of heaven and lighted on his face, and counsellors of even bloodshot eye "looking steadfastly on him, saw his face as it had been the face of an angel." And such was the effect on his own vision, of this initial ray from the paradise of God, that through all the incalculable distance between this earth and the home of the blessed in heaven; through clouds, through planets, through suns, through depths of unfathomable ether, his piercing eye beheld "the glory of God, and Jesus standing at the right hand of God!" If eyes of mortal flesh can be empowered so by one beam of that celestial glory, what will not the effulgence of noontide produce? If eyes of mortal flesh, by one blink of heavenly vision, can descry at a distance which no tongue can tell and no imagination compute, ineffable and transporting glory, what will not eyes of glorified humanity discover when admitted to the very throne of God and centre of its brilliance?

4. Faith is slow, and gradual, and successive, in making up the image of her contemplation; sight will comprehend at once, with glance of intuition. Here we glean one lineament of Jesus in this chapter, and another in that, of his holy Word; sometimes we see him in the vision; sometimes in the allegory; sometimes in the plain description. Sometimes we see him as a prophet, then a priest, then a

king; and thus, culling a flower here, and another there, one grace of his person in the Old Testament and another in the New, faith makes up her aggregate at length, and exclaims with delighted conclusion, "He is altogether lovely!" It could not be otherwise at present. A sight like that of Isaiah, in vision, of the Lord, "sitting on his throne, high and lifted up," would strike us down with terror; "Woe is me, I am undone!" Even the beloved disciple, who had reclined on his bosom familiarly in the days of his flesh, could not enjoy a glimpse of the glorified Redeemer without falling as dead at his feet.

If all the luminaries in heaven were converged into one brilliant centre, it would destroy these eyes with its flood of burning light; but distributed along the firmament, in sun, moon and stars, we drink in the mild radiance with pleasure wherever we direct the eye. If all the glories of Jesus Christ were converged into one direct and intense description, even by words, it would overwhelm and crush these feeble powers of the soul; but, diffused over the whole firmament of Old and New Testament Scripture, we survey with pleasing contemplation the truth as it is in Jesus, studded and proportioned, as one star differeth from another star in glory. But the heavenly vision will scan, with steady rapture, all that is bright in Jesus, blended and concentered in one blazing sea of glory.

5. Faith, in her highest exercise on earth, must groan, being burdened; but sight, in her lowest range of felicity in heaven, will shout with hallelujahs. "In this tabernacle we groan, being burdened."

When wings of faith and love would rise with fervor to the mount of God, a leaden body drags them down. This frame work is too narrow for the compass of faith when she reaches to Christ and swells with foretaste of his glory. "Ourselves also, which have the first fruits of the Spirit, even we ourselves groan within ourselves, waiting for the adoption, to wit, the redemption of our body." As the man whose soul is fired with enthusiastic zeal to read the starry heavens must groan impatiently, if some low vaulted prison ever prevents him from lifting his longest telescope on high; so, and more, infinitely, groans the believer, when faith lies checked and disappointed in this environed and contracted tabernacle. But the frame work of immortal life will be spacious and spiritual as its inmate; the shouts of glory in the highest will be loud, as the conceptions of the soul are grand; pure and unfailing, and inseparable, will be the powers of eye, and hand, and heart, when "we shall see him as he is," and our vile bodies will be "fashioned like unto his glorious body."

We learn from this subject how ennobling faith is, and how much dignity and excellence it stamps on human nature. Men of the world look on faith as weakness, and fancy a disparagement of reason a debility of intellectual force, an easy, erring credulity, when we speak of living by faith, walking, and fighting, and dying by faith. But so did not the Spirit of inspiration estimate the worth of human character, when beginning the notice of each Old Testament worthy, with emphatic mention of his faith. Heb. xi. So does not common sense estimate the worth of human character, when we behold a poor, short sighted, trembling worm of the dust, quailing at every change, deceived by every show, blind to the present, blind to the future, and a wretched victim of ignoble sense, suddenly stand triumphant over weakness, superior to time and change, able to value present things as they are and future things as they will be; able to comprehend eternity better than he understood one day before. Such a transformation is vastly more noble and sublime than any deification of man that heathen idolatry ever imagined. Superstition never gave to the gods an attribute so godlike as the faith of an humble believer. And if we had no other and nobler motive, the favour of God, to please whom "without faith it is impossible," peace of conscience, victory over sin and Satan, over the world and death, and an everlasting inheritance of glory—all of which are sealed to the soul the moment faith is in exercise; if we had none of these unspeakable benefits, the very enlargement of soul which it brings, empowering the human mind to see invisible things, and future things, and things substantially good, and things in all their eventful consequences, were motive enough to impel men to plead with God day and night that he would "give it to them, on the behalf of Christ, to believe in his name;" and that he would "fulfil in them the good pleasure of his goodness, and the work of faith with power."

We learn again, from this subject, how to test religion in ourselves and others, most truly; where alone is the lively oracle which gives certain responses on this all important interest. Not our frames and feelings; not our present enjoyments; not all our experience, past and present; but the exercise of faith on Jesus Christ, the reality and power of which are evinced by holy living. How many a precious hour of time have we lost; how many a pang of unnecessary anguish have we felt in standing upon bubbles which burst, in attempting to trace our hope of glory on a surface of excited feeling, which is fluctuating as the sands of the sea, shifting as the winds of heaven. It is true, indeed, that our religion is one of mighty emotion, and no man ever felt its power without feeling the most powerful of all excitement; and it is equally true that our prayers and devout endeavours must always be exercised to stir emotion and revive the power of feeling, as well as to learn its precious truths, and imbibe its sanctifying efficacy. But let us never forget, that all excitement is spurious which is not the offspring of faith, and that all faith is spurious which does not vividly apprehend the word of God, in its supreme authority and power; that faith may exist where there is but little outward manifestation of feeling, and that a conversation becoming the gospel is worth ten thousand gusts of delighted feeling; and no kind of feeling should ever be cherished for a moment which will not correspond with the soberness of a life of faith upon the Son of God. Vast inequality in the tide of religious emotion has done more to arm the power of infidelity in the world, than all the logic besides which unbelief could ever command. "The spirit of power and of love," is the spirit of "a sound mind."

Finally, we learn from this subject to anticipate

gladly the joys of that eternal world, where all the faculties of mortal and immortal man, set free from frailty and sin, restored from the debasement of the present life, and the widowed sleep of a long germination in the grave, shall become not only perfect in use, to be honoured and trusted always, but immeasurably enhanced in the original adaptation to minister happiness; by a new creation in Christ Jesus, a resurrection through the power of his life, and translation to the immediate presence of his Father and ours. " It doth not yet appear what we shall be." The pleasure of the senses, which divine goodness spared, in some degree, from the ruins of the curse, to make the present life a happy one for temperance and virtue, must rise with this identical body, which will have "slept in Jesus," not only repaired, refined, exalted, indestructible; not only re-admitted to communion with God in his direct and constant manifestation, but also advanced to the inconceivable felicity which is implied in being "partakers of the divine nature;" a destination of superlative dignity and joy, whose range of perfect happiness must be all that the glorious **Creator would** confer on any creature.

CATHOLICITY OF THE GOSPEL.

BY

CHAS. HODGE, D. D.

PROFESSOR IN THE THEOLOGICAL SEMINARY, PRINCETON, NEW JERSEY.

Is he God of the Jews only, and not of the Gentiles also? Romans iii. 29.

WE are so familiar with the truth contained in these words that we do not appreciate its importance. Accustomed to the varied beauties of the earth, we behold its manifold wonders without emotion; we seldom even raise our eyes to look at the gaudeous canopy of heaven, which every night is spread over our heads. The blind, however, when suddenly restored to sight, behold with ecstacy what we regard with indifference. Thus the truth that God is not a national God, not the God of any one tribe or people, but the God and Father of all men, and that the Gospel is designed and adapted to all mankind, however little it may affect us, filled the apostles with astonishment and delight. They were slow in arriving at the knowledge of this truth; they had no clear perception of it until after the day of Pentecost; the effusion of the Spirit which they then received produced a most remarkable change in their views and feelings. Before that event, they were Jews; afterwards, they were Christians; before, they applied all the promises to their own nation; the only Jerusalem of which they had any idea was the city where David dwelt; the only temple of which they could form a conception was that in which they were accustomed to worship. But when they received the anointing of the Holy Ghost, the scales fell from their eyes; their nation sank and the Church rose on their renovated sight; the Jerusalem that now is, disappeared when they beheld the New Jerusalem descending out of heaven; the temple on Mount Zion was no longer glorious, by reason of the excelling glory of that temple which is the habitation of God by his Spirit; old things passed away, all things became new; what they had mistaken for the building proved to be the scaffolding; the sacrifices, the incense, the pompous ritual of the old economy, which they had so long regarded as the substance and the end, were found to be but shadows. What was the blood of bulls and of goats to men who had looked upon the blood of Him who, with an eternal Spirit, offered himself unto God? What were priests and Levites to the great High Priest, Jesus, the Son of God? What was the purifying of the flesh secured by the sprinkling the ashes of a heifer, to the eternal redemption secured by Him who is a priest for ever after the order of Melchizedec? What was access to the outer court of a temple, in which even the symbol of the divine presence was concealed by a veil, to access to God himself by the Spirit? What were the tribes of Israel coming up to Jerusalem, to the long procession of nations coming to the New Jerusalem, and kings to the brightness of her rising; the multitudes from Midian and Epha; they too from Sheba, bringing their gifts with them; the flocks of Kedar and the rams of Nebaioth; the sons of strangers and the forces of the Gentiles, hastening to that city whose walls are salvation, and whose gates are praise?

This change in the views of the apostles seems to have been almost instantaneous. While Christ was upon earth, they were constantly misapprehending his doctrines; even in the night in which he was betrayed, there was a contention among them who should be the greatest in his kingdom. But as soon as they received the baptism of the Holy Ghost they ceased to speak and act like Jews, and announced a religion for the whole world.

I. In the general proposition, that the Gospel is designed and adapted for all mankind, there are several important truths involved. The most comprehensive is that contained in the text: God is the God of the Gentiles as well as of the Jews. It is obvious that the Jews generally, and the apostles, as Jews, entertained very erroneous views on this until they were enlightened by the Holy Ghost; they mistook even the spirit of the old dispensation. It is true that Jehovah chose their nation for a peculiar people, and that he was their God in a sense in which he was not the God of the heathen. He revealed himself to them as he did not unto the world; he instituted for them a system of religious observances; sent them his prophets to declare his will; exercised over them a special providence, and constituted them, in the strictest sense, a theocracy.

There was nothing, however, in the Old Testament which justified the proud and self-righteous spirit which the Jews manifested towards the heathen; they were not authorized to look upon them as reprobates shut out from the hope of salvation, as unworthy of having even the offer of the true religion made to them. The surprise expressed by the apostles that God had granted unto the Gentiles repentance unto life, that the gate of heaven was wide enough to admit more than the descendants of Abraham, shows how much they had misconceived the spirit of their own religion.

Their great mistake, however, was in supposing that the exclusive spirit, as far as it did in fact belong to the old economy, was meant to be perpetual. They mistook a temporary for a permanent arrangement, and supposed that the glory of the theocracy under the Messiah involved nothing beyond the exaltation and extended dominion of their own nation. They were blind to the plainest declarations of their own Scriptures, which foretold that God would pour out his Spirit upon all flesh; that the Messiah was to be a light to the Gentiles, to make known the salvation of God to the ends of the earth; and that the sons of the stranger were to have in his kingdom a name and a place, better than those of sons and daughters. Even the affecting parables of our Lord, designed to rebuke the narrow spirit of his disciples, failed to make any adequate impression on their minds. Though they were told that the prodigal son was to be restored to his father's house, clothed with the best robe, and rejoiced over with peculiar joy, they understood it not.

It is not to be supposed that the ancient Jews conceived of Jehovah as a local Deity, confined in his essence to any one place, or restricted in his authority to any one people. From the beginning they had been taught that he was the Creator of all things; that he filled heaven and earth; that he was almighty, doing his pleasure among the armies of heaven and the inhabitants of the earth; but they believed him to be indifferent to the welfare of other nations; they did not know that he had purposes of mercy for the Gentiles, as well as for themselves. When they called Jehovah their God, they meant not only that he was the God whom they acknowledged, but that he belonged exclusively to them, that they monopolized his favour, and were the sole heirs of his kingdom. What Christ taught them by his Word and Spirit was, that God was as favourably inclined to the Gentiles as to the Jews; that the same Lord was rich toward all who called upon him; that there existed no reason in the Divine mind, why the heathen should not be fellow heirs and partakers of the grace of the Gospel, why they might not be fellow citizens of the saints and of the household of God. This is what is meant, when it is said he is the God of the Gentiles as well as of the Jews; he stands in the same general relation to both; he is as favourable to the one as to the other; as ready to receive one as the other; as willing to receive and save the one as the other. Christ came not as the minister of the circumcision only, but that the Gentiles might glorify God for his mercy, as it is written: Rejoice, ye Gentiles, with his people; praise the Lord all ye Gentiles, laud him all ye people. This is the ground, brethren, on which we stand. We are in the Church, not by courtesy of man; not by toleration or sufferance; not as strangers or proselytes, but as fellow citizens and fellow heirs. We that were not beloved, are now beloved; we that were not his people, are now the people of God, though Abraham be ignorant of us, and though Israel acknowledge us not. It is this glorious truth, that God is the God of the Gentiles, that expands the Gospel and makes it a religion suited for the whole world. It is no longer the sluggish Jordan flowing through its narrow channel, it is a sea of glory which spreads from pole to pole. The mercy and love of God are commensurate with his ubiquity; whenever he looks down on man and says, My children, they may look up to him and say, Our Father! Praise him, therefore, O ye Gentiles, laud him, O ye people, for Israel's God is our God and our Redeemer.

II. Again, the proposition that the Gospel is designed and adapted for all mankind, supposes the spiritual nature of Christ's kingdom; that is, that the service which is now required is a spiritual, in opposition to a ritual and ceremonial service; that the government of that kingdom is a spiritual government, and that its blessings are spiritual blessings. The old economy was, from its ritual and ceremonial character, incapable of including all nations. Without the shedding of blood there was no remission, but sacrifices could be offered only at Jerusalem; there was the temple, the priest, and the altar; there was the symbol of the Divine presence; thither the tribes were required to repair three times every year. Innumerable cases were constantly occurring, which rendered attendance at the place where God had recorded his name absolutely necessary. As the Jewish ritual could not be observed out of Jerusalem, it was impossible that the whole world should be subjected to that form of worship. Those who were afar off were without an offering, without a priest, without access to God. The lamentations of David, when absent from the court of God, his earnest longings after liberty of access to the place where God revealed his glory, show how intimately the happiness of the people of God was connected with the services of the sanctuary. Our Lord announced a radical change in the whole economy of religion, and one which disenthralled it from all these trammels, when he said to the woman of Samaria, Woman, believe me, the hour cometh and now is, when ye neither in this mountain, nor yet at Jerusalem, shall worship the Father; the true worshippers shall worship the Father in Spirit and in truth, for the Father seeketh such to worship him. God is a Spirit, and they that worship him, must worship in Spirit and in truth. It was here taught, not only that the worship of God was no longer to be confined to any one place, but also that it was no longer to be ceremonial but spiritual. It is no longer necessary to go up to Jerusalem, in order to draw near to God, but wherever two or three are met together in his name, there is he in the midst of them. The temple, in which his people now worship, is no longer a temple made with hands, but that spiritual temple made without hands. Its pillars rest on the four corners of the earth, and it surmounts the heavens; the southern African, the northern Greenlander, the innumerable company of angels, and the general Assembly and Church of the first born, are all included in its ample courts. The sacrifice which is now offered is not the blood of bulls and of goats, but the precious blood of Christ, as a lamb slain from the foundation of the world. The incense which now ascends before the throne of God, comes not from brazen censers, but from living hearts.

Again, under the old economy the Church had a visible head, who dwelt at Jerusalem, by whom the annual atonement was made for the sins of the people. He was their intercessor before God; the medium of communication between God and his people; the arbiter and director of the whole congregation. Those, therefore, who were at a distance from the High Priest were necessarily cut off from many of the most important advantages of the theocracy. Under the Gospel all this is changed. The head of the Church, the High Priest of our profession is no longer a man dwelling in any one city, but Jesus, the Son of God, who by the one offering up of himself hath for ever perfected them that are sanctified; who is every where accessible, every where present to guide and comfort his people, and who ever lives to make intercession for them. The believer cannot be where Christ is not. At any time and in every place he may approach his throne, he may embrace his knees or wash his feet with tears, and hear him say, Son, or daughter, be of good cheer, thy sins are forgiven thee.

Once more, as to this point: the blessings which

the Gospel offers being spiritual are adapted to all mankind. The benefits connected with the old economy were in a great measure external and temporal. This idea the apostle expresses by saying its rites could avail only to the purifying of the flesh. Considered in themselves they could do no more than secure for those who observed them the benefits of the external theocracy. Those who were circumcised became members of the Hebrew commonwealth; those who kept the law, had the promise of fruitful seasons; those who had forfeited their right of access to the sanctuary, had it restored by offering a sacrifice; those who were defiled by any ceremonial uncleanness, might be purified within the temple by the officiating priest. Apart, therefore, from its reference to the Gospel, the blessings secured by that dispensation were exclusively of this external character, for it was impossible that its rites should take away sin. These benefits were not only of little value, but they were necessarily confined to a limited sphere; they were incapable of being extended to all mankind. How low must have been the expectations of those who considered the Messiah's kingdom as nothing but an enlargement of this system. How complete a revolution must it have produced in all their views and feelings to discover that Christ's kingdom was not of this world; that the blessings which it promised were not worldly prosperity, not a pompous ritual or splendid temple, not dominion over other nations, but the forgiveness of sin, the renewal of the heart, reconciliation with God and eternal life. These are blessings, not only of infinite value, but such as are confined to no one locality. They are not more needed by one set of men than another; they are incapable of being monopolized, for they constitute an inheritance which is rather increased than lessened by the number of the heirs. We say then that the Gospel dispensation is catholic, or designed for the whole world, because it is a spiritual dispensation; the worship which it requires may be as acceptably offered in one place as another; the head of this new covenant is every where present and every where accessible, and the blessings which he confers are suited to the necessities of all mankind.

III. Another point of no less importance, is, that the righteousness of Christ, by which these blessings of pardon, regeneration and eternal life are secured, is such as to lay an ample foundation for the offer of salvation to all men. This is a point with regard to which the minds of the apostles underwent a great change. Under the old dispensation, the High Priest, as the representative of the people, made a confession of their sins, imposing them on the head of the victim, and made reconciliation by sprinkling the blood upon the mercy seat. By that atonement the sins of the people, considered as committed against the external theocracy, were forgiven, and the blessings of that dispensation were actually secured. It is obvious that this was an atonement limited in design to that people, having no reference to any other nation. It was limited also in its value, having no intrinsic worth, but deriving all its efficacy from the sovereign appointment. It was also limited in its very nature; being attached to a national covenant, it was in its nature available to none who were not included in that covenant; it was a Jewish sacrifice, designed for Jews, belonging to a covenant made with Jews, and securing blessings in which other nations had no concern.

In complete contrast with all this, we know, in the first place, that the work of Christ was not limited in design to any one nation. Christ himself said, he laid down his life for his sheep, and other sheep he had which were not of that fold; in this sense it is said he is the propitiation for our sins, and not for our sins only, but for the sins of the whole world; or, as the same apostle expresses the same truth in another place, Jesus died not for that nation only, but that he should gather together in one the children of God that were scattered abroad.

In the second place, there is no limit to be placed to the value of Christ's righteousness; its worth is not to be measured by the duration or intensity of the Saviour's sufferings, but by the dignity of his person. In contrasting the sacrifices of the Old Testament with that of the New, the apostle says the former were inefficacious because mere animals were offered; that of Christ was effectual, once for all, because he offered up himself. It is the nature of the offering that determines its value; and as the dignity of Christ's person is infinite, so is the value of his sacrifice; if it suffices for the salvation of one man, it is sufficient for the salvation of all; it is incapable of increase or diminution. The light of the sun is not measured by the number of those who enjoy its brightness; millions can see by it as well as a single individual; it is not the less because many are affected by it, nor would it be the greater though only one enjoyed it. So also the righteousness of Christ is in value infinite and inexhaustible, because it is the righteousness of God.

In the third place, the righteousness of Christ is in its nature suited to all men. As the annual propitiation under the old dispensation belonged to the covenant formed with the whole people of Israel, and was in its nature suited to all included within that covenant; so the righteousness of Christ fulfils the conditions of that covenant under which all mankind are placed. He perfectly obeyed the precepts and endured the penalty of that law by which all mankind are bound; hence his righteousness, being what was due from every man, is in its nature suited to each and every man. As the work of Christ, as connected with the covenant of grace, has special reference to all included in that covenant, and effectually secures their salvation; but as in performing the stipulations of that covenant, he fulfilled the conditions of the covenant of works which all mankind had broken, his work is, in its nature, applicable to all who are under the covenant made with Adam.

Inasmuch, then, as the righteousness of Christ is not limited in the design of God to any one nation; as it is of infinite value; and as it is, in its nature, equally applicable to all men, we are authorized to go to Jew and Gentile, to barbarians, Scythians, bond and free, yea, to every creature, with the offer of salvation. If any man refuses the offer, his blood will be upon his own head; he perishes not for want of a righteousness, but because he rejects that which is of infinite value and suited to all his necessities.

The gospel, therefore, is not trammelled; we can go with it round the world, and announce to every creature that Christ has died the just for the unjust; that he has wrought out an everlasting righteousness, which any man may accept and plead before the throne of God.

IV. Again, the catholic character of the gospel is apparent from its offering salvation on conditions suited to all men. It does not require us to ascend into heaven, or to go down to the abyss; its demands are simple, intelligible and reasonable; it requires nothing peculiar to any sex, age, or class of men; it is not a religion for the rich in distinction from the poor, or for the poor in distinction from the rich; it is not a system of philosophy intelligible only to the learned, nor is it a superstition which none but the ignorant can embrace. It is truth, simple and transcendent; in all that is essential, intelligible to a child, and yet the object of admiration and wonder to angels. It does not suspend our salvation on any particular ecclesiastical connection; it does not require us to decide between conflicting churches which has the true succession; nor does it make grace and salvation to depend on the ministration or will of man; it is not the religion of any one sect or church, and nothing but the wickedness can equal the folly of the attempt to confine the grace of God to the shallow channel of a particular ecclesiastical organization. What the gospel demands is nigh thee, in thy heart and in thy mouth; that is, the word of faith which we preach, that if thou shalt confess with thy mouth the Lord Jesus, and believe in thy heart that God hath raised him from the dead, thou shalt be saved. For with the heart man believeth unto righteousness, and with the mouth confession is made unto salvation. Here, then, are terms of salvation which are suited equally to all men, the Jew and the Greek, the wise and the unwise, the bond and the free.

V. Again, the rule of life prescribed by the Gospel is adapted to all men, in every age and in every part of the world; it is the great law of love, which commends itself to every man's conscience, and is suited to all the relations of domestic, social, and political life. It is a principle which disturbs nothing that is good, which can amalgamate with nothing that is wrong, which admits of being acted out under all circumstances, and of accommodating itself to all states of society, and to all forms of government.

How free, how catholic, how pure, how elevated is the spirit of the Gospel, which reveals God as an universal Father; which makes known a religion confined to no locality, burdened with no expensive ritual, conferring on those who embrace it, not worldly distinctions, but the spiritual blessings of pardon and holiness; which reveals a righteousness sufficient for all, and suited for all; which offers that righteousness to all on the simplest of all conditions, that of sincerely accepting it; whose moral precepts and principles of religious duty, and of ecclesiastical organization admit of being carried out with equal purity and power, in all ages and in all parts of the world.

1. The catholic character of the Gospel, which we have now been considering, affords one of the strongest arguments for its divine origin. No reli-

gion can be true which is not suited to God as its author, and to man for whom it is intended. The Gospel is suited to God because it supposes him to be, as he in fact is, not a national God, but the God and Father of all men; and it is suited to men because it meets not the wants of any one class, nor any one class of wants, but all the wants of every class, tribe or nation. But besides this, this catholicity is the very characteristic which it would be most difficult to account for on the supposition of its human origin. The apostles were Jews, the very name for all that is narrow, national and exclusive; how could the most enlarged and comprehensive system of religion owe its origin to such men? We know that the apostles retained much of the narrow and exclusive spirit of their countrymen, as long as their Master was upon earth. When he died they were ready to despair, saying, We trusted it had been He who would have redeemed Israel. Even after his resurrection their eyes were still but half opened, for the last question which they put to him was, Lord, wilt thou at this time restore the kingdom unto Israel? Yet, a few days afterward, these same men began to preach that the kingdom of Christ was a spiritual kingdom, not designed specially for Israel, but for all mankind. This fact admits of no other solution than that recorded in the Acts, after the apostles had received the promised effusion of the Spirit; they spake as they were moved by the Holy Ghost, making it apparent that the Gospel is not the product of Jewish minds, but of men divinely instructed and inspired.

This argument may be viewed in another light.

The revelations of God, as contained in the Scriptures, admit of being divided into three portions: those written before the advent of Christ; those referring to his personal ministry on earth; and those written after the effusion of the Spirit, on the day of Pentecost. In the first portion, all, at first view, is national and exclusive; the prosperity of Jerusalem and the exaltation of the Jews would seem to be the great subject of prophecy and promise; still there is a constant gleaming through of the imprisoned glory; constantly recurring intimations of a spiritual Jerusalem and of a spiritual Israel, in whom the glorious things spoken of Zion were to meet their accomplishment.

The personal instructions of our Saviour were conveyed mostly in parables, designed to correct the misapprehension and to repress the false expectations of his countrymen, but rather intimating than fully disclosing the nature of his kingdom and the design of his mission. The descent of the Holy Spirit shed a flood of light on the whole series of divine revelations, back even to the first promise made to our first parents; it is the clear exhibition of the economy of redemption, made in the books written after the day of Pentecost, that enables us to read the outlines of the gospel in the law and the prophets; the relation of these several portions of the Scriptures to each other, written at intervals during the course of fifteen hundred years, shows that the whole is the work of one omniscient Spirit; and the fact that the catholic spirit of the gospel, as unfolded in the later books of the New Testament, is in apparent contradiction, though real agreement with the earlier portions of the Word of God, is a decisive proof that the Bible is indeed the word of God and not the word of man.

2. If the gospel, as has been represented, is designed and suited for all men, it is suited to us. We need the salvation which it reveals; we, being destitute of any righteousness of our own, must accept the righteousness which the gospel offers, or perish in our sins. That righteousness being all that any sinner needs, and being freely and sincerely offered to all who hear the Gospel, we are entirely without excuse if we refuse or neglect the invitations of mercy.

3. If the gospel is suited to all men, it should be maintained wherever it is known, and sent wherever it has not yet been preached. This is the inference which the apostle draws from this subject. If there is no difference between the Jew and Greek; if the same Lord is rich towards all who call upon him, then it is the will of God that all should call upon him. But how shall they call on him on whom they have not believed? And how shall they believe on him of whom they have not heard? And how shall they hear without a preacher? And how shall they preach except they be sent? The Gospel being suited to all men, and being needed by all, not for their temporal well-being, but for their eternal salvation, woe is us if we do not make it known; it is an inheritance in which we are but joint heirs with all mankind, and we cannot keep the knowledge of this inheritance to ourselves without manifest injustice and cruelty.

Let us, then, endeavour to enter more fully into

the catholic spirit of the gospel; let us remember that the unsearchable riches that are in Christ Jesus are an inheritance for all the poor and perishing; and while we thankfully apprehend those riches for ourselves, let us labour **that they may be made accessible to all mankind.**

CHRISTIAN SUBMISSION.

BY

H. A. BOARDMAN, D. D.

PASTOR OF THE TENTH PRESBYTERIAN CHURCH, PHILADELPHIA.

It is the Lord; let him do what seemeth him good.—1 Sam. iii. 18.

In this life we are sanctified but in part. The best of men have their infirmities. Even the most symmetrical and shining characters disclose, in one form or another, the imperfection which attaches to all things human. The case is still stronger than this. Eminent virtues are often associated with signal blemishes. Individuals conspicuous for certain Christian graces, are scarcely less conspicuous for grievous defects. The venerable Eli was an example. He was the High Priest of Israel. From the brief sketch we have of his history he would seem to have been a sincere, humble, devout man—attentive to his official engagements, and truly concerned for the welfare of the people, and the honour of their Divine king. But in one department of duty Eli was culpably remiss—he had no family government. His two sons, his assistants in the temple-rites, were profligate young men, whose conduct brought a great scandal upon religion—and yet he tolerated it. He reproved them, it is true, but in so mild a form that it produced no effect upon them—precisely, indeed, as many parents in our own day deal with the delinquencies of children whom they have, by their misplaced indulgence, trained to respect their authority only so far as it may suit their convenience. After repeated warnings had been given to no purpose, God at length informs the aged and erring priest that he had determined to destroy his sons, and to transfer the priesthood to another family—" I have sworn unto the house of Eli that the iniquity of Eli's house shall not be purged with sacrifice nor offering for ever." This threatening was first made known to "the child Samuel," who communicated it to Eli only after he had been solemnly adjured to do it. It would be difficult to conceive of a more appalling message to the heart of a pious father. To such a father, the announcement that a child was to be struck down by a sudden death, must, under any circumstances, be very afflictive; but to be told that two of his sons—sons, not in their infancy or childhood, but grown up to manhood—sons who had become notorious for their wickedness, and who neither had, nor were likely to have, the slightest preparation for death—that God had resolved, as well for *his* sin in not restraining them as for their own crimes, to cut off these sons by some terrible judgment which should "make the ears of every one that heard it to tingle"—to be told *this* must have been overwhelming. How does the unhappy old man receive it? "*It is the Lord; let him do what seemeth him good!*" Such was his answer—his whole answer; not another word escaped him. Wonderful submission! Wonderful illustration of the efficacy of Divine grace in controlling the strongest affections of the human heart, and subduing man's rebellious will into an unrepining acquiescence in the will of God!

It behooves us all to know something of this rare endowment. We, too, may have occasion to say, "It is the Lord; let him do what seemeth him good." My subject, then, is CHRISTIAN SUBMISSION.

To discuss it in detail is not my aim. All I propose is, to specify some of the chief elements which enter into it.

1. *Christian submission excludes murmuring.*

This proposition is self-evident, but the thought deserves to be dwelt upon.

It is natural to murmur under afflictions and losses. The voice of nature—that is, of our fallen nature—is not the voice of God, but contrary to it. It is as natural for us to murmur, when deprived of what we love, or disappointed in our hopes, as for holy beings to submit promptly and cheerfully to the Divine will. We are apt to feel that what we have is our own unconditionally; that when we have framed and prosecuted our plans with great prudence and energy, we are entitled to success; that when we have accumulated a fortune, we have an implicit right to keep it; that when we have collected the varied means and appliances of an elegant and graceful life, we ought to be permitted, for a period at least, to enjoy them; that when we are surrounded with a healthful and happy family, strong in each others' affections, and rejoicing in each others' companionship, no power may lawfully invade the charmed circle to strike down even the humblest or the feeblest of its loved ones. And if, in any of these cases, disappointment, bankruptcy, death, actually comes, the perverted instincts of the heart spring up in rebellion against God. I say "against God;" but the quarrel is, for the most part, not with him directly; fear prevents this. We dare not "curse God;" we deal with his instruments. Upon these the lacerated heart pours out its resentments; these it charges with injustice or cruelty.

It is not asserted that this is always done; far from it. But this is the native tendency of the heart, a tendency to set up its own will against God's will, to question his sovereignty, to cavil at his dispensations, to complain that "his ways are not equal," and that he afflicts us more than we deserve. That this disposition does not uniformly disclose itself is easily accounted for. In many it has ceased to exist. Nature has given place to a new nature. Grace has changed the lion into a lamb. Instead of saying, "Who is the Lord that I should obey his voice?" the feeling is, "Not as I will, but as thou wilt!" In other cases the tendency to murmur is held in check by prudential considerations, such as the dread of fresh inflictions, and the like. But in too many instances it breaks forth in impious complaints, or in impatient struggles to escape from the pressure of God's chastising hand. Wicked men, by their tossings and murmurings in affliction, often verify that striking image of the "troubled sea when it cannot rest, whose waters cast up mire and dirt."

It is too evident to admit of argument, that this spirit is incompatible with the temper inspired by the gospel; in other words, that Christian submission excludes murmuring.

2. *It excludes repining.*

Under great trials, it is no less natural to repine than to murmur. The heart sinks into despondency. The feeling is, "This affliction *must* crush me— God has forgotten to be gracious; He has determined, as a just punishment for my sins, to destroy me utterly." Or the feeling is, "Now that this calamity has befallen me, life is stripped of its sweetest charm; the world is a dreary void; all that remains to me is valueless; there is nothing left worth living for." And thus the oppressed soul gives itself up to the sway of sorrow, nurses its grief, and refuses to be comforted. So the Israelites, when pent up between the Egyptians and the sea, giving up all for lost, cried to Moses and said, "Because there were no graves in Egypt, hast thou taken us away to die in the wilderness?" And the prophet, in bewailing his own trials with those of his nation in the captivity, "He hath led me and brought me into darkness, but not into light. My flesh and my skin hath he made old; he hath broken my bones. He hath builded against me and compassed me with gall and travail. He hath set me in dark places, as they that be dead of old. He hath hedged me about that I cannot get out; he hath made my chain heavy. Also, when I cry and shout, he shutteth out my prayer. He hath enclosed my ways with hewn stone; he hath made my paths crooked. He was unto me as a bear lying in wait, and as a lion in secret places. He hath turned aside my ways and pulled me in pieces; he hath made me desolate. . . He hath filled me with bitterness, he hath made me drunken with wormwood. . . And I said,

'My strength and my hope is perished from the Lord; remembering mine affliction and my misery, the wormwood and the gall.'" (Lam. iii. 1—19.) In strains like these, even the believer will sometimes bemoan his miserable condition when under the rod of chastisement. The prophet, it is true, did not pause here; hope was blended with his deepest anguish, and he emerges from this thick gloom of despondency exclaiming, "The Lord is my portion, saith my soul, therefore will I hope in him." It is the *surrender* of the heart to despondency—a self-abandonment to repining and hopelessness—of which I speak in saying that it is excluded from the elements of Christian submission; for this is to "faint when we are rebuked" of God; it is to distrust his faithfulness or his power; to interpret his dispensations by "feeble sense;" to assume that he has "turned against us to be our enemy," simply because he has visited us with peculiar trials, when his word every where makes such allotments a pledge of his love and a signature of discipleship Christian submission excludes repining.

3. *It excludes insensibility.*

Here, perhaps, more persons fail than in either of the particulars already specified. They suppose themselves to be exercising submission to the Divine will, when they are simply indifferent to his chastisements. There can be no genuine submission where there is no sensibility. It seems but a mockery of God to exclaim, "Thy will be done!" where the event which elicits the sentiment involves no trial, and is felt to be no affliction. We may conceive of a case in which the conflagration of a man's warehouse would augment his property to a degree that he would sooner it should burn up than not; or of a case in which parents were so destitute of natural affection that, on mere pecuniary grounds, they would rather a child should die than live; and in examples of this sort the parties, unless they were playing the hypocrite, would manifest no sorrow under their "losses;" but who would think of calling this "Christian submission?"

So far, indeed, is this apathy under afflictive dispensations from belonging to the nature of submission, that the Scriptures hold it up as a grievous sin. Afflictions have a voice, and we have no right to shut our ears against it. They are designed to make us feel, and if we do not feel when we are smitten, we "despise the chastening of the Lord." It was one of the characteristic sins of Israel, that they would not "regard the works of the Lord, nor the operations of his hands," and he threatened, therefore, to destroy them. (Psalm xxviii. 5.) "Thou hast stricken them," says the prophet, "but they have not grieved; thou hast consumed them, but they have refused to receive correction." (Jer. v. 3.) A child that remains unconcerned under parental chastisement, who takes the reproof in a sort of stoical silence, which, being interpreted, means, "I care nothing about your displeasure, and you may punish me or not, as you see fit"—such a child is already hardened in sin. To characterize his indifference as filial submission, would be a flagrant perversion of terms, since this pretended "submission" would really have in it the essence of filial impiety. What better can be said in behalf of that "resignation" to the will of Providence, which resigns nothing, which parts with nothing it would not sooner part with than retain, which makes no sacrifice, is conscious of no loss, misses none of its customary pleasures, feels no aching void, and looks out upon a world as bright and joyous as ever? Can this be "submission?" No, my brethren. The heart must be cleft before this divine virtue can flow out. These strong affections and gentle sympathies must be crushed before they can give forth the savour of true resignation. These stubborn wills must wage a stern conflict with the hand that is stretched forth against them, before they can say in the spirit of the Gospel, "It is the Lord, let him do what seemeth him good."—Christian submission excludes insensibility.

4. *It includes a reverential acknowledgment of God's hand in the afflictive dispensation.*

Nature and unbelief eye second causes; faith fastens its eye upon the great First Cause. It is not meant by this that it is wrong to contemplate second causes; they make up a great part of the book of Providence, and we not only may but must study them. But to stop at second causes is to exclude Providence. Nothing is more certain than that his agency is concerned, directly or indirectly, in all events, afflictive or otherwise. "Is there evil in the city and the Lord hath not done it?" "I kill and I make alive; I wound and I heal." When Job's flocks and children were swept away, he does not regard the tempest, the Chaldeans, and the Sabeans, the instruments of his calamities; if he had, he might have murmured. But he looked beyond these, and in the spirit of true submission exclaimed, "The *Lord* gave, and the *Lord* hath taken away; and blessed be the name of the Lord." So, too, with the venerable Naomi, when she returned to her native town from her sojourn in Moab, a desolate and impoverished widow, and the citizens gathered around her, and said one to another, with mingled surprise and sympathy, "Is this Naomi?" "Call me not Naomi," she replied, "call me Mara; for the Almighty hath dealt very bitterly with me. I went out full, and the Lord hath brought me home again empty; why then call ye me Naomi, seeing the Lord hath testified against me, and the Almighty hath afflicted me?" To her view, all her afflictions spoke of God, and they were submissively to be referred to his providence. There can be no genuine submission without this feeling. Nor is it enough to acknowledge his agency in the event simply. He orders as well the minutest circumstances of our trials as the trials themselves. In these circumstances, there is frequently much to harass the feelings. "We could have borne the stroke, (so we are apt to ruminate upon it,) had it been ordered thus and so; had this thing been done or that left undone; could we only have known beforehand that the blow was about to fall; could we have attempted by such or such expedients to avert it; or, failing in this, could we at least have had the melancholy satisfaction of seeing it fall, it would have been less insupportable." So we reason; but how unwisely! with what unbelief! Does God notice the falling sparrow; has he numbered the hairs of our heads; and does he overlook any, the most trivial incident in the afflictions of his creatures, and especially of his own children? Let us check these fond suggestions of flesh and blood, and say of every circumstance, however slight, in the dispensations of his hand, "It is the Lord; let him do what seemeth him good."

5. *It includes a conviction of his perfect right to do what he has done.*

The Christian, under the influence of genuine submission, contemplates God as the universal Creator and Proprietor; as having a right, underived and unconditional, save as the exercise of it may be limited by his own infinite perfections, to dispose of any and all creatures, as may seem good in his sight. Ascribing to him an unrestricted sovereignty over every department of human affairs, he feels that he may, without trenching upon any real or imaginary "rights" on the part of his creatures, deal with them in the manner best adapted to promote his own glory. If he chooses to send poverty, sickness, pestilence, domestic troubles, mental disquietude, bereavements, or trials of other kinds, faith will vindicate the equity of the procedure even while the heart is bleeding at every pore, and will ask, "Shall not the Judge of all the earth do right?" I do not say that this will in every case be done without a struggle; nature is nature still, though sanctified. And sometimes the freshets of affliction burst so abruptly upon the soul, and pour themselves over it with such irresistible fury, that faith is for the time well-nigh severed from the rock, and hope's anchor drags from its fastening within the vail, and destruction seems inevitable. But presently that voice which said to the raging Gennesareth, "Peace, be still!" goes out over the tempestuous flood, and the alarmed and desponding soul again lifts up a tearful but confiding eye to heaven, and cries, "Father, thy will be done!" Only let the believer realize that it is God who is dealing with him, and he is satisfied that all his allotments are ordered in righteousness and equity. He needs no argument to convince him that even where "clouds and darkness are round about Him, righteousness and judgment are the habitation of His throne." Nor is this all. Submission not only has respect to God's perfect right to do what he has done, and to the righteousness of his dispensations, but,

6. It includes *an assurance of His wisdom, faithfulness, and love*, in the affliction he has sent.

It was a common sentiment among the ancient heathen, that great trials marked a man as an object of the Divine displeasure. Job's friends interpreted his afflictions in the same way. The Christian has been taught differently. He knows that affliction has ever been a part of the heritage of the saints. "In the world ye shall have tribulation." "If ye be without chastisement, then are ye bastards and not sons." It is the specific reason assigned for the punishments inflicted upon Israel, that they were God's children. "You only have I known of all the families of the earth, *therefore* will I punish you for all your iniquities." And herein he has reference, not simply to their aggravated guilt and consequent desert of punishment, but also to the benefits they might derive from his inflictions. They were his own people, and therefore instead of allowing them to sin with impunity until their cup was full, he would chastise them and bring them to repentance. "When we are judged we are chastened of the Lord, that we should not be condemned with the world."

This view of affliction puts another aspect upon it. To the eye of sense it is frowning and terrific; it speaks of vengeance; it forebodes destruction. But faith takes the soul up to the throne, and unveils the other phase of the dispensation—that which is averted from our mortal eyes, and of which flesh and sense can form no conception. Then it is seen that the rod is held by a Father's hand; that it is he who has cast his child into the furnace, and that his bosom yearns over him with all the love and tenderness which a fond father feels towards a son whom he is constrained to punish for his faults. He may not be apprised of all the grounds and motives of the infliction, but he will at least be conscious that he deserves chastisement. "I know, O Lord, that thy judgments are right, and that thou in faithfulness hast afflicted me." Such is the language of true submission. God has engaged to perfect his work in the hearts of his people, to withhold no good thing from them, to do for them whatever may be requisite, not for their present ease, but for their sanctification and meetness for heaven. The rod is too valuable an implement in carrying forward this process to be neglected. If he consulted simply the feelings of his children, he would seldom resort to chastisement—for what child will ask to be chastised? Or, if his affection for them partook of the infirmity which so often attaches to parental affection among men, he might suffer their sins to go unreproved; but he is a faithful and covenant-keeping God. No mistaken tenderness will ever lead him to withhold the chastisement which is essential to his people's happiness. He loves them too well and too wisely not to let them drink sometimes of the cup of sorrow.

The Christian is not often left without adequate evidence that his afflictions are ordered in wisdom and faithfulness. One of the first effects of affliction is to drive him to self-examination. Communing with his own heart, and reviewing his life, he will usually find abundant indications of infirmity and sin. He has, perhaps, been the slave of pride or of sensuality; he has cherished an irascible and vindictive temper; he has pursued his secular business with an avidity which has left no time for his soul and for God; he has floated far away from his true anchorage, on the current of worldly fashion and frivolity; he has grown remiss in watchfulness and prayer; he has undervalued and neglected the means of grace; he has failed to profit by former chastisements; and by these or other sins and omissions, he has declined in spirituality, and lost much of his enjoyment in religion, and surrendered his soul to barrenness. With these impressions of his own unfaithfulness and criminality, he will see how wisely, as well as how mercifully, his afflictions are adapted to break up his delusive slumber, recover him from his declension, and bring him back where the light of God's countenance will once more shine upon him.

And even when the affliction may be of such a nature that the grounds of it are not readily de tected, when it consists in one of those awful displays of his sovereignty with which God sometimes startles and confounds his creatures, even then the Christian will struggle against the doubts and terrors with which unbelief would overwhelm him, and bow to the rod which smites him, with the feeling—

> "God is his own interpreter,
> And he will make it plain."

7. Finally, Christian submission properly includes *a desire and determination to profit by the affliction.*

This is an indispensable test of its sincerity. There can be no genuine submission, without an earnest desire to have the lessons the affliction is fitted to suggest, written upon the heart and carried out into the life. It is not for his own pleasure that God afflicts his people; it is from no caprice or cruelty; but "for their profit." It is that they may become "partakers of his holiness," and be assimilated to Christ their Head. When we say, therefore, "Thy will be done!" it is not a bare acquiescence in the trial; it is a prayer that the gracious ends he proposes to effect by the stroke may be accomplished; a prayer that it may be so sanctified as to yield to us the "peaceable fruit of righteousness." To secure this result should be the great concern of the afflicted. The remark is as just as it is common, that trials do not leave us as they find us; they either harden our hearts or mollify them; they are either a blessing or a curse. The Christian is, or should be, too well aware of this, not to tremble at the thought of misimproving his afflictions. God has come very near to him; he is waiting to see the effect of his dispensations. How solemn, how critical a season is it in the history of that stricken Christian; how closely connected with his peace and usefulness; how vital in its bearings upon his whole future career! He sees this. He feels it. With a holy jealousy he watches over himself. He studies the Scriptures with renewed diligence. He pours out his soul, day by day, in fervent supplications for wisdom, strength, deliverance from sin, and increasing holiness. And he addresses himself with vigour and alacrity to the duties of his station, resolved, with the help of God, to live henceforth for Him who has loved him and died to redeem him.

Such is an imperfect account of Christian submission. Imperfect as the delineation is, it will readily occur to you, that it is a virtue of rare excellence and of most difficult attainment. That which constitutes its excellence, reveals the reason why it is so difficult of attainment, viz., its contrariety to our natural character. "If any man will come after me, let him deny himself, and take up his cross and follow me." True religion consists much in self-crucifixion, and self-crucifixion belongs to the essence of Christian submission.

To inculcate this virtue is easy; to practise it exceeds our unassisted powers. Blessed be God for the promise, " My grace is sufficient for thee, for my strength is made perfect in weakness." "The things which are impossible with men are possible with God." But for the "everlasting arms," his people would faint and die under the calamities of life; but he upholds them. "They that wait upon the Lord shall renew their strength; they shall mount up on wings as eagles; they shall run and not be weary, they shall walk and not faint."

There are few amongst us who have not tested the truth of these Divine promises; who have not been called, in one way or another, to say, "It is the Lord, let him do what seemeth him good." He has stripped you of your property, he has prostrated you with sickness, he has permitted your children to plant your path with thorns, he has baffled your cherished plans of worldly success and honour, he has sent death to fill your hearts and your homes with desolation. You know, then, how hard it is to say, "Not as I will, but as Thou wilt!" But you also know, I trust, that what you cannot say in your own strength, he can enable you to say; and that however painful the stroke at the time, he can so sustain and sanctify you, that you shall afterwards look back upon it with the subdued and grateful feeling, "It is good for me that I have been afflicted."

THE PRODIGAL.

BY

JOHN LEYBURN, D. D.

EDITOR OF THE PRESBYTERIAN, PHILADELPHIA.

I will arise and go to my Father.—LUKE xv. 18.

THE parable of the prodigal son is among the most interesting and affecting portions of the Word of God. Its strong pictures stand out with great brilliancy and force. Its tender associations, drawn from the family hearth-stone, grouping together a father's love, the waywardness of intractable boyhood, the prodigal's alienation from home, his spendthrift life, and what it brought him to; the coming to himself amidst the wretchedness and want his sins had induced, his return, the old father still, though years had passed, looking out for his lost one, and recognizing him afar off in his rags, the meeting, the forgiveness, the rejoicing—did ever painter have a finer succession of scenes for pencil and canvass, than inspiration has here written in its simple, telling language?

This parable, however, has other bearings, far outreaching its mere dramatic interest. Whilst it speaks of the relation of father and son, of alienation, return and forgiveness, it shadows forth under beautiful imagery great scriptural truths, which have to do with the immortal welfare of the soul. Under the person of the father is represented God, the one great Father of us all; the son is the sinner, fallen and estranged, and loving his wanderings well; the far country is the world of sin and misery, in which he makes his home; the coming to himself, his conviction of sin; his return, his repentance; and his acceptance and the rejoicings over him, his regeneration and adoption into the household of the righteous. The parable, then, has great practical bearings; and in order to bring these into such shape as that they may favourably affect you, my readers, we shall educe from the passage a few of its plain, practical teachings.

1. The first thought which the passage suggests is—that God has given to all men a portion of substance. Over and above that, which may be regarded as in some measure mediately the result of our own application and industry, we are endowed by nature with certain important gifts, which may be regarded as a capital in hand, wherewith to do our trading for time and for eternity, and of which all after accumulations are but the workings up. What greater gift could the Father of us all bestow upon one of his creatures, than a reasonable soul? This he has not given to beasts, birds, creeping things, or to any other order of creation connected with this planet where we dwell. A soul, rational and immortal, is man's possession alone. It uplifts him from the common ground on which stand all other earth-born creatures, invests him with a lofty superiority, and makes him to have dominion over them all. A great gift is this soul of man—more valuable than

gems, than mines of gold, or crowns and kingdoms—than all the world beside. Especially does this gift of a soul seem to be a valuable portion when we look at its varied faculties and capabilities.

It is endowed with an understanding. It has capacities for high intelligence. It can discern, appropriate, digest, and powerfully use knowledge. It can reason, analyze, pursue long and difficult logical processes, and fairly revel in the great fields of thought which stretch out over the vast universe of God. It has imagination, and can create from next to nothing realms of fancy, peopling them at pleasure from her vast store-houses.

The soul has a conscience also. It has capacities not only for intelligence, but is possessed of moral susceptibilities; it can discern truth and approve it; it can know evil and condemn it. Rightly educated and directed, of all the elements of a human soul, conscience is of most importance. Better could we do without any thing else than do without that which God has put within us as a sort of vicegerent for himself—sent to occupy the inner temple of ourselves, to make right suggestions, to chide us when we would go astray, to encourage and cheer us on in all right-doing. Conscience—the law written on the heart, excusing and accusing—when properly enlightened, is as if we heard the voice of God, speaking in audible terms approbation or displeasure.

And, further, to the soul also belongs a will; it has powers of volition; like the pilot of the boat, it can turn the soul about, bearing it onward or keeping it steadfast, consenting to evil or refusing, accepting the offered ways of life and walking in them, or else choosing the road to death and travelling there. In this will lies the power of the man; turn this and you turn one's whole self; fix this to purposes of good, and you have lashed the bark's helm, with her bows towards a peaceful haven, from which no adverse winds or currents can divert her.

The soul has affections too; it can love and it can hate. Among the chiefest joys life affords, are the knitting together of hearts by ties of warm affection, so that in each other they find something to approve and delight in, to enlist the sympathies and sensibilities—something to enjoy and almost live for. Men love their children, wives, neighbours—they have sympathies warm and tender beating in common with a circle in whose veins runs their blood, or in whose minds dwell kindred sentiments and purposes.

Here, then, in this soul, with its treasure of understanding, conscience, will and affections, we have the portion of goods which God our Father from on high bestows upon us all, at the outset of life. A rich inheritance truly is ours, worth infinitely more than houses, lands, ships or stocks.

2. The impenitent have taken this, their substance, and gone into a far country.

This present evil world, with its pride, covetousness, lust and self-seeking, is a country far from God. God is, indeed, in his essence and by his ever-present providence, not far from every one of us. The sinner, with all his efforts, cannot escape from the vision of the Omniscient, nor from the immediate proximity of the Omnipresent, nor from the all-powerful grasp of the Omnipotent. The wings of the morning cannot bear him from God's sight, nor can the darkness hide him, nor the uttermost parts of the earth, nor the depths of hell conceal him.

Still, as to that nearness of the soul to God, which presumes a resemblance to him in moral nature, a sympathy in the things hated and delighted in, and a close and joyful communion of spirit with him, there is none of it. It is matter of no great difficulty, impenitent reader, to prove from the actings out of your own life towards all that represents your God and Saviour here on earth, that you have wandered far from him. Here, for instance, is his Word. In this blessed book of inspiration is the very language of his utterance, placed on record for the instruction and admonition of mankind; historically it is an interesting book; poetically, strikingly sublime and beautiful; as to the times in which it was produced, it runs through the lapse of ages, and in the subjects of which it treats, extends through eternity. There is no reason, therefore, in the Bible itself, why it should not be as attractive as any other volume. But is it so? Under the suggestions of an uneasy conscience, you may at rare intervals, or perhaps even statedly, read over a chapter or two, but in these glorious themes with which its pages are enriched, and which are so well adapted to enkindle the enthusiasm and affections of the soul, how far are you from any thing of this! To the unregenerate man, God's word is not so welcome as an ordinary history, or a poem, a novel, or a newspaper; its perusal is absolutely uninteresting and irksome; if read at all, it is read under the direct stress of conscience; you do not love its truths, nor do its great principles wake up any congenial chord in your bosom. You will hence generally neglect it, treat it with practical contempt, allow it to lie until the dust accumulates on its unopened covers, ever trying to get away from what will bring God and eternity before you.

So also it is with prayer. Prayer is a direct speaking to God through the intervention of his Son. It is when the soul is engaged in earnest supplication that God, by his Spirit, deigns to visit the soul. The closet is a place of constant, sweet communion to the true disciple, akin in its pure, heart-cheering enjoyments to heaven; but the sinner has no appreciation of the privilege; he does not find comfort in pouring out his soul to Him whose ear is ever open to the suppliant's cry; if he utters what is called prayer, it is but the idle repetition of words; no wrestlings of the soul are there, no taking hold of the promises, no visions of Christ, no well-springs of consolation; all is dull, unattractive, repulsive. Hence he seldom goes through even the form of private prayer to God. He lives day after day without asking the Divine blessing upon him for this world and the next—without even thinking of it. In fact, if by any means he should be reminded that living prayerless is an offence before God, so that his conscience begins to rebuke him, he bestirs himself straightway to silence conscience or drug it to sleep. He does not wish to pray; he has no desire for communion with heaven; he has taken his portion of goods and wandered far away; he does not wish to speak with God.

In regard to the public services of God's house,

too, the same spiritual phenomena occur. This is a place where God vouchsafes to be present. His children, who love him, and desire to enjoy his favour, delight to be there. They can say, like the Psalmist, "How amiable are thy tabernacles, O Lord of Hosts!" "A day in thy courts is better than a thousand." "I had rather be a door-keeper in the house of God, than to dwell in the tents of wickedness." Not so with the sinner. He had rather dwell in the tents of wickedness. No desire has he to keep the doors of the sanctuary. Not that we would intimate that he is not a church-goer. Education, a vague sense of religious obligation, a general impression of the importance of sustaining the ordinances and influences of Christianity for the public good, and other circumstances, may have rendered him quite a punctual attendant at church. Nor is he always an uninterested hearer. When the preacher delivers his message with fine rhetorical accompaniments, it may be in his ears as the melodious sound of a pleasant instrument. When good hits are made at the short-comings of religious professors, or at general public evils, he can listen with real enjoyment, and say, That was well done. When a doctrinal point is discussed, he can follow the speaker in his logical connections, appreciate the argument, confess that he has made good his points, and give his judgment that he is an able minister of the Word of God.

But let the minister forget his rhetoric, and, leaving generalities, or abstract doctrines and other people's sins, come directly home to the sinner's own case, charging his transgressions down upon him, waking up conscience to say, "Thou art the man," and pointing to the terrible retributions threatened against such as he, then what has this hearer to say? Wearily he sits beneath such messages; no praises has he now for the preaching, and but little admiration for the preacher. He is disposed to be captious, perhaps wishes for a change of ministers, or a change of his church for one where he will hear things less unpleasant, or, it may be he forsakes the sanctuary altogether. It was not from love of the truth, or love to God, he ever went there; but from habit, interest in good speaking, or of a well-digested argument, and other extrinsic influences; and now, when these are withdrawn, and God, through the instrumentality of his Word, is revealed, he wishes to flee away and hide himself. He has left his father's house, and gone so far astray that he does not wish to have God even speak to him.

So far has he gone, too, and so fixed is he in his purpose to stay at a distance, that hitherto all means have failed to bring him back. Preaching, persuasions of friends, the example of others returning, solemn and affecting providences, and even the occasional movings of the Spirit, have all been unsuccessful. He has taken his goods and gone into a far country.

3. In the far country, whither the sinner has gone, like the prodigal, he is squandering his goods. Understanding, affections, conscience, and will, may not indeed be buried in a napkin, but they are traded with for self and this world, instead of for God. What seekings after divine truth, what flames of heavenly love, what heart-searching to bring out hidden sins that they may be slain, what self-morti-

fication, what purposes to lay out the life for Christ and his cause, are ever seen in him! Alas! to all these he is as much a stranger, and they as much strange to him, as if such things were never set forth as a part of the obligations incumbent upon him. According to that high and holy sense in which God looks upon nothing as rightly done, which has not as its prime motive a desire for his glory, the sinner's whole life has been fruitless. From the dawn of his being, to the present hour, he has not done one act, nor spoken one word, nor exercised a single affection nor volition, nor cherished a thought which heaven can approve. Neither his own soul, nor the souls of others are, by any intention upon his part, the better of his having come into this world. As to all the rich and glorious revenues, which God had a right to expect from the priceless inheritance he has given him, he has been a most unprofitable servant.

But this neglect, rightly to use his goods, is only the negative aspect of his sin. He has positively misused and squandered them; he has diverted them to ends absolutely mischievous; he has lived for self, for family, and for worldly aggrandizement. If sensual pleasures have been most agreeable, to these he has devoted himself, and, in that delusive department of things earthly, has gone the rounds of gaiety and fashionable dissipation, laying out himself for sumptuous living, worldly show, or more vulgar vice, and saying, " Soul, take thine ease." Or if his tastes have been of an avaricious cast, he has gone out into the market place, and there, with care and toil, has lived but to accumulate, and having accumulated, still abandoned himself to the same. Or if ambition has been his ruling passion, he has sought, by all devices which ingenuity could suggest, and all the industry of which he was capable, for power and place. These have constituted the one great object for which the portion of life already past has been exhausted—to which the talents given him have been devoted. Fruitless as to the chief end for which he was created, and fruitful in all that is forbidden, in the far country of this world of sin, he has squandered his substance on things which have produced no profit, either for God's glory, for the highest welfare of his fellow men, or for his own eternal interests. With such riotous living have his talents been wasted.

4. Like the prodigal, also, the sinner is in a perishing condition. Restive was the wayward son with the restraints of his father's house; puffed up with the vain conceit that he could do better for himself than could be done for him at his native home; imagining that the indulgences from which parental love withheld him were things to be desired, and wishing to be where he could revel amid such pleasures unmolested, he secured his portion of goods, and went away to lead a life of sensuality. For a season, perhaps, all went on well. Vice yielded a transient satisfaction. With money at command and none to hinder, he could betake himself to such pleasures to his heart's content. He probably wondered that he could so long have endured the mopish life at home. The freshness of sinful joys enables him to enter into them with a full relish. But soon the scene changes.

He finds that sin has a bitter as well as a sweet; that the chalice, whose delicious draughts have so exhilarated, had wormwood amongst its dregs. Hours of revelry left days of ennui, and an aching, empty, desolated heart. Soon money was gone—that which had bought the momentary pleasures—and with that went friends, and the joys of the sinful, lustful life. He has tried in vain to find the real good which he had sought for. With all his gettings, his soul is emptier than at first; and now he has not wherewith to get, at all. He lacks the very necessaries for existence—he perishes with hunger.

Now to this end has the prodigal sinner already come. With all his toil he has never been satisfied Every acquisition, however eagerly and patiently sought for, and whatever he may have hoped from it, has but left the same void within. His plans may have been well laid, they may have been judiciously prosecuted, they may have been successful. But what then? Success when achieved has been his bane instead of his lasting joy. The end attained, all the exhilaration and interest of the pursuit have vanished, and he finds himself in possession of that which, if honest, he can only hold up before his mind's eye, and look at, whilst he exclaims, "How hast thou cheated me? With hard toil, for long months, with much care and weariness, I have sought thee, and now thou art mine, what art thou? What joy canst thou give to this empty soul, thou inert thing? What sorrows canst thou soothe, what cares drive away? What am I better than before?" With all his getting, he has gotten but the chaff which the swine do eat, and is still perishing with hunger.

Is not such the experience of the ungodly world? Who amongst the throngs that crowd the broad road to the second death, have ever found that houses and lands, stocks and moneys at interest, operas, routes and gay apparel, or crowns, kingdoms, and sceptres, satisfied the cravings of the soul? Pythius, who lived in Asia Minor in the time of Xerxes, and who was, next to that monarch, the wealthiest man in the world, but who was still grinding the faces of the poor, received a most eloquent rebuke, as to the folly of so setting his heart on gold, from his wife, when she had a splendid banquet prepared with nothing to eat on the table but gold. Saladin, one of the sovereigns of Asia, after all the glories he had won, when at last his dying hour approached, could but say to his standard bearer—"Go show this flag of the dead to the army, and tell them that the lord of the East could bring nothing but a single garment to the grave." All the world's promised good, however fascinating in appearance, like the beautiful apples of Sodom, falls to ashes at the touch. Far, far have you wandered amidst such vain pursuits; long, long, has your aching heart craved for something to fill its vast desires; but all earth's resources exhausted, has there not remained the aching, empty heart still? Are you not hungering, perishing still? The priceless treasure, the immortal soul, which God gave you as your inheritance, is, indeed, still yours, but in the wanderings and squanderings it has become stupified with sin, and is of itself incapable of yielding any revenue of real good; and there, lying in your helplessness, with only the swine's chaff for your diet, you perish with hunger.

5. The only remedy in this sad extremity is, first of all, like the prodigal, to come to yourself.

Amidst the wretchedness and ruin which his reckless course had brought upon him, God's mercy still allowed him to remember that there were good things in the home he had left. At that father's house want was never known; no rags were seen even on the lowest menial who waited within its portals; none ever hungered in vain, amid the plenty with which that board was spread; all were cared for bountifully, cheerfully, and to their hearts utmost content. How does he envy the lot of the lowest who dwell there. Happy are they; whilst he, who once as a son shared the bounties of that board, is here in a far country, in the fields amidst the swine, striving to keep off famine with the husks on which the poor brutes he is tending seem to revel, but which refuse to refresh and nourish him. Why did he ever leave that home? What compensation has his riotous living afforded, for the peaceful plenty and comfort he there relinquished? How was he deluded in imagining that a life of folly and sin was more to be desired, than the gentle and wholesome restraints which prevailed in the paternal mansion. The spell which rested on him has been broken, and he now sees things in their proper light. He has come to himself; he was beside himself before.

And how truly may it be said of every wanderer from God, who is seeking his treasures among earthly things, that he is beside himself. What man in his sane mind could choose a portion such as this world affords, in preference to that offered him from the Father's house on high; and especially when his oft-repeated experience has taught him how vain are all things here below? In that house there are indeed restraints, but these are only to bar the soul from what would bring but disappointment, sorrow and shame, were they ours. With kind paternal tenderness and discrimination, and with a full knowledge of what is best for his children, our Father in heaven places his prohibitory mandate only over the gateways which lead to wretchedness and ruin. His commandments are not grievous. His ways are ways of pleasantness, and all his paths are peace. He spreads rich banquets of heavenly provision; he opens up fountains of consolation and enjoyment. such as know no poisonous intermixture; his own Son received by faith is meat indeed for the famishing soul; his word is spirit and life; he gives peace of conscience. joy in the Holy Ghost, and a hope of eternal life beyond the grave; and in the ways of obedience to him, and the fruition of the promises, there is a welling up of a fountain from which, if a man drink, he need never thirst again. With such provision all his children are supplied bountifully and freely; none need ever want; there is enough and to spare.

Why should the sinner forsake such a home to wander in the deserts of this world; and instead of this wholesome nutriment, prepared for the soul by him who made it and knew its wants, endeavour to satisfy himself with the husks of earthly good? Never can he satiate his hungerings until he come to his right mind, and sees things in their real and relative value. If this world has yielded no fruits such as the soul would have, why will he not look where alone they can be found? If wandering from God has brought only disappointment and sorrow, why will he not return to God and find real joy? Heaven's resources have not been exhausted by the glorious multitude who feed at its banquet tables. The portals of that forsaken home are open to receive him if he will but return; what folly and madness, then, to stay away! Let reason resume her throne. Let him whom God has made capable of the high dignity of a son appreciate his privilege, and seek to dwell where he properly belongs. Let him come to his right mind; let him prefer the real to the counterfeit, the substance to the shadow, the solid gold to worthless dust, the banquets of his Father's house to the poor husks of the swineherds.

6. But, unhappily, like the prodigal, the sinner, finding himself in want, often betakes himself for aid to some citizen of the country where he dwells. All his inheritance being gone, the famine pressing hard upon him, and no other prospect in view but death by hunger, unless he finds relief from some source, the prodigal seeks the help nearest at hand and most congenial. As yet he has hardly thought of returning to his long forsaken home; he does not care to go there; he fears to meet the piercing, reproachful glance of an injured father; his great object is to avert the calamity which stares him in the face; he hopes to do this by becoming a hireling, and forthwith joins himself to a citizen of that far off country, and goes into the fields as a tender of swine.

A most striking counterpart of the prodigal's

course is found in the almost uniform conduct of the sinner awakened to a sense of his perishing condition. He finds himself in want; hunger is gnawing at his vitals, the world has never satisfied him, he sees worse things in store, death is coming on and he must perish if he remains where he is. Forthwith, therefore, instead of resorting at once to the full provisions of the Gospel, he sets himself to work out some righteousness of his own, by joining himself to what at best must be regarded as belonging to the country of this present world, and not to the kingdom which is from above. He betakes himself to reformation, breaking off from his more overt sins; he abandons Sabbath breaking, profane swearing, licentiousness, attendance on places of worldly amusement and folly, and is outwardly a very different man. He hopes to be better satisfied under his new system of living. Finding this, however, unavailing, he goes further, and now opens his long neglected Bible, reading portions of it every day; he bows his knees in secret to pray; he is regular in his attendance on the sanctuary, and perhaps begins to frequent the weekly social meetings. In these he hopes to find relief for his famishing soul. But, alas! no relief comes; the Bible is a sealed book to him; his prayers seem idle words; the messages of the minister bring no comfort to his bosom. In fact the longer he continues his toilsome routine of religious services the more hopeless his prospects seem to be; his heart is hard; he cannot feel, or think, or act as he would do. He begins to despair of help from these sources. And well he may. He has been striving to work out a righteousness of his own, instead of humbly seeking that which is Christ Jesus. The means of grace, however important in their place as means, and an outward reformation, however indispensable, will not of themselves avail; he has stopped short of the right refuge, and joined himself to what are best but citizens of the country of this present world. If he goes no further for help, he must still perish with hunger.

7. And this leads to the remark, that, like the prodigal, and with the same spirit also, the sinner must return to his father's house.

Temptations, indeed, there may be to keep him where he is. Looking at the distance to which he has gone, and the steps which must be retraced, the way back seems long and difficult. In his poverty and rags he may think himself badly prepared for the journey. Should he reach the gates of the homestead, how does he know that he will be received? He erred in forsaking that home; and his career since, together with his present wretched appearance, have nothing to recommend him. Has not his father cast him off for ever? With kindred doubts and fears may the sinner, whom God's Spirit has convinced of the vanity of the world and the wretchedness of his condition, be perplexed when he thinks of returning to God. A long way, indeed, has he wandered in sin. Difficult does it seem for him to retrace his steps. With a soul all polluted and guilty—in spiritual rags and wretchedness, what has he to recommend him? He has treated with fixed and intentional neglect and contempt the calls to return which have been long ringing in his ears.

Even should he go begging to be received again, will the paternal doors be opened to him?

And yet, what would the prodigal gain by staying away? Like the leprous men at the gate of Samaria, if he stays there he will perish, and he can but perish if he goes. He will relinquish all idea of sonship; he will humble himself, and beg, as matter of special grace, to be but admitted as a servant. And so, also, we may ask the prodigal sinner thinking of a return, but kept back by doubts and fears, what will it profit you to stay where you are in your sins? You are dying with hunger; a little longer, and the famine will have clean overtaken you, and you will have perished for ever. Death is inevitable —the undying, everdying second death, should you remain in your sins; if you go to your neglected God and Saviour, seeking for mercy, you can but perish. In the whole universe there is no hope of safety but in this one thing of returning. You have no merit of your own to plead; but you can confess your sins, and beg for mercy; and peradventure pardon will ensue. So thought the prodigal, and in that dark and guilty soul the struggle was ended; the last resolve was made; the swine-herds and the husks were to be forsaken; and from his trembling lips fell the words, "I will arise and go to my father, and say unto him, Father, I have sinned against heaven and in thy sight." Such a resolution, rising from the heart-depths of a sinner, evinces the very spirit of evangelical penitence. Here is a sense of sin; a willingness frankly and fully to confess it; the conviction that it has all been against the holy and excellent law of God; an abandonment of all pretension to self-righteousness and a willingness to plead guilty, and acquiesce in the sentence which would debar him from sonship for ever; and withal, a determination to return, casting himself upon the mercy of God in Christ Jesus as his only hope. Herein is that mingled despair and rising hope—that giving up of self, and the going out of faith towards an all-sufficient Saviour, which marks the transition of a soul from the kingdom of darkness into that of God's dear Son. With such a spirit, no sinner need fear to seek an injured father's face.

8. And this leads us finally, to say, that returning with the spirit of the prodigal, a favourable and joyful reception is certain. Long though it had been since that wayward son had fled his home, the kindness of a father's heart had not grown cold. Wicked as has been his life, and wretched as he is in his poverty and rags, he will not be spurned from the homestead doors. His trembling footsteps bring him near that home; his fainting heart almost dreads to make the appeal to be received again; at the last moment he is almost ready, like Lot's wife, to look back to Sodom. But just then the Father's eye discerns him, the long lost son is recognized, the tender heart of paternal love melts in compassion; the prodigal begins his confessions, but ere they have been ended, he is embraced by a father's arms, forgiven for all his wanderings, and acknowledged as a son once more. Robes white and clean are put upon him, he is adorned with gold, the fatted calf is killed, and the whole household echoes with strains of joy. He that was as good as dead, is made alive again; the lost is found.

Such a reception, free and joyful, awaits you, **my** unconverted reader, if in your wretchedness and ruin you come pleading for mercy, at the doors of the kingdom. Through the riches of grace, which is in Christ Jesus, all your sins can be forgiven; by the Spirit which he has purchased a new heart can be put within you; and in the pure garments of his righteousness you can stand accepted. More favoured than the prodigal, you have a divine, all-powerful friend to plead your cause. God the Father, and this elder brother Jesus Christ, in the counsels of eternity, devised a plan for securing the return for such as you. The Redeemer's incarnation; his life of faithful obedience; his agonizing death on Calvary, and his intercession at the right hand of the Father in heaven, all were designed to prepare the new and living way by which the prodigal sinner may come back to God. His own honour and the compensation for the travail of his soul are involved in the rescue of the lost. Every prodigal returned is a fresh contribution to the rich revenue of glory he is to receive as recompense for his shame, dishonour and death; every wanderer brought back from sin and hell, is a new token of his triumph over his enemies—another star added to the lustre of his peerless crown. In such conquests all heaven sympathises—for there is joy among the angels even over one sinner that repenteth. Why then should you not come? The way through Christ is an open way. "Him that cometh to me," says he, "I will in no wise cast out," and in him your utmost desires shall be satisfied, for he also says, "I am the bread of life; he that cometh to me shall never hunger."

More willing is the Father to receive you, than you are to return. His yearning heart pities you, his kind voice calls you, and if you but come you shall be a son and an heir in that glorious household. No sooner will the broken utterances of your guiltiness fall from your lips, than they shall be heard, and the lofty courts of heaven shall reverberate with songs of joy.

And will you come? Let me plead with you to tarry no longer away. Does your proud spirit at last relent? Has the great resolve been made? From your troubled heart has the language gone forth, "I will arise and return?" Then, blessed, thrice blessed will you be. A Saviour's blood will wash your sins away, and your rags will be exchanged for a robe of righteousness. A prodigal returned; how great the change! No more a stranger, but a son at home; no longer away in a desert land among the swine, perishing with hunger, but here at a father's board, where there is enough and to spare. The husks all gone; the empty aching heart at last filled—the longing soul satisfied from the rich provisions of a Saviour's love; and though but yesterday an outcast beggar, now an heir of God, a joint heir with Jesus Christ, in full brotherhood with the saints on earth and in heaven, and but waiting for the mansions prepared above, for the full fruition of a kingdom and a crown. Joy, joy for ever! **The dead is made alive! The lost is found!**

THE TREE KNOWN BY ITS FRUITS.

BY

E. P. HUMPHREY, D. D.

PASTOR OF THE SECOND PRESBYTERIAN CHURCH, LOUISVILLE, KENTUCKY.

Preached before the General Assembly of the Presbyterian Church at the opening of its Sessions in Charleston, S. C., May 20, 1852.

Even so, every good tree bringeth forth good fruit, but a corrupt tree bringeth forth evil fruit.—MATT. vii. 17.

THESE words of our Lord contain a profound and comprehensive truth. As the nature of the tree, whether good or corrupt, is made known by its fruit, even so, the Master observes, false prophets may be detected. They come in sheep's clothing, yet being inwardly ravening wolves, their rapacity invariably betrays itself. Now we may give to this maxim a wider application, and suggest that a religious faith, as well as a religious teacher, whether true or false, will develope, by outward and significant marks, all its vital peculiarities. The inner life of Judaism, in its purer days, and then that life in the period of its degeneracy, clearly revealed its nature by many striking phenomena. The same remark applies to Christianity in all the phases which it assumes. These phases are determined by the peculiar theology which, from time to time, is received into the fixed and inward convictions of mankind. The true discovers itself as good, and the false as evil, by inevitable developments. "Even so, every good tree bringeth forth good fruit, but a corrupt tree bringeth forth evil fruit." The text, as thus explained, prescribes to this occasion a discourse of

OUR THEOLOGY IN ITS DEVELOPMENTS.

The purposes of this argument do not require a discussion of our theology in its sources and evidences. Nor is it needful, in this presence, to expound its peculiar doctrines. These have been made widely known through its living disciples, its written formularies, its celebrated teachers of former generations, and their powerful adversaries. Few intelligent persons are ignorant of the doctrines which its faithful disciples deduce from the Scriptures, even those touching the sovereignty of God and the dependence of the creature; his purpose as foreordaining, and his glory as the end of creation, sin, and redemption; the imputation unto all of the guilt of the first man, our federal head; the utter corruption of human nature; the election unto salvation of a certain and definite number; their redemption by the vicarious obedience and penal sufferings of the Son of God; the work of the Holy Spirit persuading and enabling them to accept of Christ; their justification by faith alone; and their infallible perseverance, secured by the immutability of the decree of election.

These doctrines are further verified as of the substance of our theology, by its celebrated symbols. Our faith is held within the brief compass of the Lambeth articles; it is stated at large in the Latter

Confession of Helvetia; it is delivered systematically in the judgment of the Synod of Dort; and it is yet more accurately defined in our own accepted standards, the Confession and Catechisms of Westminster.

Our system of doctrine is also identified closely in some things, and substantially in the most, with the names of the illustrious men who, since the days of Paul, and of Him the greater than Paul, have been masters in this school of divine learning; even Augustine, Calvin, and Edwards. We speak with reverence too, of Beza, Turretin, Owen, Ridgley, Witherspoon, Bellamy, and Chalmers; "howbeit these attained not unto the first three."

This faith is identified, still further, with the reputation of its great adversaries—Pelagius, Arminius, the Jesuit antagonists of the Port Royal, the Tridentine Fathers, and Pope Clement XI. in the Bull Unigenitus.

I may assume, therefore, that our distinctive principles are, for the purposes of this argument, sufficiently familiar to every intelligent hearer, and especially to the members of the venerable court in whose presence I am required to appear. This being assumed, I proceed at once to indicate some of the fruits of our doctrinal system.

In the first place, *it developes a peculiar type of spiritual life.* The piety which has been subjected to the influence of our theology, includes a deep sense of personal unworthiness. The man perceives that he has violated God's law in instances without number; so that he is by wicked works a sinner. Still further, he ascertains that his actual transgressions proceed from a disposition to sin inherent in his moral constitution, and that not only is his nature the source of sin, but its corruption is itself, like all the motions thereof, truly and properly sin; so that he is, in that double sense, a sinner by nature. He acknowledges, yet further, that he is wholly disabled to good, and wholly inclined to evil, so that he is a sinner only. And finally, he confesses that this death in sin is an hereditary corruption conveyed to him from the first man, Adam; so that he is a sinner of a sinful race. I spend no labour in showing that a conviction of sin fastened on the conscience by a sense of active, innate, total, and hereditary depravity, must be most thorough and pungent.

Nor is this all. The kindred feeling of utter helplessness rests on his mind. He perceives that every one of his unnumbered sins deserves the wrath and curse of God for ever; and, further, that he can offer no atonement to a violated law. He is fully conscious, also, of his absolute want of power to change his evil nature, itself being one main ground of his condemnation. Another step brings him to a knowledge of the condemnation that rests upon him with the imputed sin of Adam, our federal head. Now some may say, that his understanding is strangely perverted who accepts all these things as true; yet even they must concede that he who does in fact believe them, and believing, feels their power, will realize the ideas both of guilt and of helplessness to the uttermost. This theology brings the sinner face to face with his own inexcusable and aggravated transgressions, and face to face, also, with a condemnation, from which, as touching man or angel, every ray of hope is excluded, and in which is mingled every element of despair.

But our doctrines do not rest here. They impart to the piety of the believer the element of an undoubting faith. The Word of God, as expounded by our divines, exhibits the believer as a chosen in Christ from before the foundation of the world; so that his salvation springs from the eternal purpose of God. It further declares, that the love of God has abounded towards him in a plan of redemption; so that the believer's safety is secured by the mercy of God. Going still deeper, he learns that an atonement has been made for sin by the vicarious and infinite sacrifice of the Lord Christ, and that in this expiation, he hath fully obeyed the precept of the law, and exhausted its penalty, and now all law and all justice demand the pardon of the penitent sinner, so that he is saved from death by the act of God, not only meditating in mercy, but judging in righteousness. Still further, this expiation relieves us from the condemnation we lie under, by reason of our actual transgressions, our evil natures and our relation to the sin of the first man; so that this is an abounding salvation. The Holy Spirit, moreover, regenerates and sanctifies God's chosen ones by his efficacious grace, and secures also their perseverance unto the end; so that it is a complete salvation.

Now if the believer comprehend these wondrous truths; if he rest his soul on the unchangeable purpose of God, the finished righteousness of Christ, and the renewing power of the Eternal Spirit; if he apprehend all this to be true, planting his feet firmly here, he realizes the stupendous idea of salvation by grace, and may raise the triumphant demands of the Apostle, "Who is he that condemneth?" "Who shall lay any thing to the charge of God's elect?" "Who shall separate us from the love of Christ?"

It might also be shown, that the spiritual life, developed by our theology, is the piety of humility; that it is, further, the piety of gratitude; and further yet, that it gives to Christ, as of debt, and receives from him as of grace: "You go to receive your reward," was said to the dying Hooker; "I go to receive mercy," was his reply. If all these things be so, we may well say that our theology developes a type of spiritual life, which is not only peculiar, but the highest possible to humanity in its mortal state.

In the second place, this theology developes the principles of a *free ecclesiastical polity*.

It were easy to show that our theology, when traced to its logical conclusions, wholly divests the ministry of the sacerdotal character, denies that ordination hath any sacramental efficacy whatever, distinguishes between the right of administering sealing ordinances and the power of government, affirms that all believers are, equally, and as such kings and priests unto God, and declares for the Lord Jesus Christ as the sole and supreme Head of the Church. In these conclusions, or rather in these articles of faith, our doctrinal system developes, theoretically, the four great principles which enter into the basis of a free Church government. These are the parity of the ministry, the authority of the laity as equal and co-ordinate with that of the clergy in every ecclesiastical judicatory, the election of all church officers by the people, and the independence of the Church in relation to the State.* Now, treating this topic historically, we cannot fail to recognize a thorough alliance between our distinctive faith and each of these principles. The equality in office of all men ordained to the work of the ministry has been from the beginning invariably affirmed, and the doctrine of the prelacy has been constantly rejected, by all the churches strictly called reformed in Europe and America. Such conceptions of the ministerial office did they obtain from their theology, that the bishop's lawn or mitre would have been a spectacle, quite as rare in the French, Belgic, or Helvetian churches, as it would have been in a Presbytery of the old Scottish Kirk, or in a Puritan conventicle, or, as I take leave to add, in a company of the apostles.

* The doctrine of our ecclesiastical polity involves these two among other propositions. First, that its principles are laid down in the Word of God; secondly, that the same principles are indicated by our theology. The first proposition discovers the authority on which Presbyterianism, as a form of church government, rests; and the other discloses its logical relations. These two propositions are distinct, true, and in no degree inconsistent. The limits of this discourse did not admit the discussion of the higher topic—the authority on which our polity rests. The author was obliged to restrict himself to a brief view of the other particular—the logical relations of our theology and our polity. Not supposing that any hearer or reader of the discourse would regard the affirming of the second proposition as a denial of the first, the author is as much surprised as are the Princeton Reviewers, "to learn that some hearers took exception to his discourse, as though he placed the whole authority of our system on its logical relations." The same remarks apply to the treatment of the third head of the discourse.

The representation of the people in all ecclesiastical courts has almost invariably attended our doctrinal system. Our congregational brethren affirm this principle in its broadest sense, by investing the brotherhood in each congregation with the whole power of government. In most of the Reformed Churches, the office of the ruling elder is held to be of scriptural authority. The incumbents of this office are usually of the people, elected by the people, ordained in the name of Christ, and invested with a divine right to sit in every church court, and to share in all its deliberations. Their numbers, intelligence, and piety, give them a predominant influence in ecclesiastical affairs. Their office, at once the ornament and bulwark of a free Church, saves the kingdom of the saints from degenerating into a kingdom of the clergy.

Not less incontestible is it that our doctrinal system carries with it the free election of all church officers by the people. In the Romish establishment the sacerdotal order perpetuates itself. The Pope is the creature, and, in his turn, the creator of the cardinals. He also appoints the bishops, and they designate the priests; and this spiritual close corporation takes its charter from the dogmatic faith of the Church, as settled at Trent. In the Anglican establishment, the crown invests the bishops, the bishops appoint the priests, and the patron—it may be a profligate peer—endows them with a parish and a living. This hierarchy experiences no disturbing influences from the theology with which it is associated. But with a partial exception, soon to be mentioned, the churches which receive our peculiar faith affirm that the election of persons to preach the Word, administer the sacraments, and use authority is in the people; and that the act of power, whether civil or ecclesiastical, which places in the congregation a pastor not of its own free choice, is an intrusion which is to be for ever denounced as unscriptural, and resisted as intolerable.

The fourth principle, the separation of the Church from the control of the civil power, exhibits, in its historical development, a remarkable illustration of the vital forces of our divinity. Calvin, Cranmer, and the Scottish Reformers committed to the secular power an injurious control over spiritual affairs, because their intellects, though large and comprehensive, were not large enough to comprehend fully the immense results of their theology. They did not perceive that their own principles, when carried to their legitimate conclusions, would deliver the Church of Christ from the dominion of both kings and republics, and establish it as a purely spiritual and independent power on earth. It was their high office to fix in the convictions of men a religious faith, which, being itself true, should gradually correct the errors of its most illustrious teachers; and, being pure, should purge itself from all human ordinances; and, being free, should throw off every yoke of spiritual servitude, until it became the inner and potential life of a Church, like our own, which answereth not to the Jerusalem that then was, and was in bondage with her children, but to the Jerusalem which is above, which is free, and the mother of us all.

It may be suggested, that the Established Churches

of England and Scotland exhibit clear instances of a coalition, rather than a repugnance, between our theology and the institutions of Prelacy and Erastianism. But as to the Anglican Church, it may well be said in reply, that although the doctrinal portions of the thirty-nine articles are orthodox in terms, yet an Arminian sense has been fastened on them by the general consent of all concerned. The form of sound words is but a form; the Genevan ingredient, originally cast into the Alembic, has long since evaporated, leaving undisturbed, henceforth, the Prelatical and Erastian elements in the crucible. As a further reply, it may be stated that when the Anglican Church was most distinguished for its orthodoxy, the doctrine of the prelacy sat but loosely on the convictions of its bishops and doctors. The theological views of Cranmer, the first Protestant Archbishop of Canterbury, are made known by the fact, that his advocacy of predestination and election was as decided as that of Augustine himself; and his opinions touching the ministry are revealed in his plain avowal of the conviction, that in primitive times there was no distinction between bishops and priests. So long as his successors in the primacy perpetuated his theology, they perpetuated also his gentle views of prelacy; one of them only, Bancroft, venturing to assert its divine authority. It was reserved for Archbishop Laud to inaugurate the Arminian theology in the Church, and with that a zeal for diocesan episcopacy, as an ordinance of God, a passion for ceremonies, and a merciless persecution of those who believed, without subscribing the creed which he subscribed without believing.

The history of this establishment, therefore, instead of weakening, confirms our argument.

Not less significant is the history of the Church of Scotland, where our theology has been perpetuated for three hundred years. Its developments in the way of order have been infinitely remarkable. In the first place, the persuasions of the English court, and the bayonets of her armies, have not been able to fasten an Episcopacy on the Kirk. Secondly, a representation of the people, sitting in all the Church courts, has ever been of the substance of her polity. Thirdly, the Kirk, although condescending to be by law established, has never been Erastian; and the moderate party, so called, which verged towards Erastianism in policy, exhibited at the same time the most unequivocal tendencies towards Arminianism in doctrine; while the opposite party contended both for orthodoxy in faith, and for the rights of God's people in the free choice of their pastors. Lastly, the unexhausted forces of our theology, having delivered the Kirk from every other element of bondage, is perpetually struggling through a series of agitations and disruptions, to purge her from the remaining iniquity of patronage. These disturbances will be incessantly renewed, from generation to generation, until the venerable Kirk must take her choice between disowning her patronage, or losing all her children, or abandoning that ancient faith, which teaches them to vindicate their rights, even unto a separation from her sacraments. Either her theology, as in England, or her subjection to the State, as in this country, must disappear from the crucible, or the crucible itself will be broken by the antagonism of its ingredients. So intolerant is this theology of any other than a polity absolutely free.

In the third place, our theology developes a *simple and spiritual mode of worship*. The ritual of a religion is a most accurate expression of its system of doctrine. Comparing the Romish Church with our own, for example, we shall ascertain that their forms of worship are dissimilar, because their theologies are repugnant. The ceremonials of Rome are not accidents of the system, nor were they devised for dramatic effect alone. They embody a meaning; they express a doctrine; they address not more directly the imagination than the faith of the worshippers. It is held by that establishment that the sacrament of the supper, when rightly administered, hath an inherent power to save. It derives this power from the fact, that the elements are changed into the body and blood, the soul and divinity of Jesus Christ, and as such are presented to God, a true propitiatory sacrifice for the sins of the living and the dead. It is the function of the officiating clergymen to offer up this atoning sacrifice; he is, therefore, in fact a priest, and the table on which he lays the oblation is, in strictness of speech, an altar. The priest officiates moreover in the person of Christ. His vestments, the decorations of the altar, and all the surroundings, represent incidents in the passion of Christ. The practised eye of the devotee beholds, in the garments and bands worn by the priest, symbols of the robe in which Christ was clothed, and the cords by which he was bound. The crucifix, embroidered on the back of the robe, represents the cross which Jesus bore on his shoulders, and the tonsure of the priest denotes the crown of thorns. The altar is the figure of Calvary, and its furniture represents the linen clothes in which the body of Jesus was wrapped, the sepulchre, and the stone which was rolled against the door. The crucifix is the image of Christ's passion and death; the lighted candles are in honour of his triumph; and the ascending incense is symbolical of prayer. The circular form of the wafer denotes the perfections of the Deity. In the wafer Christ is personally present; its elevation is the fearful immolation; and the prostration of the worshippers is in adoration of the atoning lamb. Every gesture and posture of the priest embodies a theological significancy. When he kisses the altar or the book, when he spreads forth his hands, or bathes the tips of his finger, or mingles water in the wine, or breaks the bread, or makes the sign of the cross, or smites upon his breast, or bows, or kneels, he does not perform one empty ceremony, but in every, even the minutest, act of the sacred pantomime, he exhibits some one element in the single definite idea of the great apostacy—salvation by the sacraments in the keeping of the priesthood. This central idea, this interior life of the system, not only prescribes its ritual, but regulates also the form, and size, and adornments of its sacred buildings. The cathedral is not designed for the preaching of the Word, nor yet for prayer and praise, but precisely for the dwelling-place of the Lord Christ present in the sacrament, and for the work of sacrifice. It is, therefore, at once a palace and a temple. As such it must assume the form of the cross, and must be of splendid architecture. Were the conception fully realized, every stone in its walls, though hidden from mortal sight, would be hewn and polished for the eye of the Master. Its massive doors would be curiously wrought in solid brass, so that men might gaze in wonder on the beautiful gate of the temple. Within, its pillars would shoot far upwards towards the heavens; its marble pavement would resemble the solid earth, and its swelling dome the bending skies. Exquisite creations of genius would adorn its walls; gold, and silver, and all rubies, the glory of Lebanon, and the purple of Tyre, would enrich its shrines; the incense burned at its altars would breathe Sabean odours; and music would invoke its utmost melody to fill the amplitude of the temple and its mighty dome with the articulate joy of the *Te Deum*, or the dolorous wail of the *Miserere*.

Returning now to our own doctrinal standards, we are taught that the believer is first chosen according to the eternal purpose of God, then justified by the finished righteousness of Christ, and renewed by the power of the Holy Spirit. The ritual, which expresses these ideas, is too simple to be called a ritual. When the Westminster doctrine, justification by faith, takes the place of the Tridentine dogma, justification by the sacraments, instantly the priest becomes a minister, and the altar a communion table. The bread and the wine are no longer the body and blood of Christ, but the memorials of these. The impious immolation of the mass is turned into a sweet and holy feast, and the mutterings of the priest are exchanged for the pastor's prayer. The devotee, kneeling to the bread and robbed of the cup, is regenerated into the communicant, sitting, as the disciples sat, to receive the broken bread, and to drink from the cup of blessing, which in the Master's name we bless. The temple becomes a house of prayer; the preaching of Christ supersedes the elevation of the host; the hearing ear takes the place of the stupid stare; the lacerations of penance are exchanged for the sighs of penitence; the closet banishes the confessional; and the believer's act of faith, receiving Christ as the Saviour, supplants for ever the Auto de Fe of the Inquisitor, committing God's chosen ones to the flames. How quickly, how utterly does the true doctrine exterminate the idolatrous ritual of Rome! Away go surplice, tonsure, rosary, bowings, kneelings, mutterings, and antiphonies; away, away go crucifixes, paintings, images, dead men's bones, incense, lighted candles, the sign of the cross, masses for the dead, and indulgences for the living. All these symbols of a baptized idolatry do unquestionably proceed from the Romish theology; even so, every corrupt tree bringeth forth evil fruit. But how simple and spiritual the worship prescribed by our theology; the reading of the Word, the song of praise, the prayer, the sermon, the baptism, the supper, and the blessing upon the people; even so, every good tree bringeth forth good fruit.

In the fourth place, our theology developes *the intellectual powers.* Not only was pure religion revived at the period of Reformation, but the human mind was inspired with new activity. It were an easy task to trace this intellectual awakening to the theology of the Reformers. The doctrine of justification by faith alone was, perhaps, their first great discovery. Then five of the seven sacraments were discarded as fraudulent, and the two that remained were wrested from their superstitious uses. Next the Word of God was rescued both from the hierarchy and the unknown tongue which concealed its light. A step further revealed the fundamental principle that the Bible is the only infallible rule of faith and practice. A final step brought them to the knowledge of our theology. Under the increasing light and power of these successive discoveries, sacerdotalism, ritualism, the sanctity of tradition, the legends of saints, the dreams of the fathers, the insolence and fraud of priestcraft, and the credulity and servility of its subjects, withered away. The human mind, so long darkened, or intimidated, or smothered by the midiæval faith and worship, now experienced the vitalizing impulse of the apostolical theology. Other systems have inflamed the ardour of leading minds, but this communicated an upheaving force to the masses. Never since the days of the Apostles had there been such a wide spread and wonder working excitement.

It was a spiritual and intellectual resurrection. The dead were raised; the soul dead in sin, and the intellect dead in imbecility, were made alive. What was true then is true to this day. It cannot be denied that our theology, saying nothing here of its saving efficacy, is a mighty intellectual power on earth. It is an universal, unfailing educator. It planted in Scotland the free parochial school, and used the Shorter Catechism to discipline the mind of the peasant's child up to the comprehension of all liberal learning. A missionary, sent by one of our Boards to a community where there is neither church nor school, will soon establish both, and his preaching will invigorate the understanding of his hearers, while it saves their souls. A sermon on the divine decrees, delivered by a passing stranger, in a place where that doctrine was never before expounded, has been known to agitate the minds of the whole community, planting in the bosoms of many a strangely quickening power. A doctrinal book, issued by our Board of Publication and carried, we know not how, to a distant frontier settlement, has led the reader not only to pray as he never prayed before, but to meditate with an intensity he never experienced before. "Thy testimonies," saith the Psalmist, "are wonderful, therefore doth my soul keep them. The entrance of thy words giveth light, it giveth understanding unto the simple."

If we would describe the effect of our theology on the development of individual minds, we should know not where to begin, and beginning we should know not where to end our labours. The pages of history fatigue the eye with the names of illustrious men, who have arisen in every land penetrated by this doctrine. The learning of scholars, the eloquence of preachers, the irresistible logic of controversialists, the wisdom of statesmen, and the genius of great commanders have borrowed the highest inspiration from their and our accepted faith. Let us discharge this part of our duty with the mention of a single name.

John Calvin was twenty years of age before he was converted from Rome to Christ. When, soon afterwards, our theology struck its forces into his mind, it roused him to the utmost stretch of thought. It was like a fire in his bones. So vital was the new life within him, that at the age of twenty-six he had deduced our entire system of doctrine from the Word of God, adjusted its elements into a masterpiece of logical coherence, and published it to the world in his immortal Institutes. The twenty-eight years of life that remained to him were laden with affliction both of mind and body. Physical infirmities multiplied upon him, until no less than seven distinct maladies laid siege to his attenuated frame. He suffered also every private grief, even that domestic bereavement which he styled "an acute and burning wound."

It is impossible to look, without wonder, at the labours he prosecuted amidst all this weariness and painfulness. The products of his pen exist in nine huge folios of printed matter, besides several hundred letters, and more than two thousand sermons and theological treatises yet unpublished. He prepared a copious commentary on most of the Scriptures; he edited a French translation of the word of God; he disputed by tongue and pen with Bolzec on the doctrine of predestination, with Westphal and Hesshus on the sacraments, with Welsius on the free will, with Pighius on free grace, and Servetus on the Trinity. He wrote against relics and astrology, the Anabaptists, the Libertines, and the Pelagians. He employed his wit and sarcasm in assailing the Sorbonne, his powers of argumentation in confuting the Tridentine Decrees, and his noble eloquence in behalf of the Emperor against the Pope. He corresponded incessantly with his contemporaries—Farel, Viret, Beza, Melancthon, Knox, Cranmer, and the Kings of Sweden, Poland, and Navarre; projecting, by his long and masterly letters, his own intellectual and spiritual life into the leading minds of Europe. With an asthmatical cough upon him, he lectured three days in the week on theology, and preached daily on every alternate week. He presided every Thursday at the Court of Morals, attended the frequent assembly of the clergy, assisted in settling the civil and ecclesiastical affairs of Geneva; he founded there a seminary of liberal learning, and when the city was threatened with siege, laboured at the fortification. He educated preachers of the gospel; performed many journeys; was consulted on all important subjects; occupied the pulpits of his brethren in their absence; and did not neglect pastoral labour in the congregation. Besides all these things, he composed the dissensions which perplexed the Reformers, and the strifes which afflicted the churches; and aided in settling the affairs of the Reformation in Poland, France, Germany, Scotland and England. At last, being compelled by mortal disease to relinquish public duties, he received in his chamber all who sought his advice, and wore out his amanuenses by dictating to them his works and letters. When his shortening breath and failing voice terminated these labours, his kindling eye and heaving breast indicated that he was in constant prayer. On a beautiful evening in May, seven days later in the month than this the day of our solemn convocation, just as the setting sun was irradiating, with its purple light, the waters of Lehman and the

Rhone, the Jura mountains and the more distant glaciers of the Alps, this great man rested from his labours. He gave directions that his body should be buried without the slightest pomp, and that his grave should be marked by neither monument nor headstone. His commands were obeyed, and "no man knoweth of his sepulchre unto this day."

In the fifth place, our theology develops *the principles of republican liberty*. The full treatment of this topic falls more naturally into an historical discourse, than into one strictly religious. Yet a distinct mention, with a brief illustration of this part of the case, is essential to the completeness of our argument. We use no labour in showing that the principles inherent in a free commonwealth are identical with those which have been mentioned in this discourse, as inherent in a free Church. The theology, which in its full development, leaves no place for a bishop in the Church, will also rule the king out of the State. John Wickliffe understood this thoroughly when he uttered the memorable words, "dominion belongs to grace;" and Charles the First was no mean logician when he declared that "there was not a wiser man seen since Solomon, than he who said—no bishop, no king." The doctrinal system which conducts to the conclusion that all church officers should be elected by the people, will push on to the adjacent conclusion, that hereditary authority in the State is an intolerable usurpation. The creed which demonstrates the right of the people to sit by their representatives in all church courts, and which vindicates this right as divine, and which further denies that the assembly excluding the popular element is a scriptural assembly, that creed will characterize as unlawful and iniquitous any civil government whereof the people are not the masters. Indeed, our system of faith does not more conclusively sweep away the last vestige of sacerdotal usurpation from the Church, than it exterminates every anti-republican institute out of the State. The temporal must follow the spiritual, and whom Christ makes free, he is free indeed.

Such is the conclusion of logic in the premises, and such, I now add as briefly as possible, is matter of fact. Any profound examination of the history of the Huguenots, will show that their church, in its faith and order, was essentially republican, and as such, was crushed by the monarchy; and that the political position of modern France, is to be referred, first, to the life, and then to the destruction of that old predestinarian church; its life so far surviving in the heart of the nation, as to render a fixed monarchy impossible, and that life so nearly extinguished, as to render a stable republic also impossible. Even a superficial examination of the history of England, Scotland, and Ireland, will show that this divinity, expounded by its divines in the pulpit, espoused by great statesmen in Parliament, and defended by illustrious commanders on the field of battle, infused into the British constitution the soul of rational liberty, until that constitution is, with a single exception, the richest repository on earth of free principles. What that exception is, we know, and where it received its treasures we know. This same divinity came with the Puritans to Plymouth, with the Dutch Calvinists and the Scottish

Presbyterians to New York and New Jersey, and with the Huguenots and Presbyterians to South Carolina. Our fathers did not found monarchical institutions on the shores of Massachusetts bay, or on the banks of the Hudson, and the Ashley and Cooper, for the same reason that they did not set up the worship of the Virgin. Monarchy and idolatry were, both of them, repugnant to their religious faith, and they repudiated both, and established a true worship, and a free commonwealth on all these shores. This ancient faith, and the institutions rising from it, were perpetuated from generation to generation, until they culminated in the war of Independence, and in the formation of these separate commonwealths, together with their great confederacy. From that faith, as from a living root planted on our virgin soil, and by our rivers of waters, have sprung the witness bearing Church, and the republican State. These, in their turn, seeking a higher development, have flowered out with all spiritual joys, and all the fragrant charities of life:

> "So from the root
> Springs lighter the green stalk, from thence the leaves
> More aery, last the bright consummate flower
> Spirits odorous breathes."*

In the sixth place, our theology develops its life in *the patience of the confessors and martyrs*. The

---

* The conduct of the ministers, ruling elders, and communicants of the Presbyterian Church in the Revolutionary war, furnishes some remarkable illustrations of this topic. Among the ministers who were actively engaged in the struggle, were John Witherspoon, who signed the Declaration of Independence; James martyrs of Protestantism have been almost exclusively drawn from the bosom of the Reformed churches, rarely from the Lutheran or Arminian communions. A century before Luther was born, John Huss was consigned to the flames by the council of Constance, on charge of teaching, among other heresies, the doctrines of predestination and the perseverance of the saints. The charge was clearly sustained, for he had written in his book, that "no part or member of the church doth finally fall away, because the charity of predestination, which is the bond and chain of the same, doth never fall away." Jerome of Prague having avowed his faith in the preaching of Huss, was burned on the same spot by order of the same infamous Council. The works of

Caldwell of New Jersey, who was murdered by a British soldier for his patriotic exertions; William Graham of Liberty Hall Academy, Virginia, who, hearing that Tarlton was advancing on Staunton, raised a company of volunteers and led them in pursuit of the enemy as far as Lafayette's camp, below Charlottsville; President Smith of Hampden Sidney College, who repeatedly marched at the head of his pupils to repel the enemy; James Hall of North Carolina, who assembled his congregation, and besought them to take up arms for the common defence, and immediately raised among them a company of cavalry, and took both the command and the chaplaincy; Samuel Houston, who used his rifle with deadly effect at the battle of Guildford Court House; David Caldwell, for whose head Lord Cornwallis offered a reward of £200; Thomas McCaule, who led his flock to the camp, and stood by the side of General Davidson when he fell on the Catawba; and Hezekiah Balch, who, with nine ruling elders and other citizens, put forth the celebrated Mecklenburg Declaration. The military services of the ruling elders and communicants of the Church were so important and numerous that a few could not be specified, without seeming invidiousness towards the many that must necessarily be excluded from a brief note.

John Wickliffe being found by the council to contain similar doctrines, his body which had lain forty-one years was dug up and burned. As the old historian writes: "They cast his ashes into the Swift, a neighbouring brook running hard by; this brook hath conveyed his ashes into Avon, Avon into Severn, Severn into the narrow seas, they into the main ocean. And thus the ashes of Wickliffe are the emblem of his doctrine, which now is dispersed all the world over."

One hundred and forty years later brings us to the reign of Mary the bloody. On the 4th of February, 1555, John Rogers went to the stake at Smithfield, having, during his imprisonment, set his hand to a confession instinct with the Genevan doctrines. On the following day, Dr. Roland Taylor, three days later Lawrence Sanders, one day after him, Bishop John Hooper, three weeks yet later Bishop Ferrar, and in the June following John Bradford, confessors with Rogers by signing the same memorable document, became martyrs likewise with him, giving their bodies to be burned. In October of the same year, Ridley and Latimer, both bound to one stake at Oxford, testified to the truth of our divinity in their last words to the Church and their dying prayer to God. In December following, Archdeacon Philpot, and not long after him the illustrious Cranmer, in the profession of the same faith, and the suffering of the same death, entered into the joy of the Lord.

Turning now to the sister kingdom, we learn that nearly thirty years before Rogers was burned in London, Hamilton passed through the fires of St. Andrews. If the cruelty of the English Bishop justifies the historian in exclaiming, "that lion, tiger, wolf, bear, yea, a whole forest of wild beasts met in Bonner," he was well matched by the Scottish Cardinal Beaton. The priory of St. Andrews is no less monumental of Wishart's sufferings than is the gate of Baliol College of Ridley's; and the altar on Castle Hill, at Edinburgh, smoked as incessantly as that in Smithfield, with the blood of the saints. It is as certain, moreover, that the Scottish martyrs were of the faith of Knox, as that the English martyrs were of the faith of Cranmer.

I may not detain this argument with a detail of the sufferings endured for Christ, during the seventeenth century, by the non-conformists of England and the Presbyterians of Scotland. The intolerance of Archbishop Laud in the one country had its counterpart in the bigotry of Archbishop Sharpe in the other; the judicial murders of Jeffries were equalled in atrocity by the military butcheries of Claverhouse; the high commission answered to the court of justiciary; the "Bloody Assizes" of sixteen hundred and eighty-five, in England, corresponded to the "Killing Time" of sixteen hundred and eighty-four, in Scotland; and the grave yard of Bunhill Fields, in London, and that near the Grassmarket, in Edinburgh, gave rest to a multitude of "them that were beheaded for the witness of Jesus." Of the peculiar theology, to which all these gave testimony, there is no need that one should speak.

The martyrology of the Netherlands is not less decisive in support of our argument. The theology which entered these countries at the period of the

Reformation, was unquestionably the same that was subsequently affirmed by the judgment of the Synod of Dort. It is true that Holland was the original seat of Arminianism, and the birth place of its great teacher; yet it is also true that, twenty-four years before that teacher was born, William Tyndal was strangled and burned at Antwerp, having translated the New Testament Scriptures, and deduced from them the doctrine that, such is his own language, "in Christ the believer was predestinated and ordained unto eternal life before the world began." Five years before the birth of Arminius, the morose fanataeism, with which Charles V. had pursued the saints of the most High God, gave place to the wilder fury of Philip, the husband of Mary the bloody. The founder of the new theology was a lad of only eight years, playing in the streets of Oudewater, when the Duke of Alva entered the low countries and established the Council of Blood; and he was only fourteen years of age when the Duke left the Netherlands, boasting that he had, within five years, delivered eighteen thousand heretics to the executioners. If it be needful to add another word, we may observe that the Papal persecution had nearly, if not quite, spent its rage in Holland before Arminius became an Arminian.

And now, turning to the martyr Church, what shall be said of the theology which was received, and the sufferings that were endured by the Huguenots? Of the former it were enough to say, that the very germ of the Reformation was planted in France by Leclerc and Farel; that Calvin dedicated his Institutes to Francis I. as containing the precise doctrines preached by the Reformers in the kingdom; that the confession of the French Protestant Church was drawn up by the hand of the same master, and was little more than an epitome of his "Institutes;" and that as late as the year preceding the massacre of St. Bartholomew, the National Synod sat under the presidency of Beza, who was second only to Calvin in ability, and not inferior to him in attachment to the Augustinian doctrines. The story of their sufferings should begin with the punishment, in 1523, of Leclerc, the proto-martyr of France. It should describe the fete of Paris, in January, 1535, when Francis I. closed the festivities of the day by suspending six Protestants from a beam, which was so nicely balanced that its motion plunged the sufferers successively and repeatedly into a blazing furnace, until they were destroyed. It should relate how Henry II., amidst the tournaments and illuminations which graced his coronation, passed from place to place to regale himself with the mortal agonies of men dying for the faith. It should also describe the massacre of St. Bartholomew, turning the Seine into blood, choking the current of the Rhone with the bodies of the slain, and awakening *Te Deums* and merry cannonades on the banks of the Tiber. Thousands were buried alive in dungeons. Some were tortured, and then delivered, so that women received, as it were, their dead raised to life again; others were tortured, not accepting deliverance, that they might obtain a better resurrection. They were burned, they were scourged, were gashed with knives, were branded, were hanged, were drowned, were slain with the sword. But let me not wound your sensibilities with these details. I willingly turn from them, if nothing more be needed to identify our theology with the sufferings endured in all lands by those of whom the world was not worthy.

In the seventh place, our theology developes *the elements of an expanding and aggressive Christianity.*

A doctrinal treatment of this part of the case would demonstrate that a church, which incorporates into its inner life an intelligent faith in the fixed decrees of God, must become, by the necessity of its nature, a missionary church; one of these decrees, as declared by the Son of God, being that the heathen shall be given to him for his inheritance, and the uttermost parts of the earth for his possession. Indeed, our doctrines are, in a twofold sense, divinely adapted to this work; as dwelling in the bosom of the church, they sustain an intense and exalted life, even the life of God, urging his people to spread the everlasting gospel throughout the earth; as terminating on the world, they are clothed with a transcendent and mighty power, the power of God unto salvation.

The actual progress of Christ's kingdom, under the promulgation of these doctrines, confirms every word that has now been uttered. This theology entered Geneva, and in the space of thirty years caused the wrath of man to praise God, and the remainder it restrained. In France it made such headway against unrelaxing and unrelenting persecution, that within sixty years from its introduction into the kingdom, the National Synod had under its charge more than two thousand churches, the greater part of these being furnished with two ministers, and some of them with five or six; and not a few of the congregations numbering more than ten thousand communicants. Entering Holland, England, Scotland and Poland, it subdued kingdoms, "wrought righteousness and obtained the promises." Having been planted on this continent, it is the accepted faith—though in some instances less purely and rigidly held than we could desire—of denominations numbering, in the aggregate, six thousand ministers, seven thousand five hundred congregations, and eight hundred thousand communicants.

The history of its missionary undertakings is not less remarkable. Our brethren of the English church are about to celebrate the jubilee of the Society for the propagation of the Gospel in foreign parts. Yet this oldest Protestant Missionary Association on earth received its charter from William III., who was orthodox after the Synod of Dort. The enterprise of foreign missions, in this country, received its earliest impulse in a college, the theology of which is indicated by the fact that soon afterwards, our own Griffin assumed its Presidency.

The zeal for Domestic Missions originated almost simultaneously in our own General Assembly, and in churches of whose faith, at the time, the Saybrook Platform and the Shorter Catechism were the exponents. The diffusive tendencies of our theology are still further indicated by the missionary schemes of the Scottish churches, established and dissenting; the Boards of our own church; and the voluntary societies sustained by brethren of other names, who profess our faith in the "substance," if not in the "system of doctrine."

But it may be thought that the Arminian divinity, as preached by John Wesley, has developed a type of Christianity no less diffusive than our own. Now, while we may not conceal the profound conviction that our own theology, even when it differs from Wesley's, is the theology of the Bible, yet we would do all homage to the vital truths which that great man adopted into his system of faith, and to the zeal and success with which he and his disciples have proclaimed them. But the progress of this system raises several questions of immense importance. One of these respects the peculiar type of piety which it developes. On that question I do not propose to enter. Another question touches the elements of its power. It might be clearly shown, as I humbly conceive, that its past success is to be referred not to those doctrines which are peculiar to itself, but to those which are common to both theologies; not to its denials respecting election, efficacious grace, and perseverance, but to its utterance concerning original sin, justification, and regeneration.

A third inquiry relates to the continued and future efficiency of modern Arminianism. Is it a permanent, redeeming power on earth? On this part of the case I take leave, without intending any thing disrespectful towards brethren of other persuasions, to make a few suggestions.

It is now only a few years over a century since Wesley began his career. A religious system matures slowly. The truths asserted may, for a long period, hold in check the serious errors with which they are combined. The errors, if not eliminated, will at last work out the dissolution of the system. It may indeed outlast many generations, but what are even ages to the life of a true, permanent theology?

It is to be remembered, also, that the Arminian scheme has yet to be reduced to a systematic and logical form. Where are its written formularies, pushing boldly forth, to their final and inevitable conclusions, all its doctrines touching predestination, free-will, and efficacious grace? We have its brief and informal creed in some five-and-twenty articles; but where is its complete confession of faith in thirty or forty chapters? Where is its larger catechism? Nay, where is even its shorter catechism? Where is its whole body of divinity, from under the hand of a master, sharply defining its terms, accurately stating its belief, laying down the conclusions logically involved therein, trying these conclusions no less than their premises by the Word of God, refuting objections, and adjusting all its parts into consistent and systematic whole?* It has furnished us indeed with some detached negations and philoso-

* Without disparaging the ability displayed in the "Theological Institutes" of the eminent Wesleyan divine, Richard Watson, we may suggest, that the points at issue between the Arminian theology and our own, are not discussed in that work with the thoroughness, the rigid and penetrating analysis, and the scientific order which are displayed in other parts of the book, and which are demanded at the present time. Of the Catechisms No. I. and No. II., "compiled and published by the British Conference," we may remark, that these manuals contain few allusions, much less any explicit and dogmatic propositions, touching debated points, corresponding to *Questions* and *Answers* 20, 30, 36, etc., in our Shorter Catechism.

phical theories. We have, for example, its flat denial of our doctrine of predestination; but has it to this day met, for itself, the problem of foreknowledge infinite by a more plausible solution than the celebrated sophism, that although God has the capacity of foreknowing all things, he chooses to foreknow only some things? We have, also, its notion of the freedom of the will, wherein there was supposed to be the germ of a systematic Arminianism; but this budding promise was long since nipped by the untimely frost of Jonathan Edwards' logic. It is clear that an exposition of this theology, which shall satisfy the logical consciousness, is indispensable to its perpetuity; otherwise it cannot take possession of educated and disciplined minds—educated by the Word and Spirit of God, and disciplined to exact analysis and argument; otherwise, again, although it may exert a temporary influence, it will retire before advancing spiritual and intellectual culture. It is also clear that the first century of its existence has not produced that exposition. Another century may demonstrate that such a production is impossible, by showing that the logical and scriptural element is not in the Arminian system; that the law of affinity and chrystallization is wanting to its disjointed principles; that this theology, combining many precious truths, and many capital errors, resembles a mingled mass of diamonds and fragments of broken glass and broken pottery, which no plastic skill of man or power of fire can mould into a single transparent, unclouded, many-sided, equal-sided crystal, its angles all beaming, and its points all burning with light—a Kohinoor indeed!

Again, it is to be seen whether this divinity has not, on the one hand, an inherent tendency to prelacy, as in the Anglican Church, and on the other, an inherent repugnance to the popular element—the representation of the people in church assemblies—as in the Wesleyan societies in England and this country. If the case be so, we must be permitted to doubt both its soundness and its permanency.

Still further, it remains to be determined whether this divinity can abide any great day of trial. Are its vital energies equal to such a work for God as was accomplished by another theology between the birth of John Calvin and that of James Arminius? Could it survive such a century of ceaseless struggles as that which culminated in the English revolution? Not only surviving itself, could it uphold a great nation through every terrible convulsion; every exterminating war and treacherous peace; its bow abiding in strength; its quiver ever full; smelling the battle afar off, with the thunder of the captains and the shouting; lifting its brow and its war-cry undaunted in the dreadful array; its chariot plunging into the thickest of the fight, and yet bearing aloft, flaming and unextinguished, its two sacred torches—even the truth, man's heritage in the Church, and liberty, his heritage in the State? And then is that theology equal to the task of exiling itself to another and distant continent, planting there two new commonwealths, the spiritual and the civil, both free, each separate from the other, and each independent of every power on earth besides; penetrating the vast interior; founding powerful States and prosperous churches under every latitude, from the frozen to the burning zone, and under every meridian, from our own resounding sea to the golden shores of the West? Let the future age solve these momentous problems, and with them every question, touching both the Arminian theology and our own, as permanent or transient, as vital or decaying.

Here we close our inquiries into the developments of our theology. But before retiring from this vast and unexhausted theme, we should give attention to some reflections suggested both by our subject and the present occasion. The teaching and ruling Presbyters, in whose presence I stand, are about to constitute the General Assembly of the Presbyterian Church. To this judicature belong high spiritual powers, and its deliberations are of subjects infinitely momentous. Yet the most of these may be reduced to three general issues; and I take leave, in the close of this discourse, to indicate the bearings of our subject on each of these.

It belongs to the General Assembly, in the first place, to *conserve the accepted theology of the Church.* The results of the foregoing discussion apply with irresistible force to this part of our official duty. What are the fruits of this theology? At least these seven: an exalted type of spiritual life, a free church polity, a simple and spiritual method of worship, high intellectual vigour, civil liberty, the patience of martyrs and confessors, and the force of an expanding and aggressive Christianity. From each of these particulars springs an argument, pleading with us, most persuasively, to contend earnestly for the faith once delivered unto the saints. Each of these is a blessing and a heritage, and, taken together, they compose our whole heritage of blessings. **Our love for the fruitage must measure our zeal in behalf of the parent stock.** Let it come into the ears of all men, every where, that we cannot give up our theology; we can spare none of its peculiarities, not one of its "five points;" no, not one. We are jealous even for the terms in which its truths are conveyed. When the discourse is of our relation to the sin of Adam, we retain the word imputation, even with the guilt it implies, lest we lose the word, and, with the word, the blessing it speaks of when we describe the righteousness of Christ. We keep our hold upon the terms guilt, condemnation, and punishment, lest we lose our hold upon the terms righteousness, justification, and propitiation. We adhere to the expression "original sin," lest men conclude that the phrase having disappeared from our sermons, the thing has ceased out of their hearts. These terms may be condemned as antiquated, but they express ancient truths. An old oaken, iron-bound casket is quite suitable to the crown jewels of the oldest kingdom on earth, of truth and righteousness.

It belongs, secondly, to this supreme tribunal *to cherish the spiritual life of the Church.*

We should ever bear in mind that vital piety is of the very substance of faith in our theology. The assent of the understanding to our doctrines, as clear deductions from the Word, is not necessarily a faith in the doctrines themselves; it may be no more than a faith in the processes of an impregnable logic. We are not saved by receiving our catechisms as true, nor even by believing in justification by faith, but by believing in Christ. Ours is the high office to conserve our theology; but this we can do in no other way than by cherishing in the Church the spirit of genuine and unaffected piety. We should give earnest heed that we do not allow other sentiments to take the place of that in our hearts. Let us beware of the Churchmanship, which is the token of bigotry, as distinguished from the charity which is the bond of perfectness. A selfish love of the Church, as our Church, is possible; an unholy pride in its numbers, and learning, and wealth, and influence, and moral power, is possible; liberality to our Boards, because they enlarge our borders, and so give greater consequence to ourselves, as Presbyterians, is possible; a zeal for our polity as merely republican and free, while it is compact and phalanx-like, is possible; nay, these are sins that do easily beset. Let our theology teach us better things than these. Let it plant in our hearts that sweet and blessed mystery, the life that is hidden with Christ in God. Let it move us to cherish, in all our communicants, the divine life, which shall lead them to abhor their sins, to cleave to the Saviour, to frequent the closet and the family altar, to love the house of prayer and the communion of the saints—a life which shall generate in their bosoms an intelligent, perpetual zeal for the honour of God in the salvation of souls—a life which shall thirst after God, even the living God.

Our subject enforces, not less powerfully, the third great duty laid on this high judicatory, *even the duty of giving to the Gospel the widest possible extension.* We have seen that our Church derives from its theology the capacities of a free, rapid, and world wide expansion. But why does not the Church experience such an expansion? It has accomplished something; why has it not done immeasurably more for the cause of the Master? Through its four Boards, it has given no small extension to the truth at home and abroad; why has it not planted ten churches in this country where now there is only one; and why has it not preached the Gospel in every land, yea, to every creature under heaven? Whether we measure the spiritual forces with which our doctrines are clothed, or trace out their proper developments, or examine the history of their achievements, we are conducted to the humiliating, but certain conclusion, that the energies now dormant in our church immensely exceed those that are in action. We seem to resemble, by a strange anomaly, both the faithful and the unfaithful servant in the parable; the faithful, to whom the Master gave the ten pounds, and the unfaithful, who went and hid his Lord's money.

The question forces itself upon our consciences, why does not a church, which rests on such a foundation, fulfil more perfectly its office? Let the judgment, which this inquiry brings to the house of God, begin at the pulpit. Does the ministry faithfully preach our peculiar doctrines? It has been thought that such preaching is uninteresting to the hearers; or if not wearisome, disbelieved; or if not rejected, unpopular; or if not unpopular, practically powerless. But what injurious mistakes are these! Our doctrines uninteresting? When clearly expounded, they compel the attention of men. Incredible? They master the understanding of not a few by the force of a complete and irresistible demonstration. Unpopular? They are endowed with a sort of fascination, constraining those who heard them yesterday with fixed aversion, to hear them to-day with profound attention. This preaching powerless? Let no man say that within the precincts of a church which has gathered into a single grave yard the ashes of Samuel Davies, Archibald Alexander, and Jonathan Edwards; the first memorable for the awakening power of his sermons; the second trying the spirits and discerning even the thoughts of our rising ministry; and the third preaching a sermon on the doctrine of election, which was mighty in the conversion of sinners, and delivering another, so instinct with the terrors of the Lord as to bring his audience to their feet, and compel the preacher, who sat behind him in the pulpit, to start up with the exclamation, "Mr. Edwards, Mr. Edwards, is not God merciful too?" The sepulchres of these men are with us until this day, and so is their theology; but where the spirit of profound meditation and importunate prayer with which they prepared their sermons? Where is their vehemency and tenderness of utterance? Where their annihilating reply to the disputers of this world, their masterly appeal to the understanding, and their onset on the conscience?

And then let the judgment pass to our ruling elders and deacons, to all our two hundred thousand communicants, men, women, parents, children, masters, servants, all. Where are the people who are mighty in prayer, full of faith and the Holy Ghost?

Why are revivals of religion rather diminishing, than multiplying, in frequency and power? Who among the rich give heed to the apostolical charge to "do good, to be rich in good works, ready to distribute, willing to communicate?" Who among the poor imitate her example, which is spoken of in all the world where this gospel is preached? Why does our Board of Foreign Missions entreat the Church in vain to send the bread of life to starving millions? Why is our Board of Domestic Missions fainting under pecuniary embarrassments in the very heat and stress of its great work? Why is our Board of Education suffered to deplore, from year to year, the want of candidates for the sacred office? Why does not our Board of Publication expound and vindicate our faith in every mansion in the city, and in every log cabin in the wilderness? Here is our theology, not only embalmed in our standards, but received into our hearts. Here are its forces and its developments, many and mighty. Here are ministers and churches, and missions and schools, and colleges and seminaries of sacred learning. Here are all the elements of a redeeming power on earth, a paramount, permanent, expanding power. Why do we fail to realize its efficacy?

This venerable court of Jesus Christ is, by divine appointment, the tribunal to which such inquiries belong. And not less appropriate to them is the place of its present deliberations. Nearly one hundred and sixty-seven years ago, the revocation of the Edict of Nantz drove from the kingdom of France more than five hundred thousand Huguenots. They fled to all the Protestant States of Europe, to England, to the Cape of Good Hope, and to the shores of the Western Continent. Invited by the genial climate of the South to the infant colony of Carolina, large numbers of these exiled people of God found rest, some on the borders of the Santee, and others on the banks of the Cooper river. The latter company built their house of worship in a little village, a few miles distant, called Charleston. Thither, on the Lord's day, they were borne on the bosom of the river, by the gentle flow of its waters, or the motion of the oar, or the ebbing of the tide. In their forest homes, and in their humble sanctuary, they wept for joy as the voice of their supplications and the melody of their songs, rising upon the tranquil and fragrant air, stood contrasted with the carnage and terror from which they had fled. This is the ancient Carolina. This, too, is Charleston. Near us is the site of their first house of prayer. Yonder is the Cooper river. There are the fields in which they set up their dwellings and domestic altars. There the rich and odorous vegetation of the early summer repeats for us the life it lived for them. Around us lies their dust, awaiting the resurrection to meet their kindred dust, as that too shall rise from the graves of murdered saints beyond the seas. Here, in this presence, are their children. The blood which moistened the beautiful valleys of Languedoc and Tours, which stained the waters of every river, and the pavements of every city, from the English Channel to the Mediterranean, now runs in the veins of those with whom we worship God this morning. With what unanimity these adhere to that ancient faith, a stranger may not presume to inquire. But they are our witnesses, this day, that in faith, order and worship, our Church is identical with their own ancestral Church in its pure and heroic day. Not these alone; for here are they also, whose fathers brought hither, many generations ago, the living and fruit-bearing stock of Presbyterianism. Let these, our own brethren, partakers with us of the root and fatness of the olive tree, and let believers of every name, and them who believe not, discover in our proceedings, and in us, no spirit of contention, or uncharitableness, or evil-speaking. May they see nothing in this august council but a pious zeal for the theology, the spirituality, and the extension of the Church, and for the glory of its Eternal King.

Now, fathers and brethren, the God of peace that brought again from the dead our Lord Jesus, that great Shepherd of the sheep, through the blood of the everlasting covenant, make you perfect in every good work, to do his will, working in you that which is well-pleasing in his sight, through Jesus Christ, to whom be glory for ever and ever. Amen.

THE END.

www.ingramcontent.com/pod-product-compliance
Lightning Source LLC
Chambersburg PA
CBHW051738300426
44115CB00007B/616